CROSS BORDER TERRORISM IN INDIA

With Reference To International Regime

CROSS BORDER TERRORISM IN INDIA:

With Reference To International Regime

By

SHIVANI RASWAN

Vij Books India Pvt Ltd
New Delhi (India)

Published by

Vij Books India Pvt Ltd
(Publishers, Distributors & Importers)
2/19, Ansari Road, Darya Ganj
New Delhi – 110 002
Phones: 91-11-43596460, 91-11-47340674
Fax: 91-11-47340674
e-mail: vijbooks@rediffmail.com
www.vijbooks.com

Contents

Annexures

PREFACE

Over the past decade, a new player has emerged in the world affairs i.e. the cross border terrorist. The states can now unleash the terrorist activities in different capacity i.e. by pertaining the acts of terrorism in the territory of other states with the purpose of destabilising that country. Most of the countries have had violence from across the border since 1990s but never used 'terrorist violence' for it. It is now called as 'cross-border terrorism', which includes across the border violent extremism that promotes disorder, disrupts stability, and opposes freedom and State and non-state actors that sponsor terrorism, pursue nuclear technologies, proliferate weapons, and support illicit and criminal behaviour. As a multi-ethnic, religious and linguistic subcontinent, India faces many revolts backed by narrow ideologies. There is the separatist movement in Kashmir valley, Assam, Manipur and Nagaland. In addition there is an on going unrest in heartland of India where the Communist insurgents want to overthrow the state and usher in 'their' version of 'people's republic', popularly called Naxalites. All these movements indulge in use of terror tactics off and on.

In India, large number of people lost their lives in the violence and mayhem inflicted by terrorists in Punjab, Jammu and Kashmir and the North East region, at the instigation of and with the active material support from across the border.

It is a complex and difficult situation and there are no ready answers to the problems that the countries in the world are faced with. Nevertheless, Terrorism that the world faces today is essentially a power struggle and proxy war to achieve this worldly aim. Religion is used only as a cloak to hide the true intentions of the perpetrators.

It is a pity that India has yet to enunciate its anti-terrorism policy even though it has been battling with the problem for nearly five decades. The fault lies, not in the legislation, but in the system that implements the law. The implementation however calls for improvement. Delays are chronic, right from the stage of issuing summons to the defendant, which, in some cases, can take several months, as processes are delayed on flimsy grounds. Delays in civil cases hurt particular individuals and institutions; but the failure to expedite the prosecution of the accused in criminal cases – especially of serious criminal offences such as terrorism – is a cause of alarm, as it constitutes a threat to the life of the individual and to the security and stability of the state.

Today's demand is that a unified command and steps in right directions are required to curb the menace of Cross border terrorism. The Government of India has been, in the context of areas affected by terrorism, talking of winning the hearts and minds of people. It has also pumped in substantial funds for the economic development of the states. These are steps in the right direction. It is necessary however that concurrently measures are also taken to revitalise and energise the state police forces and restructure the paramilitary forces and ensure their optimum utilisation in such a manner that they are able to deliver decisive blows to the terrorist organisations trying to subvert our economy, fracture our social fabric and destabilise our polity. Therefore, it should be understood that the problem we are now dealing with requires various kinds of provisions. The various findings and suggestions have been discussed in the last chapter of the book.

ACKNOWLEDGEMENTS

There are many people behind every creative work without the help of whom the work cannot be accomplished. The same is true in case of my book. Though words are often inadequate to express the feelings of heart, one must acknowledge the genuine help and support received from others during the fulfillment of a particular task. I would therefore, like to convey my heartiest gratitude to all those people who have contributed directly or indirectly in the completion of this work.

In the preparation of the present work, I owe a huge debt of gratitude to my supervisor, Dr. Kuljit Kaur, Professor in Law, Guru Nanak Dev University, Amritsar, whose meticulous understanding of the subject has been an experience worth cherishing. She helped me in fulfilling the dream of completing this work despite the unfavourable circumstances. Her confidence and understanding of the subject always filled me with new vigour and positivity. I am also indebted to my mentor, Late Dr. M.D Singh, Professor in Law, whose deep insight and thought provoking discussions would have made possible to commence the present work. His professional commitment and personal simplicity always remained a guiding star in my academic career. I also take this opportunity to thank Dr. Madeliene Cheah, Dean and Acting Academic Director, TMC Academy, Singapore and Mr. Jonathan Davies, Military and Strategic Analyst, Chief Security Instructor for the Surviving Piracy and Armed Robbery Course, Maersk Groups on Security Issues, for their invaluable suggestions and timely inputs. I am highly obliged to them for their support when things were getting tough towards the pursuit of the research in Singapore. I also thank the staff of main library, administrative staff of the Department of Laws, GNDU, Amritsar, National library and Marine Parade library, Singapore for their multifarious and unfettered support.

I am also blessed with a supportive and motivating husband, Capt. Samar Singh Pathania, who always remained a source of inspiration. His unfailing confidence in me encouraged me to achieve higher goals in life. I am obliged to my father in law, Er. Mangal Singh Pathania and mother in law Mrs. Raj Kumari for supporting me through out and understood the potential in me and responsible for whatever little I have achieved today. I also offer my heartiest regards to my father, Mr. Shiv Charan Singh Raswan and mother Mrs. Kanchan Raswan for motivating me to be true to myself always. I am also obliged to my daughters Sanah and Sarah who always enabled me to feel the best in life and provided me their great support. I shall be failing in my duty if I do not acknowledge the great support from Manav Preet Kaur Dhindsa who is both personal friend and emotional support.

I would be failing in my duties too if I do not thank Subhash Computers who meticulously went through all the typing work towards the completion of whole work. Toward the end I shall take this opportunity to thank Almighty to provide me such a strength and zeal to make my dream come true.

As is obvious, the assistance for the present thesis has been drawn from various sources. I have, therefore taken utmost care to acknowledge those sources in the footnotes and in Bibliography. However, anything missing due to an oversight is deeply regretted.

September 2013

-Shivani Raswan

Abbreviations

ABVP	Akhil Bhartiya Vidyarthi Parishad
AC	Law Reports, Appeal Cases
ADD	Annual Defence Dialogue
AGPL	Actual Ground Position Line
AIR	All India Reporter
AJIL	American Journal of International Law
APHC	All Party Huriyat Conference
ARF	Asean Regional Forum
ASEAN	Association of South East Asian Nations
ASK	Ain-o-Shalish Kendra
BDR	Bangladesh Rifles
BOPs	Border Out Posts (Permanent Border Posts)
BSF	Border Security Forces
BYIL	British Year Book of International Law
Cr.P.C	Criminal Procedure Code
CST	Chattrapatti Shivaji Terminal
CTBT	Comprehensive Test Ban Treaty
CTC	Counter Terrorism Committee
CTITF	Counter – Terrorism Implementation Task Force
CTTC	Counter –Terrorism and Transnational Crimes
DGFI	Directorate General of Field Intelligence
DPA	Department of Political Affairs

EC	European Communities
FTO	Foreign Terrorist Organisation
HUJI	Harkat-Ul-Jihadi-Islami
IB	Intelligence Bureau
ICAO	International Civil Aviation Organisation
ICC	International Criminal Court
ICCPR	International Covenant on Civil and Political Rights
ICESCR	International Covenant on Economic, Social and Cultural Rights
ICJ	International Court of Justice
IEA	Indian Evidence Act
IIGS	Indian Insurgents Groups
IJIL	Indian Journal of International Law
IJIS	Indian Journal of International Studies
ILA	International Law Association
ILR	International Law Reports
IPC	Indian Penal Code
ISI	Inter Services Intelligence
IT	Information Technology
J&K	Jammu & Kashmir
JILI	Journal of Indian Law Institute
JKLF	Jammu & Kashmir Liberation Front
JUILS	Journal of University Institutes of Legal Studies
JWG	Joint Working Groups
KLO	Kamtapuri Liberation Organisation
LAC	Line of Actual Control

LET	Lashker-e- Toiba
LOC	Line of Control
LTTE	Liberation Tigers of Tamil Eelam
MAC	Multi Agency Centre
MCOCA	The Maharashtra Control of Organised Crime Act,(1991)
MEA	Ministry of External Affairs
MISA	Maintenance of Internal Security Act
MLATS	Mutual Legal Assistances
NDFB	National Democratic Front of Bodos
NHRC	National Human Rights Commission
NIA	National Investigation Agency
NSCN	National Socialist Council of Nagaland
NSG	National Security Guard
PCA	Permanent Court of Arbitration
PCIJ	Permanent Court of International Justice
POK	Pakistan Occupied Kashmir
POTA	Prevention of Terrorist Activities Act
SAARC	South Asian Association for Regional Cooperation
SC	Supreme Court
SCC	Supreme Court Cases
SCJ	Supreme Court Journal
SCOR	Supreme Court Official Record
SIMI	Students Islamic Movement of India
TADA	Terrorists and Disruptive Activities (Prevention) Act
UAPA	Unlawful Activities (Prevention) Amendment Act

UDHR	Universal Declaration of Human Rights
UID	Unique Identifications Numbers
UK	United Kingdom
ULFA	United Liberation Front of Assam
UN	United Nations
UNDHR	United Nations Declaration of Human Rights
UNHCR	United Nations High Commissioner for Refugees
UNTS	United Nations Treaty Series
US	United States
USR	United States Reports
UTS	Union Territories
vs	Versus
WLR	Weekly Law Reports
WTO	World Trade Organisation
Yale L.J	Yale Law Journal

Chapter I

Introduction

"Where the mind is without fear and head is held high....."

Rabindra Nath Tagore wrote these lines in 'Gitanjali' years back. Every soul under the sun wishes peace to take root, for peace nurtures an enabling environment that makes human progress possible. Even today we need to pray the same for our country. Terrorism is a curse on mankind. It has grown in form and size along with the evolution of society and common person can be a target anytime any where. Terrorism as an expression of violent dissent has always been part of most politics. Terrorism is also a convenient label, which a colonial power may choose to give a liberation movement for acts of violence directed against the power. Terrorism as a social phenomenon has a knack of spawning in different social contexts with its forms, manifestations, incidence and timing varying over time. Terrorism is uniquely offensive form of political violence, generally in response to the political importance of the ruler or some political malaise. Though terrorism has now become a buzz word used mostly for political motives, yet terrorism gnaws an enabling environment. It ought to be discouraged.

There has always been dissent against the established authority irrespective of the fact that the authority is established under a feudal system, a monarchic system or a democratic system from the rule of the dominant to the rule of the law, many stages have been witnessed in the evolution of human society. Terrorism has been identified with anarchists, with revolutionaries and with fundamentalists at different times of history. The present research, is an effort to study the new dimension of terrorism in the form of cross border terrorism in India.

Terrorism: A Contextual Perspective

Terrorism as an expression of violent dissent provides a dramatic method of highlighting a 'cause' it seeks to demoralise, terrorise and renders helpless the target group/ state; it seeks to achieve its 'cause' through coercion with total disregard of the consequences of innocent human beings as the motto is that the end justifies the means!

Terrorism is also a convenient label, which a colonial power may choose to give a liberation movement for acts of violence directed against the power. When terrorism is institutionalised in the coercive exercise of the power of a state aimed at gagging even democratic dissent, it becomes state terrorism.

International Perspective

The contexts include the age of the reformation in Europe, the American Revolution and the Latin American wars of liberation, the French revolution, and the days of Metternich's concept of legitimacy and the resultant concert of Europe and the big power politics it produced, the late 19th century guerrilla movements in the Philippines fighting against the American Colonialism, the resistance movements during the two world wars in the occupied territories, unwieldy multi ethnic empires that came to be recognized at the end of the World War I, and the European dictatorships of the inter – war period that led to the World War II. In fact the World War I ignited upon the assassination of the Archduke of Austria – Hungary by a member of an under- ground Serbian Liberation Movement.[1] The world since 1945 witnessed the cold war, during which promotion of terrorism among the dissidents of the enemy camp became the par time of the two competing super powers.

The list would be incomplete without reference to the terrorist attacks on the World Trade Centre towers in New York and the Pentagon building in United States (US). International terrorism assumed a new dimension with the assault on the World Trade Centre and the Pentagon on September 11, 2001—the biggest single terrorist strike in the history of terrorism with the largest number of casualties and the maximum economic damage. Many people were killed and property worth about twenty billion

---

1 Keiichi Aizawa, 'Strengthening the Legal Regime for Combating Terrorism',available at http://www.unafei.or.in , (Last viewed on May 17, 2009).

dollars was damaged.[2] A defining moment in the history of US and the world, the attack marked the beginning of the first major war of the 21st century and triggered off the formation of a formidable coalition against terrorism. It prompted the Security Council to take an unequivocal stand through a comprehensive resolution "with steps and strategies to combat international terrorism". [3] The heinous attack on the twin towers of the New York World Trade Centre resulted into killing so many innocent people belonging to sixty different countries has been a record of sorts achieved by international terrorism. Roundly condemned by the entire international community, this terrorism attack was perpetrated with no weapons. Two of the domestic airlines on their Trans American flights were hijacked soon after they took off from Boston airport, and the terrorist's pilots on a suicide mission rammed the aircraft in full fury against the twin towers with the full fuel tanks performing the function of lethal explosives. The result was devastating. Small wonder the US equated this to its Pearl Harbour experience, which had forced it headlong into the World War II.[4] The US investigations were reported to have indicted that the attack were imputed to the Al Qaida terrorist group of Osama Bin Laden[5], a Saudi Arabian renegade who was behind the Taliban regime in Afghanistan, where it ran terrorist training camps on a regular basis and planned and operated several terrorist missions in many parts of the world what hit the US most was the fact that Osama and Taliban, originally its own creations in aid of its anti-Soviet campaign in Afghanistan since the Soviet invasion of Afghanistan

---

2   Prakash Singh, 'Making Security Forces More Effective, Legislative Back Need of the Hour', available at **http://www.tribuneindia.com/2003**, (Last Viewed on June 7, 2011).

3   V.S Mani (2003), *International Terrorism and the Quest for Legal Controls,* pp. 41-62.

4   Ibid.

5   Osama bin Mohammed bin Awad bin Laden was the founder of **Al-Qaeda**, the **jihadist** organisation responsible for the **September 11 attacks** on the United States and numerous other **mass-casualty attacks** against civilian and military targets· He was a member of the wealthy Saudi **bin Laden family**, and an ethnic **Yemeni Kindite**. Bin Laden was on the American **Federal Bureau of Investigation**'s (FBI) lists of **Ten Most Wanted Fugitives** and **Most Wanted Terrorists** for his involvement in the **1998 U.S. embassy bombings**. From 2001 to 2011, bin Laden was a major target of the **War on Terror**, with a **US$25** million bounty by the Federal Bureau of Investigation, .After being placed on the FBI's Most Wanted list, bin Laden remained in hiding during three U.S. presidential administrations. On May 2, 2011, bin Laden **was shot and killed** inside a **private residential compound** in **Abbottabad**, Pakistan, by **U.S. Navy SEALs** and **CIA** operatives in a covert operation ordered by United States President **Barack Obama**. Shortly after his death, bin Laden's body was buried at sea. Al-Qaeda acknowledged his death on May 6, 2011, vowing to retaliate.

in 1979, had now become Frankenstein's and turned their guns against their own 'creator'.[6] The September 11 incident represented at once one of the worst crimes against humanity committed by international terrorism, it also brings home the adage that terrorism is too dangerous an ad hoist game to play even for the mightiest power on the earth.

In the east region of the globe, several instances of violence were also reported. In Indonesia, there was sharp increase in international and domestic terrorism, including several bombings, amongst two of which targeted official foreign interests. The Abu Say of Group in Philippines was also active and carried out several abductions, including those of foreign nationals.

The chain of horrific events that caused terrible devastation in US and in other parts of world have proved that no nation can claim immunity from terrorism, even if it happens to be the world's sole super power.[7] These attacks prove beyond doubt 21st century terrorism is global in its reach and nations of the world need to join hands to fight their common enemy.[8] It can only be defeated by organised international action and it should be the primary task of all open and plural societies to develop collective means for tackling the menace of terrorism.

Indian Perspective

The national liberation movements in Asia and Africa have often resorted to terrorist tactics to fight the ruthless European colonial power, taking an advantage of the elements of surprise and speed with which small bands of men equipped with improvised arms of even small arms could mount attacks on the military might of the colonial power and dissipate among the common native folk after the attack, making it extremely difficult for the colonial government agencies to apprehend the culprits, Indians for instance have adored Vir Savakar, Netaji Subhash Chander Bose and his Indian National Army, and Bhagat Singh and his friends as freedom fighters. They were, however terrorists in the British cases.

India, in fact, has suffered much more than the US could ever imagine. The foolish attack on the Indian Parliament on December 13, 2001, was

---

6 V.S Mani, 'Asia and the Twenty First Century International Law', available at http://law. nus.edu.sg/asiansil, (Last Viewed on December 21, 2009).

7 Reference of Annexure A for the List of Major Terrorist Attacks all over the World.

8 Editorial column, Chanakya Civil Services Today, (November, 2001), p.22.

a watershed in history of Pakistan-sponsored terrorism targeting this country. But for the luck being on the side of the Indian Republic, the worst could have happened. India was not able to escape for long when there prolonged terror strike on November 26, 2008 by Pakistani terrorists belonging to the Lashkar-e-Toiba (LET) in the financial and entertainment capital Mumbai[9], targeting mainly the Chattrapatti Shivaji Terminal (CST), Oberoi, Trident, Taj Mahal Palace and Tower Hotel, killing and injuring number of people. Fire fighting with terrorists actions was stopped successfully after three days in a joint operation involving the Maharashtra Police, Indian Army and the National Security Guard. The attack occurred on the 10th anniversary of the demolition of the Babri Mosque in Ayodhya. This was the worst attack in Mumbai since the 1993 Mumbai serial blasts that killed 257 and injured over 700 people.[10]

One point on which there is some degree of consensus is that terrorism is not new. Indeed, in some respects, that what is today known as terrorism predates by millennia the modern term is used to describe it. This is not to say that the acts of terrorism have remained static. Rather, as the difficulties involved in defining it reflects, terrorism has changed considerably over the years, even if retaining some of the same characteristics that have historically typified it.

While it is impossible to ascertain when it was first used, that which we today call terrorism traces its roots back at least some 2000 years. Philosophers and theologians for long have debated the question of whether it is justifiable to kill a political opponent over long time. Both Plato (429-322 BC) in his "Republic" and more fully Aristotle (384-322 BC) in "Politics" discuss the question and morality of tyrannicide (the

---

9 On November 26, 2008, in a pivotal moment that is now called "26/11", terrorists struck at a variety of locations in Mumbai on November 26, killing at least 183 people, including 22 foreigners, six of whom were Americans and 14 members of the police and security forces. Over 300 more were injured. The attacks in Mumbai targeted places frequented by foreigners and wealthy Indians. The attackers entered Mumbai from the sea and attacked people in two hotels, a Jewish center, the main train station, and additional locations, they also planted bombs in two taxis that later exploded in different locations in the city. The terrorists appeared to have been well- trained and took advantage of technology, such as Global positioning System trackers. Local and State police proved to be poorly trained and equipped, and lacked central control to coordinate an effective response. This attack was the most recent in a long list of lethal terrorist incidents the year 2008.

10 'There is no Major Threat form Saffron Terrorists', available at http://www.rediff.com news/column/ in, (accessed on January, 6, 2011).

killing of a despotic or evil ruler).[11]Therefore it is appropriate to say that Terrorism is not a new or static concept. It has evolved long back in the history also. It has changed considerably in respect to its meanings in different circumstances and situations.

Meaning And Definition of Terrorism

The term 'terror' is derived from the latin word 'terrere' meaning 'to tremble' or 'to frighten from'. It may be defined as a systematic use of violence and intimidation to achieve some goals especially political.[12] Thus it is different from all other crimes in its purpose. Its objective is to put the people in a state of terror and keep it there while forcing a government or organisation to either act or not act in a given direction. In modern times, it was first used during the French Revolution and the Jacobin Reign of Terror.[13]

At first, it was identified with the state action, but later, it was applied to individual or group violence. It covers varied form of violence, raging from indiscriminate bombing to hijacking, kidnapping, taking of hostage assassination and severe destruction of property. Terrorism is uniquely offensive form of political violence, generally in response to the political importance of the ruler or some political malaise. Literally, terrorism like other 'ism' is a system or the method or theory behind it, the method strongly believing in use of terror towards the achievement of certain objectives. Terror in the ordinary parlance means intense, overpowering fear and use of terrorising methods for governing or resisting a government.

One of the most formidable problems faced by the legal control of

---

11   David Rapport, 'Fear and Trembling – Terrorism in Three Religious Traditions', American Political Science Review, (1984), pp.668-672.

12   Webster Dictionary (1990) defines terrorism as " the act or practice or terrorising, especially by violence for political purposes, as by government seeking to intimidate a population or by revolutionaries seeking to overthrow a government , compel the release of prisoners etc. the Chambers Dictionary call it as 'an organised system of intimidation for political ends'.

13   The Reign of Terror was caused by Jacobin leadership. The rule of Maximilien Robespierre and other members of the radical Jacobin party is best remembered for the Terror, when more than thirty thousand people were executed in France between 1793 and 1794. In the following viewpoint it was criticized the Terror and disputes the arguments made by scholars wishing to defend the revolutionaries. Scholars assert that the Terror was not necessary to ensure public safety but was conducted to silence counter revolutionaries and others who threatened Jacobin rule.

terrorism is the precise definition of the term terrorism.[14] Up till now, a specific juridical definition, both from national and international perspective is not possible in view of what has been said of its dual dimensions and also because terrorism is a generic term comprising of a variety of acts including terror, barbarity or uncommon violence not only by individuals or group of individuals with in a state but also by armed forces of one state against another state. There has been a divergence of opinion between Afro- Asian states; on the other hand, and western states, as to whether states or governmental acts should be included in the category of terrorist acts.[15]

In view of the varied causes, approaches, perceptions and the diverse features of terrorism, it becomes too difficult to arrive at a definition that could satisfactorily cover all its varied interpretations. Most experts agree that terrorism is the use of threat of violence, a method of combat or a strategy to achieve certain goals that its aim is to induce a state of fear in the victims, that is ruthless and does not conform to humanitarian norms and that publicity is an essential factor in terrorist strategy.`

One of the earliest attempt to define terrorism was made by Hardman in Encyclopaedia of the Social Sciences, that terrorism is a term used to describe the method or the theory behind the method whereby an organised group or party seek to achieve its avowed aim chiefly through systematic use of violence. Terrorist acts are directed against persons who, as individuals, agents or representatives of authority, interference with the consummation of the objectives of such a group. Terrorism is unequivocally defined as the deliberate and systematic murder maiming and menacing of the innocent to inspire fear for political ends.[16]

Although scholars and diplomats continue to debate over the precise meaning of the term, recent contemporary usage, tends to restrict its meaning to either random or extortionate violence, aimed undoubtedly at the target state of a guerrilla, resistance or movements, but which strike at unarmed civilians, diplomats or non combatants.[17]According to the Oxford

---

14 N.B Grant, 'Terrorism in Search of Definition', *Indian Express*, November 2, 1996.

15 Paul Wilkinson, 'Three Questions on Terrorism in Government and opposition', *The Summer*, 2001.

16 "What did AL gained out of this Hertal", The Daily Star, available at http://www. dailystarnews.com/htm, (Last Viewed on February 20, 2008).

17 Brian Jankins (2002), *International Terrorism: A New Code of Conflict*, Los Angles, p.1.

English Dictionary, the word "terrorism" is defined as the "state" of being terrified and greatly frightened: intense fear, fright or dead, the action or quality of causing dread[18] used in this sense, the term stands for a psychic state of horror or intense fear created through a process of deliberate and systematic use of coercive intimidation.

Michael Stohl defines it as "the purposeful act or threat of act of violence to create fear and/or complaint behaviour in a victim and/or audience of act of threat.[19]Here the element of 'purposeful act' is to be taken note of as it implies that terrorism is an act of violence, done purposefully and intentionally to coerce the victims to do or not to do certain things as wanted by the perpetrators of terrorist act. From this, it can be suggested that terrorism is not a mindless act; rather it is a planned mode of keeping the target under a complete state of fear. It is not merely a nuisance but "a tool to be used rationally". There are innumerable instances of terror being used both rationally and irrationally, for non-political purpose also, particularly when it has been used by criminals and psychopaths.

After an exhaustive analysis of more than hundred expert definitions, Schmid developed an almost consensus definition, according to which, "Terrorism is an anxiety inspiring method or repeated violent action, employed by semi clandestine individual, group or state actors, for idiosyncratic individual, group or state actors, for idiosyncratic, criminal or political reasons, whereby in contrast to assassination the direct target of violence are not the main targets. The immediate human victims of violence are generally chosen randomly (targets of opportunity) or selectively (representative or symbolic targets) from a target population, and serve as message generators. Threat and violence based communication processes between terrorist (organisations), victims and main target are used to manipulate the main target audience(s) turning it into a target of terror, a target of demand or a target of attention, depending on whether intimidation, coercion or propaganda is primarily sought."[20]

The US Department of Defence defines 'terrorism' as "the unlawful use of force or violence against individuals or property, to coerce or intimidate governments or societies often to achieve a political, religious

18 *The Oxford English Dictionary*, Oxford University Press, London, 2009, p.216.

19 Michael Stohl (1988), *The Politics of Terrorism*, New York, p.3.

20 Alex P. Schmid and Albert J.Jongman (1988), *Political Terrorism: A New Guide to Actors, Authors, Concepts, Data Base, Theories and Literature*, New Brunswick, Amsterdam, p.243-248.

or ideological objectives".[21] The American Army on the other hand, defines terrorism as the "calculated use of violence or the threat of violence to attain goals-political, religious or ideological in nature".[22]

Although, the saying: "one man's terrorist is another's freedom fighter."[23] One must admit, while defining terrorism that it is very difficult to reach any consensus about it. And at the same time it is difficult to define the "terrorist" too. Those who are freedom fighters for the Palestinians are 'terrorists' to be killed and eliminated for the Israelis. In Kashmir, those who are 'terrorists for Indians but are freedom fighters for Pakistanis and even for some Kashmiris.

However, this argument is biased, as Hari Jai Singh rightly notes,

"On a contra factual expectation of unique identity. In truth, individuals have multiple identities – a man may be father and murderer; husband and rapist. We also share a multiplicity of transient identities – we are, for example, at particular times, workers, shoppers, hosts or guests. A man, on this reasoning, may be both terrorist *and* freedom fighter. The latter identity rests on his motives – what he is fighting *for*. The former relates to the methods he adopts in this fight – the targeting, specifically, of civilians, to achieve his ends. Terrorism, thus conceived, can be adopted for one among many motives – to fight for freedom, for particular environmental policies, for a ban on abortions, for animal rights, among others – and remains terrorism as long as the method or means utilized involve the intentional targeting of civilians."[24]

Even though it is difficult to define 'terrorism,' those who kill innocent and non-combatant people on a large scale could certainly be categorised as terrorists. For instance, many Pakistan-based terrorist organisations like LeT who kill innocent citizens not only in Jammu & Kashmir (J&K) but also in other cities of India are considered to be terrorists.[25]

---

21 Jason Franks, 'Rethinking the Roots of Terrorism – Orthodox Terrorism Theory and Beyond', available at http://www.st-andrews.ac.uk/interal/media/htm, (Last Viewed on May 10, 2009).

22 Prakash Singh, 'Making Security Forces More Effective Legislative Backup Need of the Hour', *The Tribune*, January 5, 2003.

23 V.S Mani(2003), *A Quest for International Legal Controls*, New Delhi, p. 161

24 Hari Jai Singh, 'Countering Terrorism', The Sunday Tribune, available at http://www.tribuneindia.com/2003/htm, (Last Viewed on June 18, 2011).

25 Ibid.

If, however, terrorism is defined strictly in terms of attacks on non-military targets, a range of attacks on military installations and soldiers' residences would escape the scope of the definition. In order to cut through the Gordian definitional knot, terrorism expert Alex P. Schmid suggested in 1992, in a report for the then United Nations (UN) Crime Branch, that it might be a good idea to take the existing consensus on what constitutes a 'war crime' as a point of departure. "If the core of war crimes – deliberate attacks on civilians, hostage taking and the killing of prisoners – is extended to peacetime, we could simply define acts of terrorism as 'peacetime equivalents of war crimes'."[26]

However, difficulties with the definition of terrorism, nevertheless, persist, many of them motivated by those who engage in, support or benefit from, activities widely perceived as such. Nevertheless, it is possible to clearly identify the essential considerations that would enter into an assessment of such acts: terrorism can, thus, generally be described as the systematic use of terror or unpredictable violence against governments, the public, or individuals, to attain a political objective. Terrorism has been used by political organisations with both rightist and leftist objectives, by nationalistic and ethnic groups, by revolutionaries, by groups pursuing particular political or ethical ends, and by the armies and secret police of governments themselves.

A clear distinction between 'ordinary crime' and terrorism is, consequently, important as is well illustrated by the Supreme Court's(SC) observations in *Hitendra Vishnu Thakur vs. State of Maharashtra*[27] that,

> 'terrorism' has not been defined under Terrorist and Disruptive Activities (Prevention) Act (TADA) nor is it possible to give a precise definition of 'terrorism' or lay down what constitutes 'terrorism'. It may be possible to describe it as use of violence when it's most important result is not merely the physical and mental damage of the victim but the prolonged psychological effect it produces or has the potential of producing on the society as a whole. There may be death, injury, or destruction of property or even deprivation of individual liberty in the process but the extent and reach of the intended terrorist activity travels beyond the effect of an ordinary crime capable of being punished under the ordinary penal law of the land and its main

---

26 Supra note 19.

27 (1994) 4 SCC 602

objective is to overawe the government or disturb harmony of the society or 'terrorise' people and the society and not only those directly assaulted, with a view to disturb even tempo, peace and tranquility of the society and create a sense of fear and insecurity. A terrorist activity does not merely arise by causing disturbance of law and order or of public order. The fallout of the intended activity must be such that it travels beyond the capacity of the ordinary law enforcement agencies to tackle it under the ordinary penal law.'

The honorable SC further added that,

"What distinguishes 'terrorism' from other forms of violence therefore appears to be the deliberate and systematic use of coercive intimidation. It is therefore essential to treat such a criminal and deal with him differently than an ordinary criminal capable of being tried by the ordinary courts under the penal law of the land."[28]

In general the criteria for defining the term terrorism has remained subjective and based mainly on political considerations. The fact, however, remains that terrorism is promoted by a wide range of motives depending on the point in time and the prevailing political ideology. It, therefore, takes different forms, is usually equated with political subversion, employed at times by governments and is used as an instruments of syndicated crime. As with any complex social problems there have been attempts to simplify critical issues in terrorism. The analysis of terrorism as a form of political violence is a problem because of lack of consensus about definition of the phenomenon itself and objective criteria free of any ideology. Walter Laqueur, an eminent authority on the subject is of the views that there is no definition of terrorism that could cover all its various manifestations in history.[29] Despite differences in approach most scholars and observers tend to agree that present day terrorism is a negative political phenomenon with grave consequences for the individual, society, political regimes, international community and the human race as a whole.

Manifestations of Terrorism

However, whatever may be the definition of terrorism; different terrorist groups of the world have different manifestations of terrorism, which

---

28   Supra note 26 at p. 603.

29   Saji Cherian, 'Terrorism & Legal Policy in India – An Overview', available at http://www.satp.org/satportp/publication, (Last Viewed on April 6, 2009).

transcend each other's boundaries very often.[30] These manifestations are:

1. Terrorism as a Caste Struggle (for instance Red Army, Red Brigade, Naxalities)

2. Terrorism as a Liberation Struggle (for instance, Abu Nidal Group, Indian Freedom Fighters, Hindustan Socialist Republican Army and Bharat Mata Association)

3. Terrorism as a Separatist Movement [for instance, Liberation Tigers of Tamil Eelam (LTTE)]

4. Terrorism as a Power Struggle (for instance movements in Lebanon, Iran, South Yeman)

5. Terrorism as a Sectarian Struggle (for instance movements in Colombia, Peru)

6. Terrorism as an Undeclared War (for instance US intervention in Nicaragua and Afghanistan)

7. Terrorism as a Revival of Fundamentalism (for instance Islamic Jihad, Mujahideen)

8. Terrorism as a Tribal Warfare (for instance North Eastern Region of India, Movements in Uganda and Zimbabwe in Africa)

9. Terrorism as a Revenge (for instance Armenian Liberation Army, New Armenian Resistance, Black June, Black September)

10. Terrorism as a Tool of Organised Crimes (for instance Drug Traffickers and Smugglers in the Andreatic Region)

In the view of the diverse manifestations of terrorism, it is too arduous to arrive at a common definition of terrorism, which can satisfactorily cover all the varied analysis. In other words, terrorism is notoriously difficult to define precisely, objectively and scientifically except that the primary act of terrorism is to terrorise. The only generally agreed definition of terrorism in the very precise form is "use of threat violence to achieve certain objectives and goals by way of inducing a state of fear or terror in the victim(s) or other target groups".

---

30   Ranjit K Pachnanda (2002), *Terrorism and Response to Terrorist Threat,* New Delhi, p.11

The Menace of Terrorism in Various Forms

One of the distinguishing features of international terrorism over the past two decades has been the resurgence and proliferation of terrorist groups motivated by religious imperative. Terrorists may use religion or religious terminology like *jihad* or *Dharma yuddh* or holy war but their objective may have nothing to do with religious teachings as such. It would, therefore, be wrong to describe a terrorist act as religious terrorism just because of religion of a terrorist and his use of religious terminology. Thus, the international terrorist, Osama bin Laden's being a Muslim and his attack on the WTC twin towers, New York, does not become an act of **'Islamic terrorism'**.[31]

Osama bin Laden had his own agenda and his acts by no means represent Islamic teachings. No religion in the world, much less Islam, teaches terrorism or inspires any one to kill innocent people. Though some Muslims may have expressed sympathy for Osama, so did some non-Muslims who resent America's policies. Osama never had any official sanction from any Islamic establishment. And in case of Osama no such institution has issued any such *fatwa* supporting his act of terrorism. It is, therefore, not justified at all to describe 9/11 attack by Osama's men as an act of Islamic terrorism. Even if any eminent *Mufti* (one who issues *fatwa*) had issued such an opinion, it would not have been binding on all Muslims. And in this case no one issued such a *fatwa.*

However, Osama bin Laden and his Al-Qaida organisation did not pretend to have any mass base. No terrorist organisation, as a matter of fact, has a mass base anywhere in the world. It would otherwise seem to be a terrorist organisation. Osama did use Islamic terminology to gain the sympathy of Muslim masses but use of such a terminology does not make it an Islamic organisation. It remains basically a terrorist organisation. The religion practiced by masses of Muslims is more spiritual than political and religion practiced by likes of Osama was more political than spiritual.[32]

Moreover, the *Koran*[33] clearly lays down that killing any person without a just cause amounts to killing whole humanity and saving one person's life amounts to saving entire humanity. This is truly humanistic

---

31 Asghar Ali Engineer, 'Fundamentalism and Terrorism: Politics of Religion and Religion as Politics', The *Tribune Online News Issue*, January 5, 2003.

32 Ibid

33 The Holy epic of Muslims.

and spiritual dimension of Islam and of any religion for that matter. Killing hundreds of innocent people can not qualify for being a religious act by any stretch of imagination. It is more of the act of '**fundamentalism**'.

Nevertheless, fundamentalism in the sense in which it is being used in the media is, in fact, a political misuse of religion in a narrow sectarian manner. In this sense, there is not much difference between communalism and fundamentalism. Both the phenomena are based on political interests. Still there is a subtle difference between the two. While communalism is all about political or economic interests of a particular community, fundamentalism is enforcement of sectarianism with all rigidity for political mobilisation of a community for the power-goals of its elite. While communalism is the exploitation of sentiments of a religion-based community for a secular goal (i.e. political power) fundamentalism is enforcing narrow sectarian practices for strengthening religious orthodoxy as well as achieving political power.[34]

In fact whether fundamentalism and terrorism are linked together or not, but both are curses for humanity. No truly religious person should approve of such a gross misuse of religion. A religious attitude has to be of humility, distance from political power and of non-violence. The Sufi Islam which was truly spiritual Islam always maintained its distance from power centers and believed in the doctrine of what is called *sulh-i-kul* i.e. peace with all. True religion is one, which does not get politicised.

Undoubtedly, political Islam or political Hinduism became a great danger for peace and tranquility in the society. It is political Hinduism (*Hindutva*) which caused havoc in Gujarat[35] and many other places and

---

34   Asghar Ali Engineer, 'Fundamentalism and Terrorism: Politics of Religion and Religion as Politics', *The Tribune Online News Issue*, January 5, 2003.

35   Reference of the Godhra Kand, in Gujrat, where there was Gujarat violence which describes the Godhra train burning and resulting **communal riots** between **Hindus** and **Muslims**. On 27 February 2002 at **Godhra City** in the state of **Gujarat**, the **Sabarmati Express** train was forcibly stopped and attacked by a large Muslim mob. As a result, 58 Hindu passengers — mostly women, children and seniors returning from the holy city of **Ayodhya** — were burned alive. The attack prompted retaliatory massacres against Muslims on a large scale, in which 790 Muslims and 254 Hindus were killed. 223 more people were reported missing. 523 places of worship were damaged: 298 dargahs, 205 mosques, 17 temples, and 3 churches. Muslim-owned businesses suffered the bulk of the damage. 61,000 Muslims and 10,000 Hindus fled their homes. Preventive arrests of 17,947 Hindus and 3,616 Muslims were made. In total 27,901 Hindus and 7,651 Muslims were arrested. Nearly 10,000 rounds of bullets were fired by the police, killing 93 Muslims and 77 Hindus. In August 2002 a plot by **Lashkar-e-Toiba** to assassinate

it is political Islam which has resulted in bloodshed in New York or in Kashmir for that matter. It is American media, which started using 'Islamic fundamentalism' when the Islamic revolution was taking place in Iran in the late 1970s.

The 1990s have witnessed a new dimension to international terrorism i.e. **suicide terrorism**, a new phenomenon in the sphere of international relations, mainly in North and South Asia. The threat of suicide bombings is likely to spread to other areas. North America and Western European Security and intelligence agencies assess suicide terrorism as a threat to Western Security.[36]

Nuclear Terrorism is yet another important and latest development in international relations. The ever increasing proliferation of nuclear weapons and materials makes the threat of this is to be stolen by or supplied to terrorists. Besides nuclear weapons, terrorists are now seeking biological and chemical weapons of mass destruction is also practicing **cyber terrorism.**

The menace of terrorism and abuse of drugs has adversely afflicted the world during the past two decades. That the activities of narcotic gangs and clandestine arms deals through covert support from different intelligence agencies were causing international concern was also clear from the US of 1997.[37] Elaborate international networks have developed among organised criminals, drug traffickers, arm dealers, money launderers, creating an infrastructure for catastrophic terrorism around the world.[38]

According to Brain Jenkins a terrorism expert, 1985 has proved to be "the worst year, yet" and claimed as many lives world wide in hijacking, bombing, assassinations and sabotage. These terrorist activities involved

---

Narendra Modi, Praveen Togadia, and other **Sangh Parivar l**eaders was unearthed by Indian police. The terrorists were planning to set up a base in Gujarat and were trying to lure some of the riot-hit people into taking up "so-called jihadi activities-In September 2002, at least 29 people were killed when **Islamic fundamentalist** gunmen engaged in the **Akshardham Temple attack** in the city of **Gandhinagar** in **Gujarat.** The Pakistani **Inter-Services Intelligence** and Islamic terrorist group **Lashkar-e-Toiba** were accused of supporting the terrorists, available at **http://en.wikipedia.org/wiki/2002_Gujrat_violence/ html.**, (accessed on January 27, 2011).

36   Frontline, (Februry, 4, 2000), p.14.

37   Kenis Kari Markers (1996), *International Terrorism: Unsolved Problems of International Community*, New York.

38   Editorial column, 'A Strton carter and others, Catastrophic Terrorism: Tackling the New Dangers', Foreign Affairs, (November- December, 1998), p.81.

as many as 77 countries.[39] As pointed out by US Ambassador to the UN Vernon Walters,[40] "there is today no people, no government, no diplomat, and no traveler who can count himself immune from the terrorists." Though the malady of terrorism has become universal and its dangers are present everywhere irrespective of race, religion, nationality, ideology or sex, the efforts made so far have been far from satisfactory.

State Terrorism which is directed by those in power and carried out by state organs against a certain populations is yet another dimension to international terrorism which has been, of late, causing much worry and making it further difficult to counter terrorism effectively, in a multi color world where states are guided by different political philosophies, ideologies etc. State terror may include not only terrorist type acts by a government against its own population but also government support of individual terrorist activity. State terrorism is also involved when a government support acts of terrorism by supporting terrorists group, providing them with training and financing them.

It is pertinent to note that the gravity of the problem of international terrorism has been assuming serious proportions, with some states exporting terrorism or sponsoring the use of various forms of terrorism, through financial assistance, arms supply and militancy training to third world countries.

Though several attempts have been made by the international community through various international conventions to enforce human standards of behaviour, abolition of torture etc., yet several states continue to indulge in the practice of torture and other forms of state terrorism.[41]

Cross Border Terrorism: A New Dimension

It is to be noted that there are different dimensions of international terrorism which is having a wider scope includes those acts where two or more States are involved, i.e. where the perpetrator and victims are citizens of different States, or where the act is performed in whole or in part in more than one State. Over the past decade, a new player has emerged in the world affairs i.e. the cross border terrorist who is responsible for cross border

---

39   S. K Kapoor (2008), *International Law*, Allahabad.

40   Ibid.

41   T. S Rama Rao, "State Terrorism a Response to Terrorism: National and International Dimensions", 1987 *IJIS.183*.

terrorism which is one form of international terrorism. Since the States can unleash the terrorist activities in different capacity i.e. by pertaining the acts of terrorism in the territory of other states with the purpose of destabilising that country. They may use their own directly recruited and controlled terror squads, or may choose to work through proxies and client movements across the border. They almost invariably work covertly in such support so that they are able to plausibly deny their involvement.

Commonly called 'Cross border terrorism', it is geared to facilitate foreign policy, covertly bringing pressure to bear on country across the border through violence, short of open warfare. Unlike the national liberation movements of old, like the Palestine Liberation Organisation or the Irish Republican Army, cross border terror groups do not confine themselves territorially or ideologically to a particular region. Instead, in the words of one foreign policy expert, they are explicitly global in orientation, happy to move funds, men and material from one location to another. In this form of terrorism a State is involved in the act of terrorism, directly or indirectly for the fulfillment of certain objectives, may be a matter of policy. Involvement of a State in such acts may be in different ways in varied degrees. For instance, firstly, the act may be committed by the authorities of a State in respect of some of its citizens residing inside or outside the territory with a view to intimidating them, or against colonialism, or against national liberation movement. Secondly, an act may be committed by a Sate in the territories of another State by way of giving assistance to the latter. The range and intensity of the act may be different from case to case. It is to be noted over here that the above ways of terrorism have not only been condemned by the national and international communities, they are contrary to the well established rules of International law. Further they are contrary to many international conventions and declarations.[42]

The term 'terrorism' too has its origin in American media after 9/11. Most of the countries have had violence from across the border since 1990s but never used 'terrorist violence' for it. Generally it was called either

---

42 For instance, see Article 6, Para C of the Charter of the International Military Tribunal; convention on the Prevention and Punishment of the Crimes of Genocide of 1948; International Convention of the Suppression and Punishment of the Crimes of Apartheid of 1973; International Covenant on Civil and Political Rights of 1966, and the Charter of the United Nations. Also see principles of International Law concerning Friendly Relations and Co-operation among States; Declaration on the Strengthening of International Security of 1970.

extremism or militancy. It is now termed as **'cross-border terrorism'** which includes across the border violent extremism that promotes disorder, disrupts stability, and opposes freedom and State and non-state actors that sponsor terrorism, pursue nuclear technologies, proliferate weapons, and support illicit and criminal behaviour.

Consider Al-Qaida, the best known of the new breeds of terrorists and increasingly a kind of brand name used by an assortment of Islamic terror groups. Al Qaida has become famous for its sporadic attacks, for moving its bases from failed states to failed states and for its networks of individuals distributed around the globe. Whether in South London, South Florida or South Asia, Al Qaida has been severely weakened by the post – September 11 war on terror, but recent attacks in Saudi Arabia, Morocco and other unstable parts suggest that disparate elements are keen to keep on bombing.[43]

Terrorism Poses A Challenge

At the dawn of the twenty-first century, there are very few countries immune from terrorism. Its internal dynamics and external linkages have made it a formidable challenge not only to national security but even to world peace. Undoubtedly, there are many prime ministers or heads of states in various parts of the world who have lost their lives in terrorist incidents since the conclusion of World War II. These include John. F. Kennedy of US, Olaf Palme of Sweden, Anwar Sadaat of Egypt, Aldo Moro of Italy, Indira Gandhi and Rajiv of India, besides several others.[44]

Terrorism has been assuming grave dimensions, endangering or taking innocent lives or otherwise, jeopardizing human rights and fundamental freedoms. The internationalisation of the problem of terrorism has been associated with the extension of the terrorist's zone of actions as well as the qualitative changes in the terrorist's means and methods of actions.

In Central Asia, the Middle East, the horn of Africa and the Balkans, there are small Islamic fundamentalist groups who respect no borders, no boundaries and no state institutions. From the remains of Al Qaida along the Afghan/ Pakistan Border to Al-Wa'd in Egypt to Jemaah Islamiah in South East Asia (whose members are currently on trial for the Bali

43 'Dimensions of Terrorism', Available at http://www.aljazeerah.info/articles/html, (accessed on May 15, 2008).

44 Prakash Singh, 'Making security forces more effective Legislative backup need of the hour', *The Tribune Online Special Issue*, January 5, 2003.

nightclub bombing of October 2002), cross border terror groups loom large in the western mind, as a new and dangerous threat to world peace.

Today's cross border groups have no such attachment to territory. They view territory expediently, as a base from which they can organise their campaigns and plot their attacks. The new breed of Islamic terror groups are, explicitly global – in the sense that they have broadly anti western views rather than locally defined objectives, and their members hail from different states rather than from a distinct community with distinct interests. For these global terrorists, territory is merely a place from which they can plot.

Indeed, it was Western intervention in the third world, specifically the 'humanitarian intervention' of the post Cold war period that encouraged the emergence of today's cross border terrorists. By undermining state authority and notions of sovereignty, humanitarian intervention created the space for the rise of non state actors. And by internationalising local conflicts, Western intervention did much to encourage the flouting of traditional borders and the movement of armed groups between territories.

Cross Border Terrorism and India

As a multi-ethnic, religious and linguistic subcontinent, India faces many revolts backed by narrow ideologies. There is the separatist movement in Kashmir valley, Assam, Manipur and Nagaland. In addition there is an on going unrest in heartland of India where the Communist insurgents want to overthrow the state and usher in 'their' version of 'people's republic', popularly called Naxalites. All these movements indulge in use of terror tactics off and on.

However, in India, many people are estimated to have lost their lives in the violence and mayhem inflicted by terrorists in **Punjab, Jammu and Kashmir and the North East region,** at the instigation of and with the active material support from across the border. Apart from the loss of human lives and the extensive damage to public property, India lost a Prime Minister, an ex-Prime Minister and a former Army Chief.[45]

In addition to the above, since last two years, a motley group of Hindu extremists have taken to 'retaliate' for the past acts of terror attributed to Islamist terror groups located in Pakistan and who receive some support from fringe element of Indian Muslims. The groups like the

---

45 Supra note 42

Students Islamic Movement of India (SIMI) or its latest avatar, the Indian *Mujahideen,* are essentially an extension of the Pakistan-based LeT.[46]

A brief look at statistics shows that in the last five years the LeT-led combine has carried out ten major attacks in which over 625 Indians have been killed and over 3,000 have been wounded seriously (approx. figure). Equally startling is the fact that so far not a single terrorist involved in these activities has been punished. Most of the investigations have reached a dead end or the perpetrators have fled to Pakistan.[47]

Although even more telling is the fact that the LeT-led campaign against India is essentially a joint enterprise with Pakistan Army [through the Inter Services Intelligence (ISI)]. While in all the types of across the border intrusions including the one in Kashmir valley, there is an element of external support (The Naga rebels do receive Chinese help), the LeT-led campaign is unique in that it is a virtual proxy war launched by one state against the other by using the tactic of deniability.

It has been 23 years since first shots of Kashmiri Hindus' ethnic cleansing were fired loud and clear from the ramparts of mosques in the Kashmir valley. And it has been 23 long years of neglect, apathy and carelessness on the part of all the successive governments both in the state of Jammu and Kashmir and the capital New Delhi. Kashmiri Hindu refugees who were overnight made homeless on January 19, 1990 have been moving from pillar to post, demanding their fundamental rights. It is the day when 23 years ago final nail in the coffin of forsaken community of Kashmiri Hindus was hammered. It was the day when Islamic terrorists and their sympathizers gave 24 hours eviction notice to Kashmiri Hindus. It was the day when the threats of *Raliv, Galiv Ya Chaliv* (Convert, die or escape) replaced the sounds of evening Azaan (prayers) from majority of mosques in the valley of Kashmir. It was the day when so-called secularism died in Kashmir. It was the fateful day when humans lost and beasts took over. It was the day that will remain etched in the memories of Kashmiri Hindus worldwide because on this day they lost the most precious thing they had -- their homeland. But no one cares. No one has time for this community because they are too small a number to matter. It is a shame that the one and only symbol of India in the valley, the Kashmiri Hindus,

---

46   'There is no Major Threat form Saffron terrorists', available at http://www.rediff.com/news/column/ in, (accessed on January, 6, 2011).

47   Reference of Annexure B for Major Islamic Attacks on India

are treated as pariahs by the government. This is such a community who has been living in the tents and camps like refugees from so many years in the miserable condition till the date.[48]

It is a complex and difficult situation and there are no ready answers to the problems that the countries in the world are faced with. For a country like India, it is all the more agonizing since it has the world's second largest Muslim population in its midst and they are part of the Indian nation. But New Delhi's major headache is that Pakistan is exploiting the Islamic card to create conditions of destabilisation through terror tactics. Terrorism that the world faces today is essentially a power struggle and proxy war to achieve this worldly aim. Religion is used only as a cloak to hide the true intentions, be it Osama or the LeT. Similarly, even the Tehrik-e-Taliban-e-Pakistan (TTP) is out to grab power in that country. It is unfortunate that the current political power struggle got the 'Islamist' tag because the terrorist's themselves invoked religious sanction for their acts by selectively quoting from the holy book. However, surprising, for the Indian subcontinent, the fact that in Pakistan in last five years there have been over 42 attacks on mosques and over 530 worshippers have been killed while performing *Namaaz*. In the entire period of 63 years these many attacks have not taken place in India.[49]

India has to be on high alert to keep intact its social fabric, communal harmony and brotherhood among various communities. It will be futile on the part of the Pakistani regime to think that India will give Kashmir to it on a platter or China's Claim for the territory of Arunachal Pradesh. For this country, Jammu and Kashmir or Arunachal Pradesh is not merely a piece of territories; infact, it is a symbol of all that India stands for. However, mere rhetoric cannot make Indian leaders fight the deadly menace of terrorism successfully. They have to gear up themselves and work out new plans and strategies to eliminate militancy not only from Jammu and Kashmir but also from the rest of the country. This can be done provided our political leaders show the requisite will and act on the ground instead of talking in the air.

---

48 Lalit Kaul, 'Kashmir Hindus: Forsaken, forgotten for 21 years', available at http:// www.rediff.com/news/column/ , (assessed on January 19, 2011).

49 'There is no Major Threat form Saffron Terrorists', available at **http://www.rediff. com/news/column/ in**, (accessed on January, 6, 2011).

LEGISLATIVE BACKUP

International Aspect

The US and United Kingdom (UK) have both effective anti-terrorism laws. The **United States Anti-terrorism and Effective Death Penalty Act of 1996** made terrorism a federal offence expanded the role of the Federal Bureau of Investigation (FBI) in solving such crimes and imposed death penalty for terrorism. The Uniting and Strengthening America by Providing Appropriate Tools Required to Intercept and Obstruct Terrorism **(US Patriot Act) Act of 2001** aims to deter and punish terrorist acts in the United States and around the world. It gives sweeping powers to both domestic law enforcement and international intelligence agencies.

The UK has a stringent **Terrorism Act, 2000**, which has widened the definition of terrorism and recognised that it may have religious or ideological as well as political motivation and would cover actions which might not be violent in themselves but which can, in a modern society, have a devastating impact. The Act has also expanded the definition of terrorist organisations to include those who plan violent protests in the UK (even if the protest takes place abroad) and brought the members of and fund-raisers of such organisations within the ambit of law. The police have also been given the wider powers under this Act. Despite having stringent Acts and enactments at international level, no State could eradicate the curse of terrorism completely.

National Aspect

However, India too worked hard for the anti terrorist laws, but in India, several political parties and the Human Rights' groups opposed the enactment of an anti-terrorist law. The **Terrorists and Disruptive Activities (Prevention) Act (TADA)** was allowed to lapse and there was no anti-terrorism law for about five years. The government, after great difficulty, was able to pass the Prevention of Terrorist activities Act. In 2002 March session of the Indian parliament the **Prevention of Terrorist Activities Act (POTA)** was introduced. It was termed as Indian version of U.S Patriot Act. It was nothing more than the reincarnation of TADA with largely cosmetic changes. The Act was considered as a draconian piece of legislation as it curtailed various rights of a citizen which were recognized since long and were contrary to Article 21 of the Constitution. It was repealed in 2004 with **Unlawful Activities (Prevention) Amendment**

Act, 2004 (UAPA).[50] The POTA had widespread opposition not even in the Indian parliament but throughout India especially with the human rights organisation because they thought that the act violated most of the fundamental rights provided in the Indian constitution. The protagonists of the Act have, however, hailed the legislation on the ground that it has been effective in ensuring the speedy trial of those accused of indulging in or abetting terrorism. POTA was considered useful in stemming state-sponsored cross-border terrorism. POTA was seen as a controversial piece of legislation ever since it was conceived as a weapon against terrorism.

The UAPA was designed to deal with associations and activities that questioned the territorial integrity of India. When the Bill was debated in Parliament, leaders, cutting across party affiliation, insisted that its ambit be so limited that the right to association remained unaffected and those political parties were not exposed to intrusion by the executive. So, the ambit of the Act was strictly limited to meeting the challenge to the territorial integrity of India.

It is a pity that India has yet to enunciate its anti-terrorism policy even though it has been battling with the problem for nearly five decades. The fault lies, not in the legislation, but in the system that implements the law. Delays are chronic, right from the stage of issuing summons to the defendant, which, in some cases, can take several months, as processes are delayed on flimsy grounds. Delays in civil cases hurt particular individuals and institutions; but the failure to expedite the prosecution of the accused in criminal cases – especially of serious criminal offences such as terrorism – is a cause of alarm, as it constitutes a threat to the life of the individual and to the security and stability of the state.

Curbing Cross Border Terrorism: The Way Forward

Today's demand is that a unified command and steps in right directions are required to curb the menace of Cross border terrorism. A unified command of the civil and defence forces is absolutely essential to deal with any terrorist situation. The concept has already been accepted and applied in J&K and in Assam in India. The implementation, however, calls for improvement. There is generally either inertia from the civil side or reservation from the army side. Problems of ego are a great hindrance. These need to be sorted out and we would have to ensure that the civil services and the defence forces act in unison.

---

50 Awantika Manohar, 'Terrorism, How to Control it', Lawz, Vol.VI, (June, 2006).

The Government of India has been, in the context of areas affected by terrorism, talking of winning the hearts and minds of people. It has also pumped in substantial funds for the economic development of the states. These are steps in the right direction. It is necessary however that concurrently measures are also taken to revitalise and energise the state police forces and restructure the paramilitary forces and ensure their optimum utilisation in such a manner that they are able to deliver decisive blows to the terrorist organisations trying to subvert our economy, fracture our social fabric and destabilise our polity

Therefore, it should be understood that the problem we are now dealing with requires various kinds of provisions. Legitimate power has to be given because this is an extraordinary situation. Extraordinary situations require extraordinary remedies. Terrorism has several consequences that have to be faced in the context of a growing threat to the country. References have repeatedly been made to laws in other countries. It is very dangerous to quote selectively. We should deal with it under the normal procedure. Learning from experience from various terrorists attacks time and again, the people who are opposing this law to once again reconsider their stand because posterity eventually will decide that this country, for its integrity, sovereignty and unity certainly needs this law. Quite clearly, there is a crying need to fight the menace of terrorism united.

As the philosopher Slavoj Zizek wrote in the wake of September 11, 2001 *"the only way to ensure that it will not happen here again is to prevent it going on anywhere else"*. Only then will the war on terrorism see victory.

The book has been covered in chapters dealing with various issues. After the first chapter of Introduction, the second chapter deals with India's stand on cross border terrorism and various conditions responsible for the emergence of terrorism in India. As a multi-ethnic, religious and linguistic subcontinent, India faces many revolts backed by narrow ideologies. There is the separatist movement in Kashmir valley, Assam, Manipur and Nagaland. In addition there is an on going unrest in heartland of India where the Communist insurgents want to overthrow the state and usher in 'their' version of 'people's republic', popularly called Naxalites. All these movements indulge in use of terror tactics off and on. In India, large number of people lost their lives in the violence and mayhem inflicted by terrorists in Punjab, J&K and the North East region, at the instigation of and with the active material support from across the border. Undoubtedly, cross border terrorism targets India's democracy and secular character.

Chapter three deals with the problems and challenges faced by the government of India and its neighbouring countries in combating cross border terrorism, for instance the management of the borders and internal political security environments. Control of cross border activities on borders require some of the important strategic heights important for the security of the nation. Both external and internal situations of the country are changing at a fast pace with the developments in nuclear weapons and missiles, increasing cross border terrorism, the emergence of non-state actors, the growth of Islamic fundamentalists, the narcotics arms nexus, illegal migration and left wing extremism, gravely impacting upon the security of the country and thus posing challenge to management of borders. The Indo- Pakistan Border is a long one and heavily inhabited and inhabitants have a common history of growth, culture, language and rich heritage. Today, most of the problems are the manifestation of this fact. The problem of border management on this border is not just of securing the border but of doing so without causing harm to the economic interest of the people, long dependent on mutual trade and various other forms of interdependence.

The next chapter four of the book has discussed different aspects of International and National laws. The first part provides a close analysis of the international provisions to curb terrorism with reference to international law and the international institutions like United Nations (UN), International Criminal Court, South Asian Association for Regional Cooperation (SAARC) and ASEAN Regional Forum (ARF). It is quite interesting to know as to what extent International efforts are successful in curbing the terrorism. It brings out the loopholes present in the international law and their main concerns for further efforts to curb this menace.

It further finds that the greatest hurdle in the implementation of International treaties and conventions are that these are not binding on the member-nations and many a time even the signatory take the escapist route in the name of ethnic, cultural and religious grounds. Thus it is proposed that these Conventions once passed must be clubbed with the development grants and loans to the member-nations and the defaulters must be refused the same.

The second part of the chapter has undertaken the study of the legal regime in India to curb terrorism. There is an analysis of Indian initiatives at various levels is undertaken in particular. However, in India, there is an element of overlap in the anti-terrorist operations. Forces are deployed not so much according to their suitability for particular terrain or the nature of operations called for but more according to their availability. Therefore there is a need to review the effectiveness of specially trained forces to tackle terrorism. Organisational support to the security forces should be given. The state police forces should be strong enough to deal with terrorist movements in initial stages. Therefore it is suggested that it is required to reform and energise the state police forces and also our set up for the collection of technical signal and human intelligence.

Chapter five deals with the case study of India's Anti terrorism laws and their implications and the hurdles of their implementation in the domestic territory. This chapter is also highlighting upon the pertinent issues like weaknesses and limitations pertaining to these anti terrorism legislations. India is facing multifarious challenges in the management of its internal security. There is an upsurge of terrorist activities, intensification of cross border terrorist activities and insurgent groups in different parts of the country. Terrorism has now acquired global dimensions and has become the challenge for the whole world. The reach and methods adopted by terrorist groups and organisation take advantage of modern means of communication and technology using high tech facilities available in the form of communication system, transport, sophisticated arms and various other means. This has enabled them to strike and create terror among people at will. The criminal justice system was not designed to deal with such type of heinous crimes. In view of this situation it was felt necessary to enact legislation for the prevention of and for dealing with terrorist activities.

The last chapter draws certain conclusions and suggestions to look forward on the prospects of rapprochement of India with its neighbouring countries in peace keeping and curbing the menace of terrorism from its roots with the unified efforts and appropriate steps in right directions.

Chapter II

India's Stand On Cross Border Terrorism

Throughout history, large and small States have constructed walls and fortifications in their frontier areas. They have been put up in China, Central America, Britain, Denmark, Somalia, Algeria and Vietnam. In Asia, the Great Wall of China was built to exclude which could not be included and was the first physical expression of a linear boundary. Japanese Sakai, which meant crest of divide or water parting, was probably the first example of use of natural features as a boundary.[1]

Boundary problems, difficulties and hence border security and defence are universal phenomena. Borders mark the extent of sovereignty which a State can claim in relation to another. As such, they are usually associated with defence arrangements and often wars. For most parts of the world in the past, especially in Europe, boundary disputes and boundary determination were the major causes of international conflicts. Today the problem has reached an alarming proportion in some parts of the world and in particular in Asia where the concern of leaders has been to formulate and implement their foreign policy objectives towards the permanent resolutions of these border problems in their interactions. These interactions can either be co-operative or confliction depending on factors such as relationship between border populations, presence of resources along the borders and of course the nature of regime.

India's Land Borders – An Evolution

Historically, India's boundaries extended over a vast geographical area stretching from the Himalayan Mountain ranges in the North to the Indian Ocean in the south including the territory between the Strait of Hormuz and the Strait of Malacca.[2]South Asia is distinctive: Stephen Cohen classifies

---

1   N.S Jamwal, 'Management of Land Borders', Strategic Analysis, (July- September 2002).

2   Ibid.

it as an independent geopolitical region not within a geo- strategic region. It is big enough to be a sub- continent in its own right. It has been, and is guarded from the Eurasian powers by the massive wall of the Himalayas, from the middle – East by the Hindukush Mountains of the Northwest frontiers, and from Burma and Indo – China by lower but heavily forested jagged mountain ranges. India has absorbed many people and endured many invasions, expansions and disintegrations of empires that have shaped its land boundaries. The Indian subcontinent of more than one and a half million square miles was considered to be an "intelligible isolate."[3]

Since the period of ' Aryan Invasions' and migrations which occurred during the second millennium, India's land boundaries have been subject to constant changes and by 6th century B.C sixteen kingdoms or tribal republics had come into being in Northern- India and jostled for more territory.[4] In classical antiquity there was no option of frontiers as linear state borders. Local administrative boundaries certainly did exist and indeed, were often linear, marked by lines of boundary stones or rivers. The Aryan territory in the early Vedic period (about 4500 years ago) seems to have extended roughly from the 28th to the 7th parallel North latitude and from 68 to 80 degree longitude[5](This is approximately present day Afghanistan, Pakistan and up to Uttar Pradesh). Territorial boundaries were never fixed because the Aryans were moving in all directions and further extending their colonization.[6]

Alexander the Great of Macedonia attacked from the North- Western direction in 326 B.C after crossing the Hindukush Mountains defeated Porous on the banks of the Jhelum River and extended the territory up to the plains of Punjab. The Kingdom of Magadha, situated in the middle Ganges region, expanded into a vast empire covering three quarters of India–from present Kashmir to Mysore, from Afghanistan to Bangladesh. The Kushans controlled sectors of the Silk Route that was the crucible of lucrative trade between the Indian, Persian, Chinese and Romani Empires as well as the highway for the outward spread of Buddhism.[7]

The contours of India's land boundaries further changed with the

---

3   Surjit Man Singh (1998), *Geographic settings*, New Delhi, p.4.

4   Ibid

5   B.L Sukhwal(1991), *India: A Political Geography*, New Delhi, p.23.

6   Ibid.

7   Supra note 3.

thrust of Islam which came from the Turkish people of Central Asia, newly converted to Islam and the Persian culture. For 200 years the new Muslim rulers of Delhi defended borders and staved off Mongol attacks, which had devastating effects on China, Persia, Russia and Eastern Europe.[8]

The British Raj and Independent India

British motivations for expansion stand out as economic gains, culture mission, and considerations of military – political security.[9]The later included perceptions of threat were not only from various Indian powers, but from Burma, Nepal, France, Russia and Germany. These threat perceptions spurred the British to establish direct and indirect control over the land and sea routes to India as well as the strategic outposts of the subcontinent.

Subsequently, at the time of partition in 1947, Sir Cyrill Radcliff, assisted by two boundary commissioners, demarcated boundaries between India and Pakistan (i.e. east and west). The boundaries so demarcated are devoid of any natural and geographical features and continue to be afflicted with unsettled border disputes till date.[10]Sir Radcliff did not deal with the boundary of J&K between India and Pakistan because it was a princely state – not under British India had the option of remaining independent.

The evolution of the threat perception in India over the centuries has stressed on the geographical unity of the sub–continental land mass, the importance given to internal and external threats and the resources available to tackle them. External threats have been assessed to arise over time from raiders and plunderers to nations seeking a place under the British imperial sun. There were various concrete ways in which rulers attempted to higher their control over their boundaries, and thus to clarify the division between their spheres of authority and those of neighbouring rulers. All the major invasions, except those by the Europeans, came through the north western passes of the Hindukush. This explains why the Mughal emperors, notably Akbar and Aurangzeb, expended so much energy and treasure to secure these passes against later invaders. The geographical reality influenced their strategic thinking.[11]

---

8   Id.

9   Ibid, 6.

10 Alistair Lam(1992), *Kashmir – A Disputed Legacy 1846-1990*, Karachi, p.103.

11 N.S Jamwal, 'Management of Land Borders', Strategic Analysis, (July- September 2002), p.26.

Present Geo–Strategic Scenario

In the present scenario, India faces threat from all the countries with which it has its land borders, in one or the other form. The form of threat through varies from purely military to a combination of military and non – military. India has land borders with Pakistan, China, Nepal, Bhutan, Myanmar and Bangladesh, out of which two are nuclear powers one is Pakistan and the other is China.[12]

India has a total of 15,106.70 Kms. of land border running through 92 districts in 17 States and a coastline of 7,516.60 Kms. touching 13 States and Union Territories (UTs). India also has a total of 1,197 islands accounting for 2,094 Kms. of additional coastline. All Indian states in the country, barring Madhya Pradesh, Chhattisgarh, Jharkhand, Delhi and Haryana, have one or more international borders or a coastline; and thus can be regarded as frontline States.[13]

Stretch of Indian Land Borders

The length of India's land borders with neighboring countries is as under:[14]

Name of the country	Length of the border
Bangladesh	4,096.70 Kms
China	3,488 Kms
Pakistan	3,323 Kms
Nepal	1,751 Kms
Myanmar	1,643 Kms
Bhutan	699 Kms
Afghanistan	106 Kms

These borders comprise a vast variety of terrain encompassing deserts, plains, hills, mountains, high altitude and riverside areas.

Main Border Contact Points.

- **Pakistan Stretch.**

    ○ Wagah, Amritsar – This is made famous in numerous

---

12 Prakash Singh, "Border Management", (July 2, 2001), *BSF Journal* 11.

13 The Ministry of Home Affairs Report, Border Management Department, Defence India www.mapsofindia.com/india.../india-defence.html - India, (accessed on September 10, 2009).

14 Ibid.

Bollywood movies and the contact entry point for the Buses and Train routes from Amritsar to Lahore.

- ° Hussainiwala, Ferozepur – This is made famous by the annual fair held at a Muslim Fakir's grave that sees pilgrims from both sides making a beeline to pay their respects.

- ° Aman Setu – This is considered as much revered and embattled bridge in Kashmir.

- ° Siachen – This is famous as the world's highest and coldest battleground.

- **China Stretch**

   - ° Nathu La pass – This pass is a part of the Silk Route, recorded history by traveler Huen Tsang.

- **Bangladesh Stretch**

   - ° Salbagar-Akhaura

   - ° Karimganj-Suthargadi

   - ° Petrapole

   - ° Dauki

- **Nepal Stretch**

   - ° Sanauli, Gorakhpur district, made famous by Dev Anand, in Hare Rama Hare Krishna.

   - ° Naxalbari on the Indian side and Dulabari in Nepal

- **Bhutan stretch**

   - ° Transit from Darang Area

- **Myanmar stretch**

   - ° This is made famous as the last route taken by Bahadur Shah Zafar.[15]

---

15 Ibid.

Sensitivity of Land Borders With India

However, five of the six states in South Asia have borders with India, and this has resulted in inevitable complications since all the states are in their infancy and in several cases the boundaries are not yet firmly settled. India, which looms large as the centre piece shares ethnic religious and cultural affinities with all its neighbors. In times of conflict in neighboring countries, this becomes a source of acute tension. A spill over crisis across the borders is not uncommon.[16]

The problem of cross border terrorism over the last fifty years in India has occurred in three regions – **Punjab, Kashmir and the North – East**, where people are on the social and physical fringes of India. Language, religion and the feeling of alienation set these people apart from the people of the heartland of the country. All the three are concentrated at the outer limits of India adjoining a neighbouring country that has the desire and the ability to create problems in India's internal security.[17]

North – East India is in a strategically vulnerable geographical situation and is surrounded by countries like China, Myanmar, Bhutan and Bangladesh from three sides. It is linked with the rest of the country by a narrow corridor (20 km wide Siliguri neck). North – East India is anthropologically a paradise, which is inhabited by races of Mongoloid stock, besides Indo – Aryan groups. Barring the Khasis and Jaintias who belong to the Austric linguistic group (now branded as Mon-Khmer cultural groups of Myanmar), almost all hill tribes belong to the Tibetan–Chinese linguistic family and Tibet – Burman sub family. The non– Aryan population, being prominent in this region, shelter more than 125 major groups each having district cultural traits. In the case of the North- East, terrorism arises from a strong feeling of alienation from the mainstream of northern India plus a conviction, that the central government should be more active in north- eastern affairs.[18] Essentially, their economic backwardness stems from the unexploited natural resources, inadequate infrastructure development, rampant corruption and the strong nexus among politicians, contractors and insurgents in the region. Economic hardship due to poor and underdeveloped agriculture, alarming mass

16 N.S Jamwal, 'Management of Land Borders', Strategic Analysis, Vol.XXVI, (2002).

17 N.S Jamwal, 'Counter Terrorism Strategy', Strategic Analysis, Vol.XXVII, (2003), pp. 56-78.

18 Supra note 16.

unemployment problem, rampant corruption, and lack of educational and medical facilities, exorbitant prices and shortage of essential commodities in the far flung areas of the North-East forced the promising youth to turn to extremist activities. The employment situation lent an edge to the separatist tendency by creating numerous insurgent outfits in all the States of the North- East.[19]

The dynamic nature of the problems concerning borders is brought out by the manner in which the sensitivity of Indo-Nepal and Indo-Bhutan borders has changed over a period of time. These borders which have been open were once peaceful and trouble free. However, with the increasing activities of the ISI in Nepal and frequent movement of Assam militants into Bhutan, the nature of the borders has changed completely.

The events unfolding as above are the result of a subtle and well planned initiative to encircle India by a nexus of China- Pakistan and Myanmar. They have done so by applying the concept of 'Engagement after Encirclement'. The strategic encirclement extends from the Karakoram Highway, Aksai Chin, the China- Indian border and Myanmar down to the Bay of Bengal. By doing so, India's ability to threaten their borders has been diffused.[20]

Indo-Pakistan Border

The border to be guarded on Indo- Pakistan borders is running along the States of Gujarat, Rajasthan, Punjab and J&K. It is clearly demarcated except for about 900 kms of borders in J&K categorized as Line of Control (LOC) and Actual Ground Position Line (AGPL) which divides the State, held of India and Pakistan – further helps it to threaten the security of the State.[21]

The borders have a variety of problems and issues and need a comprehensive focus for durable settlement. At many places, the social contours of the border are mercilessly cut across and divided into various ethnic groups. In time of conflict in neighbouring countries this becomes a source of acute tension.

---

19 Supra note 17 at pp76-78.

20 Surinder Singh (1999), *Evolution and Growth of Border Security force of India*, Jammu, p.31.

21 N.S Jamwal, 'Terrorists' Modus Operandi in Jammu and Kashmir', Strategic Analysis, Vol.XXVII, (2003), pp. 382-402.

The Pakistan sponsored border terrorism in Punjab remained active for over a decade broadly, from 1980- 1990. The conflict was caused due to a number of reasons ranging from the future of Chandigarh, territorial adjustments with neighbouring States, river water allocations, protection as well as promotion of Sikhism, reducing landholdings over the past few decades which resulted in the progeny of marginal farmers being converted into owners of economically unviable land holdings, and unemployment reaching a new peak in the early 1980s, which gave rise to disgruntled youth who took to militancy. During the period when militancy was at its peak, about 15,000 people died in the militant attacks. Pakistan exploited the dissatisfaction borne out in the State and gave covert and overt assistance for their struggle. External support also came from influential/ prosperous members of the community who resided abroad.[22]

It is true that turbulence in Punjab and Kashmir was a consequence of Indian economic, social and political failures but Pakistan had no right to deliberately fish in troubled waters to exacerbate conditions. Further Pakistan's terrorists intrusion on Indian land was not only directed against India but had tentacles in several Islamic countries like Algeria, Egypt, Tajikistan and even Xinjiang province of China, which continues to witness terrorist violence from Islamic cadres trained in Pakistan. There was an active ISI programme of using the institution and infrastructure created for operations against the Soviets in Afghanistan to devise Islamist violence in Kashmir and terrorism in Punjab. Specialist training was imparted by supervision specialists from Sudan, Libya, Iran and Pakistan. The weapons and materials provided to militants operating in Kashmir were identical to those provided by the ISI to *Mujahideen* in Afghanistan.[23]

Indo-Pakistan relations are characterized by existence of number of bilateral disputes some of them rooted in historical past such as Kashmir issue, others in current dynamics of bilateral issues viz. Baglihar Dam dispute. Pakistan continues to occupy illegally large areas of Kashmir and lays claim over whole State of Jammu and Kashmir. Both countries have sections at both the ends of the borders which are yet to be settled.

The situation in the State of J&K has almost always been more

---

22 N.S Jamwal, 'Counter Terrorism Strategy', Strategic Analysis, Vol.XXVII, (2003), pp. 56-78.

23 A Congressional Report to the US House of Representative by the Task Force of the Republican Research Committee presented in February 1993 available at http// www. usiofindia.org/html (Visited on July 29,2006)

vulnerable than that of any other State in the country. This is the only State which Pakistan has never accepted to be a part of India. It is the only Muslim majority State of India which Pakistan believes should have belonged to it like all to her Muslim majority parts of the subcontinent.[24] Although the dispute originated in 1947 along with many other complex problems that were the product of hasty and badly planned partition, Kashmir dispute is perhaps one of the very few and the most important dispute that has survived over the years in somewhat original form. While India is known to have made innumerable efforts to burry the issue, the efforts for a peaceful and lasting solution of the dispute is still carried out by the Pakistanis.[25] Compared to the Pakistanis, the Kashmiris, being disappointed by the world community's apathetic attitude has opted, in recent years, for more violent course of action. Pakistan claims that her stand on Kashmir is not motivated by any considerations of territorial ambition, and that she asked for nothing more than the extension to Kashmir of the principle that determined the division of the rest of the subcontinent, the said principle requiring that contiguous Muslim majority areas should be separated from contiguous non- Muslim majority areas to form the two dominions, Pakistan and India respectively. Pakistan demands that India should permit the people of Kashmir to decide their future through an internationally supervised plebiscite. While recognizing that vast majority of the Kashmiri people are the followers of Islam, India justifies her possession of Kashmir on the basis of the Maharaja's[26] instrument of

---

24 Balraj Puri, 'Security Situation in Jammu and Kashmir', Strategic Analysis, (July-September, 2003), p.32.

25 Pervaiz Iqbal Cheema, 'Assessing the Role of Confidence Building Measures in the India Pakistan Tangle' available at http://www.ipripak.org/IPRI(Islamabad Policy Research Institute), (Last modified June 30, 2004)

26 Like India, the State of Jammu and Kashmir also becomes independent on August 15, 1947. Maharaja Hari Singh, then ruler of Jammu and Kashmir, initially did not like to become part of India and Pakistan. He thought of independence. He offered to sign a Stand Still Agreement with both India and Pakistan aimed at continuing the existing relationship pending his final decision regarding the future of the State. However for variety of reasons the Stand Still Agreement was not signed between Kashmir and India. When the people of the State saw that independence has come in India, they raised their heads and demanded the establishment of a responsible government. In the absence of a formal agreement between India and Maharaja, Pakistan interpreted it to mean other that Kashmir would ultimately become part of Pakistan. The people of the State were tired of uncertainty and even there occurred the Poonch Revolt against the authority of Maharaja. The Maharaja now realized that he could no longer hold the Kashmiri people in subjugation through reliance on his army and police. On October 20, 1947 several thousand tribesmen supported by Pakistani army attacked the frontiers

accession, the legality and validity of which cannot be questioned, at least of all by Pakistan.

As regards India's undertaking to ascertain the Kashmir through a plebiscite, India claims that she promised to do so long before the dispute was referred to the UN Security Council. Hence, it was a promise to the people of J&K and not to Pakistan or the UN and as such it does not involve any international commitment as far as the validity of accession is concerned. Still although India was prepared to fulfill her promise to the people of Kashmir, the holding of a plebiscite was constantly obstructed by Pakistan's refusal to withdraw her troops from such parts of the state which were under her illegal occupation. In these circumstances, India had no alternative but to let the Kashmiri decide their future through a duly elected representative body. The Constituent assembly, having meeting on 17 November, 1956, confirmed the State's permanent accession to India. This being its people's voluntary verdict, Kashmir's accession to India is therefore final, complete, perfect and irrevocable[27] Pakistan of course does not accept the arguments advanced by India, and her attitude thereon is generally shared by most other members of the UN.

Due to India Pakistan conflict on Kashmir, the subcontinent has experienced four wars and continues to face proxy war, low intensity conflict and limited war, Pakistan having failed to grab Kashmir despite fighting wars resorted to the strategy of terrorism. Not only have the conventional wars proved quite expensive but also the chances of achieving political objectives through wars have diminished due to the development of nuclear weapons and the possible international reaction. The three wars between India and Pakistan, although ended without settlement of dispute, proved Indian conventional superiority which convinced Pakistan that it could never achieve its mission in Kashmir through conventional warfare. Since conventional war has lost its utility as a tool of foreign policy, nations, particularly military weaker nations, try other means to achieve their objectives. Therefore, Jay Millan defined "Terrorism" as a substitute

---

of the State. The riders were fast approaching Srinagar. The Maharaja was extremely nervous and he saw his dream of independence shattered. It was the only as a last resort then the Maharaja approached the Dominion of India to accept accession. In order to save his State from ruin, the Maharaja of the State decided to accede to Indian Union and an instrument of accession was signed by him on October 26, 1947, as a result of this, the State of Jammu and Kashmir become part of Indian Union.

27   Balraj Puri, 'Security Situation in Jammu and Kashmir', Startegic Analysis, (July-September, 2003), p.25.

of overt warfare. According to him when diplomats fail, soldier take over, when soldier fail, terrorists take over.[28] This view is quite suitably applicable in case of Pakistan's strategy in Kashmir.

Pakistan continues to illegally occupy Kashmir and lays its claim over the whole State of J&K and hence does not recognize even the international border in the Jammu sector. Unsolved border disputed with Pakistan in the area of Sir Creek in Gujarat, the LOC in J&K, AGPL portion in Siachen are the outstanding issues between India and Pakistan on boundary demarcations.[29]

Pakistan supported terrorism across the border in Kashmir has become more intensified in the post- cold war scenario. Pakistan has been supplying arms to terrorists in Kashmir and continued to do so even after the end of cold war. Pakistan having won the convert war against the Soviets in Afghanistan feels emboldened that if it could win against a super power, terrorism can certainly be a successful strategy against a lesser powerful country like India. Pakistan is in a position to supply a large member of armed militants and insurgents in Kashmir because it is still in possession of weapons supplied by US had supplied arms, ammunitions and equipment worth millions of dollars to Pakistan. About ten thousands of tones of small arms were supplied to Pakistan by America, China, Saudi Arabia, Egypt, Israel, Turkey and Britain.[30]Portable weapons like automatic rifles, Kalashnikov with rate of fire of 600 rounds per minute, were of highly accurate and lethal nature. It is estimated that at least 4000 Kalashnikov assault rifles had been supplied to the Inter Service Intelligence and about 900 stinger shoulder fired surface to air missile to the Afghan *Mujahideen* according to the Auditor- General of Pakistan, Rs. 94.90 million was spent by the ISI Director- General in February 1993 for purchase of arms and ammunitions. India has been affected mostly by these developments because Pakistan and Afghanistan became the centre of gravity for terrorism.[31]

Pakistan is not using terrorism as a last resort but as a shortcut to

---

28 Jay Millan, "Terrorism as a Military Weapon", (January- February, 1999), 28 *Air University Review54.*

29 N.S Jamwal, 'Management of Land Borders', Strategic Analysis, (2002), p.26.

30 Ibid

31 P.R. Chari (1999), *Perspectives on National Security in South Asia,* New Delhi, p.161. And also available at http://www.mcpr-bhu.com/jindal.htm (Visited at July28, 2004)

attain strategic and political objectives. Terrorism in Kashmir through initially(1989) supported by some disgruntled youth, can be defined as cross border or international terrorism because it is sustained only with external financial support, cross border training campus and sanctuaries. National phenomenon, using mercenaries, organised crime cartels, sophisticated weaponry and into various countries. They operate in an international organised structure which is spread all over the world. Cross border terrorism has exacerbated due to one nation's terrorist groups not recognizing the boundaries.[32]These terrorist groups try to acquire the legitimacy for religion or ethnic identity. Pakistan tried to project its terrorism as the Kashmiris fight for the right of self determination and uses religious ideological doctrines like '*Jihad*' by *Jihadis*[33]to promote terrorism in Kashmir. Thus Pakistan sponsored terrorism in Kashmir is politically motivated and built around religious fundamentalism. Pakistan has been using Islam as a tool of its domestic and foreign policy since its creation. It justifies its claim on Kashmir on the basis of the two nation theory and has been using religious ideology as the basis of terrorism in Kashmir.

The main objective of Pakistan's sponsored terrorism across the border in Kashmir is to use violence to affect the psychology of India so that it gets exhausted and surrenders. Pakistan sponsored terrorism is a well – planned strategy. They specifically target political leaders of institutions to malign the creditability of a government. The main aim of Pakistan's proxy war against India is to ensure that the Indian Army and central paramilitary forces remain engaged in counter insurgency and internal security operations in Kashmir. In religious terrorism, though the target is the State, the victims are civilian. Jihad has killed more than 100000 people in Kabul and more than 10000 in Kashmir. The objective is to bleed India by thousands cuts to destabilize and dismember it. [34]

---

32 Ibid.

33 Jihadis – The concept of jihadis have been debated, over the centuries by a number of Islamic theologians. Some of the Sufi thinkers have emphasized the importance of a higher Jihad against one's lust, but in the perception of the militants groups it is incumbent on every Muslim to fight war against the infidels and the unbelievers. Unlike other terrorists their goals are definable in distinct political terms; the goals of the jihadis are no less than to establish "Islam" over the globe and especially to liberate regions which were once ruled by Muslims.

34 Tara Katha, 'Countering Transnational Terrorism', Strategic Analysis, Vol. XXIII, (February, 2000), p.4.

Pakistan resorted to the strategy of cross border terrorism because it appeared to be a more cost–effective option. It was a low–cost option that has greater chances of success. It also does not involve the risk of conventional was as it is fought on the victim's territory. It appears that due to these advantages the option of proxy war through terrorism has increasingly replaced the option of conventional war in South Asia. It enables Pakistan to keep the conflict at low costs, less intense and at low level to avoid the possibility of full-fledged conventional war. Lieutenant General Chandra Shekhar, Vice Chief of Army staff, explained that proxy war is a low- cost and no- case option but best suited to promote Pakistan's geo political, diplomatic and military interest, not only to wrest Kashmir but also to gain forward strategic depth.[35] Pakistan's main objective is to keep India involved in protracted 'proxy war' to degrade India's conventional superiority through a process of strategic fatigue.

In order to understand the rationale behind cross border terrorism in J&K and other parts of India, reference of some active terrorist organisations is necessary. There are various terrorist organisations operating in State of J&K, having their own objectives. This trend is of great concern to humanity in its fight against terrorism.[36] Some of the organisations which are actively working in Kashmir are:

- Jammu & Kashmir Liberation Front (JKLF): Pro–independence Kashmir group mainly comprising of the local Kashmiri Muslims. Set up in 1960 by Maqbool Bhatt and Ammanullah Khan [now in Pakistan Occupied Kashmir (POK)]. Revived in the late 1980s. Presently led by Yassen Malik. Though a moderate group and no more an active militant outfit.

- Al-Umar Mujahideen: Deadly group of downtown, Srinagar. Founded by Mustag Zargar. Struggling to gain prominence.

- Al-Jihad: Emerged in 1991. Most active in South Kashmir. Non-existent.

- Al-Barq: Founded in 1994 and seen as the armed wing of Peoples Conference. Founded by Abdul Ghani Lone. Non Existent. (Mr. Lone was killed in Srinagar on May 21, 2002)

---

35 Ibid.

36 Amitabh Matto (ed.) (2007), *India and Pakistan*, Jammu.

- Harkat-ul-Mujahideen: Pan-Islamic group formed in 1993. This is also known as Harkut-ul-Ansar and Al Faran. Very active and ruthless.

- Pan–Islamic Group: Formed in 1994 operates from Pakistan. Very active and ruthless. Introduced '*fidayeen*' (suicide attacks).

- Al Badr: Formed in 1999 and mainly composed of foreign mercenaries. Operates from border areas under the direct control of Inter Services Intelligence.

- Hajib-ul-Mujahideen: A militant group of ethnic Kashmiris. Wants an honourable settlement of the Kashmir issue.

- Jaish-e-Mohammed: Pan- Islamic group formed in Jan 2000 by Maulana Massod Azar (Killed on 28 March 2001). Gets lavish patronage of the ISI and notorious for human bombs.

Among these organisations, two important organisations, Harkut-ul Mujahideen and Lashkar-e-Tayeba (LET) are provided for waging an irrational war called as Jihad against thousands of innocent Kashmiris. Earlier known as the Harkat-ul-Ansari, Harkat-ul-Mujahideen was designated has a Foreign Terrorist Organisations (FTO) by the US government in October 1997. This is an Islamic militant group based in Pakistan operates primarily in Kashmir. Its leader Fazlur Rehman Khalii has been linked to Bin Laden and signed his '*Fatwa*' in February 1998 calling for attacks on US and Western interests. Harkut-ul-Mujahideen operates terrorist training camps in eastern Afghanistan and suffered causalities in the US. Missile strikes on Bin Laden associated training camps in Kowst in August 1998. Fazulur Rehman Khalil subsequently said that his organisation would take a revenge on US. It conducted a number of operations against Indian troops and civilian targets in Kashmir and is linked to the Kashmir militant group. Al- Farhan that killed and kidnapped five western tourists in Kashmir in July 1995; one was killed in August 1995, and the other four reportedly were killed in December of the same year.[37] Maulana Masood Azhar, organisation ideologue freed in January by India in return for hostages on a hijacked Indian Airlines plane, has vowed to recruit half a million men to fight Indian rule in Kashmir," we are going

---

37   Editorial column, 'Terrorism – A Great Menace', *The Times of India,* March 27, 2006, p.5.

to organise a 500,000 Mujahideen force to fight against Indians", Masood Azhar told thousands of his supporters.[38] Azhar said the force would be recruited from all over Pakistan. The parent organisation of Lashker-e-Tayeba is Markaz Ad- Da'wah Wal Irshad which claims to be committed to Islamic education and jihad. It also claims that thousand of its militants are fighting the Indian security forces and 600 have been killed during encounters with the security forces. The head of the Lashkar, the so called Ameer Markaz is Hafiz Mohammad Saeed. At a congregation in Muridke near Lahore, Lashkar leaders spewed venom against India and the US. For instance, "addressing the annual congregation one of the leaders said that "the next target is New Delhi". Lashkar is probably the strongest *jihadi* organisation today. As with all such organisation, it is supported by various agencies within Pakistan.[39]

According to Indian Intelligence agencies, terrorist training camps in Pakistan training North- West insurgents get patronage and protection from both Pakistan and Afghanistan. The crisis situation in Kargil[40], was managed by India's restraint and American diplomacy, which led to cease fire and status quo in Kashmir, Pakistan however continues its policy of cross border terrorism in Kashmir post Kargil, the ISI is trying to expand its network to execute its network to execute its plans. During the war, a

---

38   Editorial column, 'Fight to Continue' *The Tribune,* available at www.http://www. tribuneindia.com/- (Last modified on January 11, 2000).

39   Ibid

40   Pakistan intrusion in Kargil was a desperate attempt on the part of it to capture Kashmir in the year 1999 in which Pakistan failed in its attempt. In mid 1999, Islamic fighters from Pakistani in Kashmir infiltrated and took control of the Kargil range overlooking the highway in Indian Kashmir connecting Srinagar to Kargil and Leh in the east. Their objective was to severe the main Srinagar- Leh road which runs north south in Indian Kashmir. Had they succeeded, they could have effectively cut the Indians held Kashmir in two, since south of this highway, the inhospitable Zanskar range prevents any communication between Kashmir proper and Ladakh. Pakistanibacked forces made great gains initially. However, India deployed a massive force, to dislodge the infiltrators. At the same time, fears of the Kargil war turning into a nuclear war, provoked the U.S president Bill Clinton to pressure Pakistan to retreat. The conflict ended with the withdrawl of Pakistani backed forces, with some irregular allegedly being left stranded in the Kargil Peaks, and India reclaiming control of the peaks which they now patrol and monitor at considerable cost. It was claimed that Kargil infilteration was ordered by the Pakistani Army without clearance of the civilian government. Prime minister Sharif was blamed by the Army for forcing them to withdraw though the withdrawl order was also seen as a escaperoute for the military which was ill- equipped to deal with the operation's political fallout and this was a significant factor in the overthrow of the civilian government by the Army Chief, General Pervez Musharraff, who is actually responsible for Kargil operation.

large number of Pakistani trained militants and agents were reported to have been pushed into the Indian side of the LOC. Pakistan continued to support Taliban in Afghanistan due to vested interests. Kashmir is the prime mover behind Pakistan's policy towards Afghanistan. On October 12, 1999, Musharraf staged a coup against Nawaz Shariff because the latter was portrayed as having betrayed the cause of Islamic Jihad in Kashmir. The military coup after Pakistan's withdrawal from Kargil suggests that Pakistan's army and religious leaders do not want Indo- Pakistan relations to normalize. Pakistan's army has flourished on an anti India stand. It intends to continue during so otherwise it might loose the power vantage it enjoys in Pakistan. In other words, the army does not want the political solution of the Kashmir problem.[41]

Pakistan continues its strategy of cross border terrorism as it neither leads to conventional war nor an escalation of the situation nor yet keeps India constantly engaged in interval squabbles that impact its socio-economic and political conditions. Clearly cross border terrorism is and effective strategy that gives an added advantage to the sponsoring country by giving it an option of denying its role if international reaction becomes too hot for it to bear; in order to camouflage its real intent, Pakistan is using the plea of supporting Kashmir's cause for self determination and trying to Malign India's image by projecting the Indian Army's actions as violation of human rights in Kashmir.[42]By resorting to terrorism under the grab of Kashmir's movement of self determination, Pakistan has sought to internationalize the issue to get it resolved in its own favour.

Pakistan has been indulging in the nefarious games of cross border terrorism against India from its inception by exploiting the sensitivities of India's religious and cultural communities. There are number of training camps in POK in which terrorists are trained and sent inside J&K. Direct accessibility of the borders allows insurgents groups tactical flexibility. Some technological developments enabling quick passage of info, transfer funds, underworld criminal gang's links with terrorist groups have

---

41 R.S, Siwach, 'U.S Strategy to Counter Global Terrorism', Mainstream, (December 6, 2003).

42 Nirmal Jindal, 'Kashmir Issue in Nucleotides South Asia', Foreign Affairs, (January-February, 2005), p.183. and also by Sanajai Singh, 'Strategic Perspectives: Border Management of Western Borders of India' available at http://www.usiofindia.org/pers/.htm (Visited on July28, 2005).

changed the focus and tenor of border security.[43] It is also worthwhile to mention that terrorists and subversive elements are using soft borders of India touching countries like Nepal and Bangladesh to enter India.

Pakistan has used covert action in the guise of terrorism as an instrument of State policy against India. It has recruited, trained, financed, armed and infiltered terrorists in India and has provided sanctuary to anti- Indian elements. Despite global outcry against terrorism and not withstanding a string of confidence building measures adopted by two governments, Pakistan has not yet dismantled the terror infrastructure in the territory under its control. This infrastructure is continued to be used by Pak- ISI to recruit, train and finance terrorists and infiltrate them into India. Strategies of ISI are to intensify proxy war operations, espionage, destabilising the economy of the country by circulation of fake currency notes and raising the pitch of high voltage disinformation campaign to discredit India's security forces for alleged violation of human rights.[44]

North–East India is in a strategically vulnerable geographical situation and is surrounded by countries like China, Myanmar, Nepal, Bhutan and Bangladesh from three sides. It is linked with the rest of the country by a narrow corridor (20 km wide Siliguri neck). North-East India is anthropologically a paradise, which is inhabited by races of Mangoloids stock, besides Indo- Aryan groups. Barring the Khasis and Jaintias who belong to the Austric Linguistic group (now branded as Mankhmer cultural groups of Myanmar), almost all hill tribes belong to the Tibetan – Chinese linguistic family and Tibeto- Burman sub- family. The non- Aryan population, being prominent in this region, shelter more than 125 major groups each having distinct cultural traits. In the case of the North- East, terrorism arises from a strong feeling of alienation from the mainstream of northern India plus a conviction, that the central government should be more active in north- eastern affairs. Nagas argue that **Clause 9** of the **Hydari Agreement** promised them the option of freedom. Essentially, their economic backwardness stems from the unexploited natural resources, inadequate infrastructure development, rampant corruption and the strong nexus among politicians, contractors and insurgents in the region. Economic hardship due to poor and underdeveloped agriculture, alarming mass, unemployment problem, rampant corruption, lack of educational and medical facilities, exorbitant prices and shortage of essential commodities

---

43 Ibid.

44 P.S Bhatnagar, 'Managing Borders of the Country', *Sainik Samachar*, 2008.

in the far flung areas of the North – East forced the promising youth to turn to extremist activities.[45] The employment situation lent an edge to the separatist tendency by creating numerous insurgents outfits in all the States of the North- East. In the case of Assam and Tripura, unabated infiltration of Bangladesh nationals into these two States with the ulterior motive of upsetting the demographic balance first, and then swallowing up big chunks of territory has the blessings of Dhaka.[46] According to the group of Ministers Report of February 2001, "illegal migration from across the borders has continued for over five decades, today, we have 15 million Bangladeshis, which has implications to national security."[47]

Indo-Bangladesh Border

India shares a long boundary with Bangladesh (earlier East Pakistan). The Indo- Bangladesh border, which came into existence after India's partition in 1947, gave rise to many questions as to the interpretation and implementation of the boundary so drawn. Millions of Bengalis in erstwhile East Pakistan fled across the borders to India in 1971 to escape the atrocities of an invading Pakistan Army.[48] Since the mid 1990s *Chakmas* from the *Chittagong hill* tracks have south asylum across the border to avoid genocide by Bangladesh security forces.[49]

Some of the indications of illegal immigrants available from the Indian census of 1981 are that early 40 lakhs people originally from Bangladesh, including 20 lakhs in Assam, are in India. Since the change of regime in 2001, Bangladesh National Party Government came to power with the support of fundamentalist parties like Jamait – e- Islami and Islamic Oikya Jote which have an anti- India agenda.[50] There are about 127 training camps sponsored by ISI functioning in Bangladesh under the patronage of Jaimait -e- Islami, Harkut-ul-jamait-e-islami, and Islamic Morcha. These training camps co-ordinates with the activities of Lashkar-e-tayeba, Jaish-e-Mohammad and Al-Qaida. These insurgents target trunk

---

45 N.S Jamwal, 'Counter Terrorism Strategy', Strategic Analysis, Vol.XXVII, (2003), pp.56-78.

46 Ibid.

47 Ibid.

48 N.S Jamwal, 'Border management: Dilemma of Guarding the India- Bangladesh Border', Strategic Analysis, (January1, 2004) available at http://www.idsa.in/ Publications/strategic-analysis/2004/jan/jamwal/-(Last viewed at April 30, 2009).

49 Ibid.

50 Ibid

routes, railway tracks, bridges, telephone exchanges, power stations etc. Safe heavens have been offered to insurgents in lieu of an assurance that no harm is to be caused to Bangladeshis in India.[51] Bangladesh has been used by insurgent groups in the north east like United Liberation Front of Assam and Nationalist Socialist Council of Nagaland, who crossed the border and started getting training in Bangladesh from 1992 onwards.[52]

One of the most serious and long standing problems is illegal migration of Bangladeshi nationals to India. Even prior to partition, a substantial number of immigrant's cultivators, primarily Muslims, came into Assam from Mymensingh district in the 1930s and 1940s. Another main problem across the border is atrocities on the Hindu minority in Bangladesh. These atrocities forced Hindu families to migrate to India in waves since the creation of East Pakistan. There is urgent need to take action to protect the country's religious minorities from terrorist attacks and harassment. The atrocities committed against nearly 30 million minorities including about 20 million Hindus. The atrocities have resulted in the decline of the Hindu population from 24 percent in 1947 to 10 percent as of now.[53] An analysis of population growth of Hindus in Bangladesh reveals that the decadal growth rate has been 3.1 percent for 1974, 9.3 percent for 1981 and 5.8 percent in 1991, which is far below average 24 percent growth rate of Hindus in the subcontinent. If this (24 percent) decadal growth rate is to be applied in case of Bangladeshis, the Hindu population should have been approximately 14.7 million while it is 10.5 million as per the census. Obviously, these have illegally crossed through the porous borders and settled in India.[54]

According to Indian intelligence agencies, terrorist training camps in Bangladesh training North- East insurgents get patronage and protection from the Bangladesh Army. Most of the important camps are in *Dhaka, Chittagong, Sylet, Habiganj, Mymensingh, Rangamati, Khagrachari, Bandarban, Sherpur, Moulvi Bazar, Netrakona* and *Sunamganj* districts. *Cox bazaar* in *Chittagong* district is used for the trans- shipment of

---

51 Madhav Godbole, 'Management of India's International Borders: Some Challenges ahead', Economic and Political Weekly, (December 1, 2001), p.36.

52 N.S Jamwal, 'Border management: Dilemma of Guarding the India- Bangladesh Border', Strategic Analysis, (January 1, 2004) available at http://www.idsa.in/ Publications/strategic-analysis/2004/jan/jamwal- (Last viewed at April 30, 2009).

53 Ibid.

54 Ibid.

weapons and explosives. Intelligence sources put the figure of terrorist training camps in Bangladesh as 130 (43 of them are for the National Liberation Front of Tripura- NLFT). There are several 'joint camps' that involve the NSCN (IM), NSCN (Khaplang), United Liberation Front of Assam (ULFA), National Democratic Front of Bodoland (NDFB), NLFT, All- Tripura Tiger Force (ATTF), People's Liberation Army (PLA) and United National Liberation Front (UNLF), for example, ATTF and ULFA cadres operate from camps in Khagrachari and Satchari in Habiganj districts. An NDFB-NSCN (I-M) training centre exists at Alikadam in Bandarban district. While ULFA has 24 camps, mostly in Dhaka, Sylhet, Khagrachari, Maulavi Bazar and the Chittagong Hill Tracts (CHT), the NLFT's camps are located mostly in CHT and Khagrachari. The ATTF is active in Maulvi Bazar, Habiganj and Comilla. The evidence is based on electronic and technical intelligence.[55]

The Indo- Bangladesh border is a long one and heavily inhabited and the inhabitants have a common history of growth, culture, language and rich heritage. Today, most of the problems are the manifestation of this fact. The problem of border management on this border is not just the one of securing the borders but of doing so without causing harm to the economic interest of the people, long dependent on mutual trade and various other forms of interdependence. Being on the extreme corner of the country, the border areas have remained underdeveloped and were economically and politically ignored for a long time. The negligence by the mainland forced the people of the border area to indulge in and depend on the traditional systems for their survival and this gave rise to cross border movements.

Indo-China Border

India and China are neighbours and their borders are common for thousands of kilometers. India has been a great supporter of the Chinese Revolution since long. When India became independent two years before China, India had developed very good relations with China. But unfortunately there was Indo- China war in the year 1962 for the border disputes. This made the relations between India and China bitter. The Chinese leadership tried to exploit the Indo- Pakistan and Indo- Nepal lack of cordiality to its advantage and gave assistance to Pakistan even in the manufacturing of nuclear bomb and tried to do harm to the Indian interests. But the new

---

55 Chandan Nandy, 'Delhi Ready with Dhaka: Terror Report', *The Hindustan Times*, December 1, 2002.

Chinese leadership which has emerged in the post Mao period has been quite pragmatic and has kept the border dispute in the background and is making sincere efforts to improve Indo- China relations.

In the 1990s Sino- Indian relations were strained mainly due to the territorial issue and the Chinese annexation of Tibet. Pakistan had been successful in drawing China closer which multiplied India's problems. The military ties between China and Pakistan have progressed since India was targeted as the common enemy. With the end of the Cold war, China is accommodating to the changes in the international sphere. Along with other factors its aspirations for regional and global supremacy have facilitated a conciliatory approach in its relationship with the Asian countries including India. But the detonation of the nuclear device by India in 1998 and the 'China threat' resulted in strong reactions in China, which was evident from the way it mobilized world opinion against India's nuclear weapon status. Inherent in China's anxiety is the military capability of India which it perceives to be an attempt to catch up with China and upset the strategic balance in the region. Line of Actual Control continued to be the de fact international boundary for both the countries though till 1970 China gained some Indian territory and claimed large tracts of Indian Territory, which was also claimed by India. The disputed areas in the India- China border are about 125,000 sq,km out of which 90,000 is in the eastern sector, 2000 in the middle sector and 33000 in the western sector. In 1993 when the Peace and Tranquility Agreement was signed, this was helpful towards reaching a solution to the Sino- Indian border dispute.[56] Following the agreement, regular meetings were held between the soldiers on both sides, a hotline link between the two countries was set up, an agreement to maintain peace and security on both sides of the Line of Actual Control (LAC) was signed. An accord was signed for the partial demilitarization of the disputed border of 4500 km. both the countries endorsed that neither India nor China "shall use force against the other by any means and seek unilateral military support".[57] The agreement has its significance in forging a new relationship between both the countries; a 'constructive co-operation' though it does it does not indicate total dispersal of troops from the border or a constructive discussion on ending the dispute, which is the core to improve relationship between both the countries.

---

56 Snehalata Panda, 'Sino Indian Relationship in a New Perspective', Strategic Analysis, Vol.XXVII, (January- March, 2003), p.1.

57 Ibid.

China's military and economic support to Pakistan an Myanmar in the form of nuclear and military assistance, development of airfields, roads and equipping the armies with Chinese – made weaponry send across the borders are issues which are of great concern to India's national security and border management.

Indo-Nepal Border

Like most of the countries of the world, the existence of Nepal had been recognized even before the international boundaries had been fully and finally established. Mention of Nepal is found in the ancient history of both China and India. Nepal- India boundary has a recent origin and its present boundary demarcation and delimitation took place after the Anglo-Nepal war of 1814- 16. Nepal-India border is unique in the world in the sense that people of both the countries can cross it from any point, despite the existence of border check posts at several locations. The number of check posts at several locations. The number of check posts meant for carrying out bilateral trade is 22. However, only at six transit points out of them, the movement was permitted to nationals of third countries, who require entry and exit visa to cross the border.[58] As the whole length of the border except police does not patrol and check the posts or paramilitary or military forces of either country, illegal movements of the goods and people is a common feature on both sides of the India- Nepal border.

There has not been any formal treaty between Nepal and India on Nepal- Sikkim boundary after the independence of India, and even after the annexation of Sikkim with India in 1975. It is to be noted that Nepal has not yet formally recognized the annexation of Sikkim by India. And, at the same time, India has not sought recognition from Nepal.[59]

There is no denying of the fact that it is not unusual from the practical point of view to have illegal smuggling of goods, trafficking of girls to brothel in Indian cities, trafficking in narcotic drugs, arms and ammunition and movement of criminals and terrorist across the border. The most serious adverse impact of open and uncontrolled Nepal- India border has been in the form of growing and anti- social and lawless activities.

---

58   Vidya Bir Singh Kansakar, 'Nepal India Open Border: Prospects, Problems and Challenges', available at http://www.nepaldemocracy.org/documents/treaties_ agreements/html (Last viewed on March 28, 2006).

59   Ashok K.Mahata (2005), *Problem of Terrorism and Other Illegal activities on Indo-Nepal Border: Issues in effective Border Management*, Delhi, pp.1-14.

The ever increasing crimes along the border have been a major concern for both the governments since early nineteenth century. However, the policy of open border has rather enhanced such activities. The unrestricted movement across the border has indeed been responsible for all sorts of criminal, anti- social and illegal activities such as robbery, theft, murder, smuggling of goods to evade custom duties, narcotic drugs trafficking, trafficking of girls, arms smuggling of archaeological arts and artic rafts and manuscript, kidnapping for ransoms, etc. since 1980s, Nepal-India border has developed into a thorough passage for the cross border movement of terrorists. In view of growing terrorism in Uttar Pradesh-Tarai border in Nepal, there is a demand for the sealing of the Nepal India border. When Nepali political leaders and intellectuals raised their voice for controlling and regulating the movement of people across the border, their counterparts in India termed the Nepalese concern as an anti- Indian stand. In recent years, there has been sudden spurt in crimes such as theft, robbery, kidnapping and murder on both sides of the border as well as increase in terrorist activities on the Indian side. Open border has provided safe passage to criminals and terrorists. It has been alleged that criminal elements have been harbored and provided protection by the political leaders and influential persons on either side of the border. Apart from tampering with the Nepal India border by the local people in the Indian side, the Indian government itself has been involved in violating the norms of international boundary.[60]

Indo-Bhutan Border

Nepal and Bhutan are separated by a wide stretch of Indian Territory, Darjeeling district of West Bengal State and Sikkim State. Being a landlocked, mountainous country, Bhutan's trade routes and access to the sea pass through India and it is thus largely dependent on the latter for its economic security. While Bhutan has diversified its political and economic relations and had attained a good level of socio- economic development, the reality of its position and shared borders with India means that destabilising elements from external sources continue to pose threats to its stability. These have been evident from the spillover effects of militancy from Assam, and of cross border economic migration driven by regional poverty.

---

60 Vidya Bir Singh Kansakar (2001), *Nepal India Open Border: Nature, Pattern and Socio- Cultural Implication,* Delhi, pp.1-14.

Bhutan and India have no open borders. In reality, the first place of asylum for the Bhutanese refugees is India. However, because of the open border between Nepal and India could easily enter into Nepal via Indian Territory. Under international convention, it is the responsibility of India to settle them in India by establishing refugees represents different Nepalese ethnic and caste groups, but it does not mean that they have directly migrated to Bhutan from Nepal. Lots of them have migrated from different parts of eastern and north eastern India as well. Nearly 100,000 Bhutanese refugees are resettled in the camps in Jhapa and Morang districts. Though they live in the closed camps with barbed wire fencing, their movements outside are not restricted, and they are also able to cross the barbed wire fencing easily. This has affected the natural, social and economic environment of the surrounding areas, because they are engaged in illegal cutting of trees in the government forests, are engaged in business and work as cheap labour thereby affecting the business and employment of the local community.[61] It is also alleged that a lot of Bhutanese refugees have been able to secure Nepalese citizenship through illegal means. Moreover, a lot of the Indians of Nepalese origins have also migrated to Bhutan, and naturally a large numbers of them must be Indians.[62]

India and Bhutan can be seen to be supportive of each other. While Bhutan has not always voted identically with India over every issue, thereby expressing its own choices, it has maintained a consistent pattern of support to India on many occasions and significant issues. To name a few, these include the vote on the Comprehensive Test Ban Treaty (CTBT), the establishment of Nuclear Weapons Free Zone in South Asia, India's aspirations to be a permanent member of the UN Security Council, India's candidature to various international bodies, negotiations in World Trade Organisation (WTO), and the importance of India in the success of South Asian Association of Regional Countries (SAARC).[63]

India and Bhutan share an extraordinary warm friendship, issues such as the state of relations with China continues to be a cause of some concern

61   Tashi Chodan, 'Indo – Bhutan Relations: Recent Trends', Paper presented at Regional Conference on Comprehensive Security in South Asia, Institute of Foreign Affairs, Kathmandu, Nepal available at http://www.himalaya.socanth.com.ac.uk/collections/journals/jbs/pdf (Last viewed at October 8, 2007).

62   Jayanta Kumar Ray (1997), *India- Nepal Cooperation: Broadening Measures*, Calcutta.

63   Permanand (2007), *The Politics of Bhutan*, Delhi.

to both the countries. Considering the importance of Bhutan's economic relations with India, the liberalization policies in India and its implications for Bhutan is an additional development to take into account. Recently, the illegal presence of militants using Bhutan as a base and hideout while rebelling against the Indian government resulted in the Bhutanese army taking military action to flush out the insurgents.[64]

Over the last decade or so, the illicit establishment of camps by the ULFA, NDFB and the Kamtapuri Liberation Organisation (KLO) militant outfits in the dense jungles of south–east Bhutan has been a matter of great concern and security threat for Bhutan.[65] In addition to hampering businesses and implementation of development activities in many parts of the country, the presence of these militants was a potential cause of affecting the friendly relations enjoyed by Bhutan and India. In consideration of the close ties between Bhutan and India, and recognizing that the militants (despite their actions) are nonetheless Indian citizens from the neighbouring States of Assam and West Bengal, the Bhutanese government repeatedly urged the militants to leave the country peacefully. But in spite of the Bhutanese government having spent almost six to seven years to find a peaceful solution to the problem, it was apparent by the last months of 2003 that the militants had no real intention of leaving Bhutan until their own objectives had been fulfilled. In December 2003, with the talks with the ULFA and NDFB having failed, and the KLO not even responding, the Bhutanese government's repeated attempts at a peaceful solution came to an end. On the morning of 15 December 2003, the Bhutanese army finally launched military operations to flush out the militants. Even as 67 security forces took over all thirty of the militant's camps into the second day of offensive, the combing process and the implications of the operations have brought forth the reality, that long spell of peace and tranquility that has been the proud inheritance of the present Bhutanese generation can no longer betaken for granted. Although the operation was considered successful, Bhutan has come into realize the need to be wary of possible repercussions following such action.[66] Having

---

64 Supra note 61.

65 The ULFA, fighting for the independence of Assam, NDFB, fighting for an independent State of Bodoland, and KLO, fighting for an independent State of Kamtapur had an estimated 1560 militants in 13 camps, 740 militants in 12 camps, and 430 militants in 5 camps respectively, as reported by Bhutan's Home Minister to the 81 session of the National Assembly prior to the launch of military operations in December 2003.

66 Manorma Kohli (2003), *From Dependency to Independence- A Study of Indo- Bhutan*

long kept the military option at bay in consideration of possible retaliation against Bhutanese from the militants as well as their relative's supporters from Assam, Bhutanese have recently had to be much more cautious than usual while traveling through Indian Territory.

Indo-Myanmar Border

Myanmar shares common borders with five countries: Bangladesh 193 km, China 2,185 km, India 1,463 km, Laos 235 km, and Thailand 1,800 km. India dominates Myanmar's western borders. Its 1930 km long coastline dominates the eastern arch of the Bay of Bengal, leaning on to the Malacca Strait. Thus Myanmar provides China the shortest land and sea access to South Asia, just as it provides convenient external land and sea communication options to India's landlocked northeastern States.[67] During the British colonial period Myanmar was administered as apart of British India till 1935. Till the end of the World War II, Indian traders, professionals and administrators had followed the British to work in Myanmar. The Indian freedom movement inspired the freedom struggle in Myanmar.

After liberalisation of Indian economy from 1992 onwards, India started looking at the lucrative markets of ASEAN region as part of the 'Look East Policy'. Following the admission of Myanmar as a member of Association of South East Asian Nations (ASEAN) in 1996 its importance in furthering India's trade with ASEAN increased. Development of the seven northeastern States has remained stagnant resulting in the alienation of sections of society and encouraging the growth of intruders across the border. Development of land and sea links for through Myanmar could end their isolation and wean them away from insurgency. Some of the insurgents groups like the National Socialist Council of Nagaland (NSCN) and ULFA operate from sanctuaries in Myanmar.[68] Better relations and coordination with the regime in Myanmar could put an end to the operation of such across the border activities. Myanmar's abundant reserves of natural gas waiting to be exploited, could help India in meeting its ever increasing demand for energy resources as the economy keeps growing at a fast pace.

Relations, New Delhi.

67   Editorial column, 'The National Socialist Council of Nagalim Rider to Ceasefire – Outfit Demands Delhi Commitment', *The Sanagai Express*, available at http:// www. nagalim.nl/news/00000673.htm, (Last Modified July 28, 8 ,2007).

68   Ibid.

Myanmar has a great deal of strategic significance for both India and China. Over the last two decades the Chinese has built very close economic, political, military and development relations with Myanmar. Myanmar's role in providing China a shorter access route to Indian Ocean and South Asia is going to be crucial in the strategic scene of South Asia. The Chinese have used the geophysical advantage they enjoy to gain access to Myanmar's mineral and natural gases resources. Following a policy of non- interference in internal affairs of the country, china has become the main supplier of arms of Myanmar. This has enabled the military junta in power to beat the western sanctions for democracy going under the leadership of Aung San Suu Kyi since 1990.[69]

India has embarked on a policy of building closer relations with Myanmar to counter the Chinese influence and facilitate the growth of trade and commerce with ASEAN as part of its look east policy. It is financing road and port development projects in Myanmar which would improve connectivity of India's north eastern States and help their development. India has also been selectively arming Myanmar despite the military regime's dismal record in human rights and governance. With a friendly regime in Myanmar, India hopes to evict Indian insurgents groups from sanctuaries in Myanmar. The military regime has welcomed these efforts to broaden its relationship with India and ASEAN countries in the interest of its own strategic security.[70]

India's current Myanmar policy appears to be largely copying the methods adopted by the Chinese. However, India as the largest functional democracy has a larger role to play in encouraging the restoration of democracy in Myanmar. Considering this, India's relationship should aim at building better economic and developmental relations with the military regime while exploring all avenues to help the military regime and the democratic forces evolve a viable solution to build a democratic society.

However, sacrificing India's fraternal relations with Myanmar's democratic forces by itself is unlikely to increase India's influence as the military regime is using the competing interests of India and China to its own advantage. Apart from the lead it has gained in Myanmar,

---

69 Col. R Hariharan (retd.), 'Emerging India- China- Myanmar Relations', Paper presented at the Chennai Centre for China Studies and the Department of International Relations of Stella Maris College, Chennai, on July 19, 2007 available at http:// www.nagalim. nl/news/00000673.htm, (Last Modified July 28,2007).

70 Ibid.

internationally China has greater economic, political and military clout than India in helping out the military regime. Given this advantage, India is unlikely to replace China's position as the most influential country in Myanmar under the military regime.

The military regime has been able to weather international sanctions for nearly 20 years. However, as Myanmar's ties with India and ASEAN countries grow and economic liberalisation touches the younger generation of military officers, we can expect a desire for change among armed forces. Similarly, the student movement holds the potential to take over a leadership role for political rapprochement with the military regime. When these developments come through perhaps there is scope for evolving a democratic society through different from the western concepts but meeting Myanmar's needs. India and China are indispensable in enabling this process that could stabilize the society in their strategic neighbourhood. Thus in the interest of India's strategic security, helping the creation of a stable and democratic regime in Myanmar should be India's long term policy rather than mere economic goals.

Right of Self Determination: A Cause of Cross Border Terrorism In India

Self determination is one of the most important as well as the most obscure principles of contemporary international law and practice. Basically, the right of self determination is the right of people to determine its own destiny, to choose particularly, its own political status and its own form of economic, cultural and social development. It is powerful and innovative concept, inspiring and threatening, frequently cited yet rarely defined. As a principle, it has achieved almost universal support, but this support rarely translates into encouragement from the international community for the break up of States. Infact, Statehood and self determination have an ambiguous relationship. On the one hand, self determination supports Statehood by giving a rationale for the acceptance of existing State boundaries and leadership.[71]

In the present day context, the meaning of the right of self determination has changed considerably. Now it is not just the right of a nation as a whole but an individual right also. Earlier it was used to apply only to the States under colonial rule but since it is a human right now, can be applied

---

71   Dr. Shalini Marwaha, "Delimitation of Right of Self determination", (Chandigarh, Punjab, 2007), *IJUILS* 107.

to the people of the States against their parent States. Now this right can be available to every human being who wants to revolt against their parent State. It is something against the norms that this principle being applied to every individual and not to a nation as a whole. The principle should not be applied to bring about the fragmentation of a country or its people.[72]

In its present state, self determination has been domesticated to serve the interests of ruling classes, it is a right which has been defended in lofty terms when it is politically advantageous and is rejected when it is not so. And these ambiguities in self determination have been often proved useful for harassing political support, both by State and indigenous, minority groups, seeking to increase their independence. Today, self determination means much more than the right to secede.

In contemporary South Asia, the claimants to self determination against the established States are many, but undoubtedly the most well known is the Kashmir dispute where the favourite argument put forward by Pakistan against India for Kashmir is the right of self determination. It has tried to elicit world support on the pleas that the people of J&K have been denied the right of self determination.

National Integrity

Pakistan sponsored terrorism targets India's democracy and secular character. The goal of Pakistan promoted border terrorism is to affect India's **national Integrity**. The secessionist movements in Kashmir and the North- East aimed at independence from the Indian union. Punjab militancy also aimed at disintegration from India and establishment of independent Khalistan.[73] So, it is not only J&K that Pakistan is aiming at, but the larger design of Pakistan is to ultimately work for the disintegration of India through promotion of terrorism. Towards this objective the ISI is fully supporting various secessionist groups within India and outside.

Political Independence

Terrorists operating against India are under the belief that by means of violence they can achieve their goals, and that no instrument of conduct of international relations like international organisations, international law, diplomacy or even war works as effectively as terrorism. India is targeted

---

72 Radhika Salathe, "Right of Self Determination of People in National Context: Kashmir Issue", (Chandigarh, Punjab, 2007), 1JUILS *99*.

73 Ibid.

for alleged violation of human rights in Kashmir and the North- East by the national and international human rights watch groups. Continuous fight against terrorism in Kashmir and North- East is expected to weaken the nerves of the Indian government. In present context of terrorist attacks on the US, the latter has sought Pakistan's cooperation in its war against global terrorism. Pakistan had really no choice given its present economic situation and close relationship with the ruling Taliban in Afghanistan. But US Pakistan cooperation since September 11 has already reduced Pakistan to the status of a client State in a patron- client relationship. The government of India had given unsolicited support in the war against global terrorism. Now, the war against international terrorism, says the US, first will be fought against Osama bin Laden and Afghanistan and later it will be extended elsewhere.

Government Institution

Government institutions in the terrorism affected areas like the judiciary, civil administration; press/media etc. have either ceased functioning, or are forced to tow the pro-militant line. They were the instant causalities of terrorism. Democracy as a value system is under threat in India as a result of continued cross border terrorism. The constant use of armed forces to maintain peace in Jammu and Kashmir and elsewhere not only raises the question of human rights violations both nationally and internationally but also creates a credibility gap between democracy as a value and its practice. Human rights are violated in the process of fighting terrorism. There is always a dilemma- should a government violate human rights to preserve the nation's integrity or sacrifice integrity to protect human rights?

Finally, Pakistan promoted terrorism questions the multi- ethnic and multi religious Indian State's right to exist. Pluralism itself is under attack, since terrorism, in its latest phase, after Musharraf took power, has been presented as jihad to liberate Kashmir.

National Security

National security embraces not only external security contours, but also internal security, which is equally important. Deployment of forces in Jammu & Kashmir, and North- East to combat militancy and insurgency is at the cost of army's preparation for war. It is also a drain on the economy forcing the State to divert scarce resources to a non- productive fight to eliminate it. Terrorism is a low cost, high yield, option for the militants and Pakistan. It is conflict of low intensity only from the viewpoint of the perpetrators of conflict. But it brings about maximum destruction and death in India. This is brought out clearly by its prolonged continuation in India and the government diverting and spending crores of rupees from the development projects to fight it. This aspect is also brought out by the fact that if only 19 committed terrorists could bring about destruction and death of the magnitude of the 9/11 attacks in US< nations need not maintain a standing army at all.[74]Also, it is difficult to identify and separate terrorists from civilians and fight them. If the Americans could be led to his position with one single attack, one could easily imagine the effect on ordinary citizens in India of their living with decades of Islamic terrorism.

The threat from terrorism to India's national security is real and alive. Contemporary terrorism carries out acts of violence mostly as sponsored large- scale operations surpassing all national boundaries. From isolated individual acts, the groups are resorting to mass murders. Other contributions to the changing nature of terrorism are attributable to radical changes occurring in the attitudes of different groups in society towards each other, particularly with regard to attitudes and authority. When participation is denied, authority may be challenged with terrorism as a viable option.

Thus, it can be easily concluded that as far as Kashmir issue is concerned, the principle of self determination is a weapon used by Pakistan against India to attract world sympathy. When all the issues have failed for Pakistan to claim Kashmir, it has chosen the favorite principle of self determination as it is well defined right these days.

Therefore it is important to understand that self determination is not one time choice, it is an ongoing process for the achievement of human security and fulfillment of human needs with a broad scope of possible outcomes and expressions suited to different specific situations. We should not reduce such sacramental, basic principle merely as a weapon of political rhetoric.

Conclusion

An analysis of these movements brings out some of the common aspects

---

74 N.S Jamwal, 'Counter Terrorism Strategy', Strategic Analysis, *Vol.XXVII*, (2003), pp.56-78.

among them. The secessionist movements occurred in bordering States/ regions, have external sponsors/supporters and occurred in the population mix which is culturally and ethnically different from the heartland. The demographic profile in these regions is minority- dominated compared to the rest of the country. As the problem remained confined more or less within the State boundaries, it was allowed to be dealt with by the Sates which treated insurgency and cross border terrorism- related issues as law and order problems. Each State initially responded with the resources available at its disposal and allowed the situation to grow worse quite fast. The problem has been met with a mix of hard and soft responses from the government and a pro-active national policy to give a clear direction to the counter- terrorism mechanism is yet to be implemented. National consensus to deal with terrorism, an analysis of insurgencies in India brings out violence, mass support, external assistance and wide publicity, as the common factors for their growth and lack of education, development, employment and religious tolerance produce insurgents. External assistance to terrorism/insurgents has been possible due to the national internal conflicts and weak response. 'Secularism' the very foundation of the nation is being questioned. The threat to the nation has very deep-rooted implications, which can be successfully fought if all the issues are addressed jointly and there is consensus to convey a strong message to secessionists. In a democratic set up, consensus on vital issues is a must. India, being a secular, democratic country, cannot fight cross border terrorism effectively without popular support. Within the constitutional and sovereignty framework, all the political parties should raise above the vote bank politics and treat cross border terrorism as a threat to national security. Terrorism threatens the national security of the nation. Territory integrity, political independence, fundamental political institutions and cultural values are the targets of terrorists in India.

Ethnic disharmony, rebel movements and insurgencies threaten approximately one-third of all the present member- countries of the United Nations. It is necessary to correctly perceive the intricacies of the changes taking place in the international order and their repercussions on the political, socio-economic, cultural and ideological components of society so that meaningful strategies can be formulated for the future progress, development, well-being and survival of mankind. As long as terrorism was considered a type of criminal behaviour, counter terrorism was considered a task of the police. This view point was entirely appropriate for incidents of domestic terrorism. Unfortunately, terrorism that India is facing is international terrorism and it has assumed more and more the characteristics of unconventional conflict. Obviously, dealing with international terrorism, especially the state sponsored type calls for radically different responses from those that the police use in handling criminal offenders. In the US war against terrorism, President George W. Bush signed an Executive Order on Terrorist Financing on September 24, 2001 and the US Congress passed the USA- Patriot Act 2001 which deals with terrorist funding among other issues. Further, on September 28, 2001, the Security Council unanimously adopted Resolution 1373 under Chapter VII of the UN Charter. Its provisions require, among other things, that all member States prevent the financing of terrorism and deny safe havens to terrorists. States also need to review and strengthen their border security operations, banking practices, customs and immigration procedures, law enforcement and intelligence cooperation as well as arms transfer control regulations.

Therefore, keeping in view the welfare and development of people of all the countries, there is an urgent need to check and regulate the free as well as illegal movement of people and goods across the un-patrolled open border through intensive research, joint reviews and fruitful dialogues on diverse aspects of open border so that India and its neighbours friendship can be further strengthened.

Chapter III

Problems In Combating Cross Border Terrorism

The scourge of terrorism has haunted Indian policy-makers since independence. Some of the states, particularly the bordering states, having different cultural and ethnic composition from the heartland, suffered from a real or perceived sense of neglect and misgovernance. Inimical powers exploited this aspect and sowed seeds of sedition and secession amongst some sections of society of these states-particularly the states of the North-East, Punjab and J&K-by providing them with arms training and financial support and instigated them to take up arms against the state machinery. India's experience in combating insurgency/terrorism in these states has mostly been of finding a military solution to a political problem. Central and state governments have responded with various actions, mostly military, within own borders but lacked a coherent counter terrorism policy.

According to Prakash Singh, former Director General, Border Security Force (BSF): "The level of security arrangements along a particular border would depend upon the political relations, the economic linkages, the ethno- religious ties between people across the borders and the configuration of the border itself."[1]

Controls of cross Border activities on borders require some of the important and strategic heights important for the security of the nation. Both external and internal situations of the country are changing at an incredibly fast pace with the developments in nuclear weapons and missiles, increasing cross border terrorism, the emergence of non- state actors, the growth of Islamic fundamentalists, the narcotics arms nexus, illegal migration and left wing extremism, gravely impacting upon the security of the country and thus posing challenge to management of

---

1 Prakash Singh, 'India's Border Management Challenges', Asthabharthi, Vol. VIII, available at http://www.asthabharthi.org/-DialogueApril (Last modified on October 1, 2006).

borders.[2]

The dynamic nature of the problems concerning management of borders is bought out by the manner in which sensitivity of the Indo-Pakistan, Indo- Bhutan, Indo- Nepal and Indo- Bangladesh borders have changed over a period of time. These borders, which have been open, were once peaceful and trouble- free. However, with increasing activities of the ISI in Pakistan and frequent movement of militants in other States, the nature of the borders has changed completely.[3]

Globalisation, media revolution and technological development in various fields have immensely impacted the border management framework. Now more comprehensive planning is needed to achieve peace and progress on borders. Geo-centrality of India and the fear of the smaller neighbouring States of India's size, economic resources and military strength has impacted on mutual relations. India faces military and non military threats from all countries with land borders. Land borders with Pakistan and Bangladesh have witnessed rapid security affecting changes. Borders with Myanmar and Nepal are also causing serious concern. Pakistan and India have fought four wars over the issue of J&K.[4] The problems persist and proxy war unleashed to wrest J&K continues. Without peaceful borders with its neighbours India can hardly play its legitimate role in global affairs at this time of seminal global change. Now these days there are many problems on the border management irrespective of the security measures in order to combat cross border terrorism.

The conventional definition of border management that we are familiar with may not be able to comprehensively explain what the terms stands for. An ideal definition should exhaustively cover the steps to be taken by all concerned agencies (not just military) to ensure not only the sanctity of the border but also the well being of all the border encompass.[5]

Challenges To Border Management

Our borders have a variety of problems and issues and need a comprehensive

---

2   N.S Jamwal, 'Management of Land Borders', Strategic Analysis, Vol. XXVI, (2002), pp. 406-426.

3   Ibid.

4   Sanajai Singh, 'Strategic Perspectives: Border Management of Western Borders of India' available at http://www.usiofindia.org/pers/.htm (Visited on July28, 2005).

5   Ibid.

focus for durable settlement. At many places, the social contours of our border are mercilessly cut across and divided into various ethnic groups. In time of conflict in neighbouring countries this has becomes a source of acute tension. Indo- Pak relations are characterized by existence of number of bilateral disputes some of them rooted in historical past such as Kashmir issue, others in current dynamics of bilateral issues viz Baglihar Dam dispute. Pakistan continues to occupy illegally a large area of Kashmir and lays claim over whole State of J&K. Both countries have sections at both ends of the border, which are yet to be settled.

Despite India's centrality, different geographical areas require different standards of security. There can be no horizontal stratification for accessing the standard of border security; on a specific segment of the border one has to go through many factors and not just geographically induced threat perception. Other trigger elements are: strategic importance of area, population pattern, and incidence of trans- border crime, disputability and security posture of opposing country.[6]

However, at border guarding level, reduction of tension amongst the neighbouring countries is of utmost importance. It helps, as administrative machinery can continue border regulation even in disputed areas. Border misunderstandings and clashes which has potential to trigger major confrontation can be reduced and borders can be better managed. A decisive posture, coupled with preparedness and constant vigil will help generate respect for us and reduce tensions.

Therefore, proper management of borders is vitally important for the national security. Different portions of extensive border have a variety of problems specific to them which have to be appropriately addressed. These problems have become aggravated in recent times with Pakistan's policy of cross- border terrorism along with its intensely hostile anti- India propaganda designed to mislead and sway the loyalties of the border population.[7] The intensification of cross- border terrorism targeted to destabilize, India has thrown up new challenges for border management policy.

---

6   Supra note 2..

7   Editorial Column, 'Managing Borders of the Country', *Sainik Samachar*, available at http://www.mod.nic.in/samachar/nov1-01/html. (Visited on October 20, 2009.

General Constraints

External threats to India's security are not the only border management issue dealt with at present by the national security apparatus. India's rate of growth has far outpaced that of most of its neighbours and this has generated problems like mass migrations into India. Other threats and challenges have also emerged. The border security scenario is marked by; increased cross- border terrorism; infiltration and ex- filtration of armed militants; emergence of non- State actors; nexus between narcotics traffickers and arms smugglers; illegal migration; left- wing extremism; separatist movements aided and abetted by external powers; and the establishment of madrasas (training schools), some of which are potential security hazards.[8]

Undemarcated Borders

One of the important problems in managing the borders is their delimitation and demarcation on the ground. India has an undemarcated border with China, Pakistan and Bangladesh. The problem of the undemarcated border is more acute in the case of Pakistan and China.[9] The fact is that the boundaries are a mix of well recognized demarcations; International Border, LOC, LAC, Working Boundary, AGPL, McMohan Line, Disputed borders etc.

India's border with Pakistan remained with various State police till 1965. K.F Rustamji, the first Director General of BSF, writes that in context of developments after Pakistan's deliberate intrusion in Kanjarkot area in Rann of Kutch in January 1965, the then PM, Lal Bahadur Shastri, wanted a review of security arrangement of borders with Pakistan and wanted a force controlled centrally to guard the borders. General J.N Choudhary, the then Chief of the army staff, L.P Singh and K.F Rustamji, were closely associated in the raising of a central force viz. BSF on 1 December 1965.[10]

The total length of border to be guarded on Indo- Pakistan borders is 3223 kms running along the States of Gujarat, Rajasthan, Punjab and

---

8   "Internal Security and Border Management", Indian Defence Review, available at http://www.indiandefencereview.com/-IndianDefenceReview/html   ,(Last modified on April 17, 2010).

9   Madhav Godbole, "Management of India's International Borders: Some Challenges ahead", Economic and Political Weekly, (December, 2001), p.36.

10 Sanajai Singh, 'Strategic Perspectives: Border Management of Western Borders of India' available at http://www.usiofindia.org/pers/.htm (Visited on July28, 2005).

J&K categorized as LOC and AGPL. Pakistan has used covert action in the guise of terrorism as an instrument of State policy against India. It has recruited, trained, financed, armed and infiltrated terrorists in India and has provided sanctuary to anti- Indian elements.[11] Despite global outcry against terrorism and not withstanding a string of confidence building measures adopted by two governments, Pakistan has not yet dismantled the terror infrastructure in the territory under its control.

When a border is not demarcated on the ground and when there is no common understanding between two sides as to what constitutes the LAC due to the Chinese reluctance to exchange with us maps indicating their understanding of the LAC, such intrusions are bound to take place from both sides. Such intrusions used to be a recurring feature across the Sino-Myanmar border in the Northern Shan State and the Kachin State before the Sino- Myanmar border was demarcated in the 1970s except in the northern tri junction where the borders of India, China and Myanmar meet, which remains undetermined and undemarcated till today.[12]

Recently, the government of India, incidentally, is now conducting a fresh survey of the northern plateau in Sikkim to counter claims by China, as China continues to needle Indian forces all along the 4057 kms LAC. In the latest set of incursions across the LAC, Chinese patrols once again transgressed into the Indian side in eastern Ladakh as China wants the border to be drawn in a straight line to gain strategic advantage.[13] But eastern Ladakh is not the region where Chinese patrols have been flexing their muscles in an aggressive border management policy to put pressure on India and lay claim to disputed areas along the LAC. Similar Chinese moves have been witnessed in the eastern sector in Arunachal Pradesh and Sikkim in recent months. With over 80 incursions across the 206 km Sikkim Tibet border being recorder since January 2008, the Indian establishment is especially worried about so- called 22.1 sq km 'finger area', the northern most tip of Sikkim, which China is claiming as its own territory.[14]

---

11   Ibid.

12   B.Raman, 'China's Strategic Intrusion in India's Neighbourhood', available at http://www.southasiaanalysis.org/papers34/html, (Last viewed on September 15, 2009).

13   Ibid.

14   Rajat Pandit, 'Fresh Chinese Incursions across LAC', *The Times of India*, New Delhi, September 11, 2008.

Before the independence of India, there existed a system of regular survey and supervision of Nepal- India boundary jointly conducted by the officials of both countries every year to oversee and find out encroachment, if any, on the boundary, ill- defined boundary, missing and broken as well as displaced boundary pillars with the objective to fix and place them in their original position. Accordingly, while Nepal has been entrusted to look after the pillars having odd number, India looks after the pillars having even number. After the independence of India, no joint boundary survey has been conducted until the formation of a Joint Boundary Commission in 1981 with the composition of six boundary survey teams. Delay in the formation of a Joint Boundary Commission resulted in several boundary disputes, which remain unresolved, because the activities of the Commission are going on at a very slow pace. There is a provision for two meetings of the Joint Boundary Commission every year. Twenty years have been elapsed since the formation of the Commission in 1981 and accordingly, there should have been 36 meetings up to 1999, but so far only 22 meetings have been convened.[15]

Boundary survey of almost all the districts bordering India has been completed except for Darchula, Dadeldhura and Kanchanpur as well as the border with Sikkim State of India. Moreover, there have been several cases of encroachment on and tampering with the boundary makers and damage, destruction and removal of boundary pillars in the areas already surveyed by the joint boundary teams. As a result, there exist several cases of boundary disputes with resulting claims and counter claims. There are reportedly 8 disputed areas along the Nepal India border with a total of six along the rivers of *Mahakali*, the *Narayani/ Gandak (Susta)* and the *Mechi* and the other two are in *Pasupatinagar* and *Thori*.[16] There are several areas along the Nepal- India border where no man's land has been encroached on both sides.

According to Mr. Buddhi Narayan Shrestha, the former Director General of the Department of Survey of Nepal, there are 53 disputed and encroached areas along the Nepal- India boundary. However, the All Nepal Free Students Union affiliated with the Nepal Communist Party (Marxist and Leninist) has indicated 61 disputed areas along the Nepal-

---

15 Ibid.

16 Vidya Bir Singh Kansakar, 'Nepal India Open Border: Prospects, Problems and Challenges', available at http://www.nepaldemocracy.org/documents/treaties_ agreements/html (Last viewed on April 25, 2009).

India boundary. Out of the 26 districts of Nepal bordering India, the map indicates 22 districts having encroachment (problem) and the only 4 remaining districts have no boundary problem are Baitadi, Bara, Mahottari and Dhanusha. The map also indicates boundary problems in the districts bordering the Sikkim State of India.[17]

Undemarcated areas continue to remain a source of tension and pose a hindrance towards normalization of relations between two nations. India had to defend its territory by going to war over these issues.

Porous Nature of Border

India's borders comprise a vast variety terrain encompassing deserts, plains, hills, mountains and riverine areas. By and large, these borders are very porous due to the terrain and ethnic affinities of population on both sides of the borders. Illegal migration, infiltration of anti-national elements, smuggling of arms/explosives and drug trafficking are some of the serious problem.

Pakistan has been indulging in the nefarious games of cross border terrorism against India from its inception by exploiting the sensitivities of India's religious and cultural communities. There are number of training camps in POK in which terrorists are trained and sent inside J&K. Direct accessibility and the porous nature of the borders allow insurgents groups tactical flexibility.[18] Some technological developments enabling quick passage of info, transfer of funds, underworld criminal gang's links with terrorist groups have changed the focus and tenor of border security. It is also worthwhile to mention that terrorists and subversive elements are using soft borders of India touching countries like Nepal and Bangladesh to enter India.

The Indo- Bangladesh border is highly porous making the illegal movement of people and goods a perennial problem. In fact, the border area between India and Bangladesh is not completely fenced and leaves a fringe area under open territory. Forty six patches have been identified along the border, which cannot be fenced due to territorial problem. These patches have half fringe of their land along the Indian part while the other

---

17 Ashok Mehta (2001), *Problem of Terrorism and Other Illegal Activities on Indo- Nepal Border: Issues in Effective Border Management*, Delhi, pp.1-14.

18   Sanajai Singh, 'Strategic Perspectives: Border Management of Western Borders of India' available at http://www.usiofindia.org/pers/.htm (Visited on July31, 2005).

half is in Bangladesh. Therefore to avoid problems, decision has been taken jointly visit these areas and take decisions regarding the type of fence that should be constructed. Therefore, though relations between Bangladesh and India are usually friendly but they have occasional disputed, mainly related to cross border trespassing and smuggling through their 4000 km border, a relatively porous one that runs through rivers, hills and marshes. Therefore India proposed several times for coordinated patrolling of its border with Bangladesh to curb trespassers who cross over at night, leading to many of them was being shot by the BSF – the bone of contention at talks between the top brass of the border guards of the two countries. The killing of unarmed civilians, as Bangladesh puts it, has become a sensitive issue between the two neighbours that ultimately create impediments in the over all bilateral relations. But Bangladesh always vehemently denied Indian charges on harbouring either Indian insurgents groups or providing assistance to other extremist forces. They see this Indian attempt to malign them in the international community and insist that there is no earthly reason for Bangladesh to support terrorism against India. Dhaka has shown the political will to crack down on these groups that operate on its small border with Myanmar. A similar gesture on the Indian border would boost mutual confidence.[19]

The terrain and the demographic composition of the border area make it conducive for Bangladeshis to sneak into India and also to get easily assimilated into the local populace. Migration from Bangladesh into India, especially in Assam and Tripura has primarily been driven by the quest for better economic opportunities. Many Bangladeshis have also crossed over into India to escape political and religious persecution. Over the years, the magnitude of this illegal migration had reached such an astounding proportion that it had begun to alter the demographic profile and threaten the socio- political fabric of the Border States. The porous nature of the border and the constant floe of the people have also made it easy for Indian Insurgents Groups (IIGs) to cross over into Bangladesh, where they have set up safe houses and training camps under the benign eyes of Pakistani and Bangladeshi intelligence services.[20] The increasing influence of

19 Editorial Column, 'Coordinate Border Patrolling – India tells Bangladesh', *Sindh Today Online*, available at http://.www.sindhtoday.net/news/1/30728.htm, (Last Viewed on June 30, 2010).

20 Pushpita Das, 'The India – Bangladesh Border: A Problem Area for Tomorrow', IDSA Comments available at http://.www.idsa.in/idsastrategiccomments/theIndiaBangladeshBorderAProblemareaforTommorrow/Pdas. (Last Modified

Islamic fundamentalism in Bangladesh has resulted in the large- scale push into India, of not only economic migrants, but also the foot- soldiers of jihad terrorism and pan- Islamic fundamentalism, all of which have the potential to destabilize the country and threaten national security.

Nepal and Bhutan are separated by a wide stretch of Indian Territory, Darjeeling district of West Bengal State and Sikkim State. Bhutan and Indian have no open border. However, because of the open border between Nepal and India they could easily enter into Nepal via Indian Territory. In reality, the first place of asylum for the Bhutanese refugees is India. Under international convention, it is the responsibility of India to settle them in India by establishing refugee camps, but India drove them into, Nepal. The Bhutanese refugees represent different Nepalese ethnic and caste groups, but it does not mean that they have directly migrated to Bhutan from Nepal. Lots of them have migrated from different parts of eastern and north- eastern India as well. Nearly 100,000 Bhutanese refugees are resettled in the camps in *Jhapa* and *Morang* districts.[21] Though they live in the closed camps with barbed wire fencing, their movements outside are not restricted, and they are also able to cross the barbed wire fencing easily. This has affected the natural, social and economic environment of the surrounding areas, because they are engaged in illegal cutting of trees in the government forests, are engaged in business and work as cheap labour thereby affecting the business and employment of the local community. It is alleged that a lot of Bhutanese refugees have been able to secure Nepalese citizenship through illegal means. Moreover, a lot of the Indians of Nepalese origins have also migrated to Bhutan, and naturally a large numbers of them must be Indians.[22] It is not known when the Bhutanese refugee problem will be solved.

Therefore porous nature of the border is another major problem with the Indian borders where dense population is residing, allows free movements of national criminals of neighbouring countries. This problem gets severely compounded in the riverine and jungle areas where patrolling is difficult.

---

at June 6, 2011)

21 Vidya Bir Singh Kansakar, 'Nepal India Open Border: Prospects, Problems and Challenges', available at http://www.nepaldemocracy.org/documents/treaties_ agreements/html (Last viewed on April 25, 2009).

22 Ibid.

Over Population in the Border Areas

Density of population in the border areas at some places is approximately 700-800 persons per sq km on the Indian side and about 1000 persons on the Pakistan side. Such an overpopulated area with a porous border poses problems in detection and apprehension of criminals who have the option of crossing over to the other side to evade arrest. Since many villages are located so near the border there are approximately 187 villages in Kashmir where houses are located within 150 yards of International Border where the density of the population is far more than the rest of the country.[23]

Compared to India's western border, conditions have become more difficult on Indo-Bangladesh border due to increase in the density of population, firstly, because of the overall increase in the population of the country and secondly, due to the influx of illegal migrants from Bangladesh who have settled in the border area. A major problem with the Indo- Bangladesh border is the habitation of the border belt. Both sides are yet to exchange certain enclaves. Despite the limited nature of dispute, there have been conflagrations on the Indo- Bangladesh border at regular intervals. Things have worsened with the increasing population pressure in Bangladesh. With pressure on their land Bangladeshis are trying to enter into Indian Territory to cultivate land with the tacit support of Bangladeshi border guards. This has increased the problems for Indian Border Security Force who is supposed to manage the Indian side of the border.[24] They are now demanding that border issue should be sorted out with urgency so that it can be sealed off efficiently.

The riverine border, mostly in *Dhubri* district of Assam and Southern West Bengal, presents peculiar problems, as it is difficult to locate Permanent Border Outposts (BOPs) in the area due to swelling of the *Brahmaputra* and other rivers that increases the depth of the river by about 30 feet.[25] The 'Char' areas thrown up during the dry season and which people inhabit are almost completely submerged. Patrolling in such areas is problematic. The nature of the border configuration affords an easy opportunity to the infiltrations and smugglers to cross over to India. The crossing is further facilitated because the border is thickly populated. The

---

23 N.S Jamwal, 'Management of Land Borders', Strategic Analysis, Vol. XXVI, 2002, pp.406-426

24 N.S Jamwal, 'Management of Land Borders', Strategic Analysis, Vol. XXVI, 2002, pp. 420-26.

25 Ibid

southern frontier of the West Bengal border is much more vulnerable, and so the number crossing is larger. Several areas of Kolkata have already been saturated with Bangladeshi nationals to spread to other parts of India. The density of population on the Indo- Bangladesh border varies from State to State. In West Bengal it is 766, in Assam and Meghalaya it is 181 and in Tripura and Mizoram it is 268.[26] The boundary passes through the middle of the villagers/houses. The houses are scattered almost along the entire stretch of the boundary. Another problem is atrocities on the Hindu minority in Bangladesh. These atrocities forced Hindu families to migrate to India in waves since the creation of East Pakistan. A news report by Ershadul Huq, states that the Bangladesh High Court has asked the government to explain why it should not be ordered to take action to protect the country's religious minorities from terrorist attacks and harassment. The petition submitted by Ain-o-Shalish Kendra (ASK) states the atrocities committed against nearly 30 million minorities including about 20 million Hindus. The atrocities have resulted in the decline of the Hindu population from 24 percent in 1974 to 10 percent as of now. An analysis of population growth of Hindus in Bangladesh reveals that the decadal growth rate has been 3.1 percent for 1974, 9.3 percent for 1981 and 5.8 percent in 1991, which is far below the average 24 percent growth rate of Hindus in the subcontinent. If this (24 percent) decadal growth rate is to be applied in case of Bangladeshis, the Hindu population should have been approximately 14.7 million while it is 10.5 million as per the census. Obviously, these have illegally crossed through the porous borders and settled in India.[27]

A recent survey revealed that as much as 15 percent of the total Bangladeshis population has reportedly illegally migrated to India. Now the heftiest intellectuals of Bangladesh have floated the idea of handing over a part of Indian Territory along the 4000 Km Indo-Bangladesh border to it for accommodating the ever increasing population. In 6 districts of Assam, these illegal migrants constitute 6 percent of the population and in another six, they form 40 percent. Armed with voting rights, now these illegal migrants are influencing the policy of the State, which poses a great threat to country's security.[28]

---

26 Id. at p. 406.

27 Supra note 24

28 Editorial Column, 'Indo Pak Border Route of Terrorists', *The Times of India*, October 21, 2008.

In 2002, seven people have lost their lives in every 10 days to terrorist attacks in the western side of India. A survey revealed that 81 percent of the country's citizen feared for their safety in the face of terror in India, the country's own weakened response to control this menace had helped in its rapid growth. The ISI has succeeded in attracting fringe elements from Muslim community of the country towards terrorist activities and the emergence of technology- savvy extremist's elements is a dangerous trend. The impregnable ghettos that had emerged in various metropolitans and other towns posed a serious challenge to security agencies.[29]

Given the history of ethnic violence in Assam, we run the danger of rushing to conclusions about motives and culprits. But it is not half as premature to debate the portent of the serial blasts in Assam in the year 2008 that have shaken *Guwahati, Barpita, Kokrajhar* and *Bongaigaon*. The blasts have claimed more than 50 lives and injured hundreds of people in a State that was the victim of bombs and guns long before Indian cities elsewhere began to see bombs going off every second day. Much blood has blown down Brahmaputra, spilled in clashes caused by ethnic and linguistic strife in violent project determined to carve up the State, through attempts to even secede from the Indian Union. And the United Liberation Front (ULFA) is synonymous with gore in the dictionary of terrorism.[30] This terror attacks in Assam killed so many people and had the stamp of Lashkar-e-Taiba (LeT) and Harkat- ul- Jihadi- Islami's (HuJI) involvement.

Illegal migration is emerging as a migraine for the country and threatening to alter Northeast's demography. With tacit support from political parties, particularly in Assam, illegal immigrants are not only a burden on the state's resources but also a breeding ground for Pak-sponsored terrorism. Though there are no official figures of actual numbers of illegal Bangladeshis in Assam, their population, according to a rough estimate could be over 2 million of the state's 30 million people.[31]

Border Fencing

The primary aim of fencing along the Indo- Pakistan border was to check the ingress of criminals, prevent smuggling and provide a sense of security

---

29 Ibid.

30 Editorial column, 'Watch the Aftermath', *Indian Express*, October 31, 2008.

31 Dipanjan Roy Choudhury, 'Avoid another J & K like Problem', India Today. (January 10, 2009).

to the border population. There are wide gaps as fencing is not complete. This is due to slow progress in acquisition of land, resistance by locals, flaws in conceiving the project and lack of sincerity. The fencing however, has not resulted in curbing the menace to significant degree. By itself, the fencing is not a barrier. It can be effective only when it is vigorously patrolled and kept under surveillance round the clock. The terrain, climatic conditions, dense vegetation, improper design and alignment without taking into consideration the traditions and culture of the border population, has further led to its repeated breaching. The BSF, deployed to guard the border, is stretched too thin along the border, resulting in large unmanned, unguarded gaps, which are exploited by the criminals. High snowfalls results in large stretches being waterlogged, dense vegetation and undergrowth immediately after the winters. This has severely affected the fencing which got rusted and damaged within a few years o fits commissioning. Moreover, there are many villages between fencing and the International Boundary, where people are in collusion with the criminals, making detection of illegal migrants and criminal difficulties. Fence has also resulted in virtually giving away the land lying between the fencing and the International Border to Pakistani criminals. The government has adopted a well coordinated and multi- pronged strategy tackle ISI activities. Border has been strengthened to check illegal cross- border activities by fencing IB and creating obstacles along LOC along terrorist's routes. So far 159 kms of fencing work has been completed in Jammu sector.[32]

Any discussion on cross border fencing problem, especially in the Indian context, would be incomplete without mention of China's role in promoting Trans national's activities on Indian soil. The Chinese have two major claims on what India deems its own territory. One claim, in the western sector, is on Aksai Chin in the northeastern section of Ladakh district in J&K. The other claim is in the eastern sector over a region included in the British designated North- East Frontier Agency, the disputed part of which India renamed Arunachal Pradesh and made a State. In the fight over theses areas, the well trained and well armed troops of the Chinese People's Liberation Army overpowered the ill- equipped Indian troops, who had not been properly acclimatized to fight at high altitudes. India accuses China of illegally occupying 43,180 sq km of territory in

---

32 Sanjai Singh, "Strategic Perspectives Border Management of Indian Borders", available
     at http://www.usiofindia.org/Pers1.htm, (Last Modified on June1, 2009).

Jammu & Kashmir, including 5,180 sq km Beijing has illegally ceded to Pakistan in 1963. On its part, Beijing accuses New Delhi of occupying some 90,000 sq km of Chinese territory, most of it the northeastern Indian State of Arunachal Pradesh.[33]

Evidence collected by the police in many recent terrorist incidents including the Mumbai blasts in July, the Varanasi serial blasts in March and attack on the Indian Institute of Science, Bangalore in December 2005 point to an increased use of Bangladeshi territory by ISI backed terrorist groups like Harkat-ul-Jihad-al-Islami (HUJI).[34] It is suspected that the bomb blasts in Jalpaiguri and Guwahati in 2006 were also carried out by the persons on the behest of ISI stationed in Bangladesh. The incident of weapon hauls in various Northeastern Sates indicates that Bangladesh has also become a conduit for arms trafficking.[35] Smuggling especially of cattle, human and narcotics trafficking, counterfeit currency, kidnapping and thefts are quite rampant along the border.

Construction of fences at eastern borders has been undertaken in two phases, with phase I sanctioned in 1987 and phase II in 2000. Phase I ended with the fencing of only 20 percent (857 km) of the border, and even this was of limited utility since much of the fencing was subsequently damaged as a result of faulty construction designs and vagaries of weather. Under phase II, an additional 2429.5 km offence was sanctioned and by 31 January 2005, 1275.4 km had been completed.[36]

In a survey conducted by a team of the Akhil Bhartiya Vidyarthi Parishad (ABVP), on the Indo- Bangladesh borders in northeastern States revealed that fencing of only 30 percent of border has been done, which is also in a poor condition due to the alleged use of substandard material. The team surveyed 1,074 km long International Border in 12 border districts of four north eastern States, Assam, Meghalya, Tripura, and Mizoram. The members of the team covered 78 km long remote areas by foot and 45 km through boats.[37] From the last few years, a large scale infiltration from

---

33 James Heitzman and Robert L. Worden 'India, China to Maintain Peace and Tranquility in Border Areas', available at http://www.globalsecurity.org/military/world/war/indo-prc1962.htm, (Last Modified on May 31, 2011).

34 Reference of Annexure C for the Banned Organisations in India.

35 Pushpita Das, 'The India- Bangladesh Borders – A Problem Area for Tomorrow', IDSA Strategic Comments, New Delhi, (December8, 2006)

36 Ibid.

37 Editorial column, 'Fencing of Indo- Bangladesh Border', *The Tribune*, September 26,

Bangladesh has been taking place in north eastern States. A detailed report to this account by the former governor of Assam S.K Sinha was submitted to the President of India. The growing terrorism, smuggling and various illegal activities have posed a serious threat to the national security in the north eastern States.

However, at most of the places in Meghalaya, the fencing is old and in poor conditions. The gates erected at some places are badly damaged. Similarly in Tripura, most of the border is open and the old fencing at certain places has worn out. Out of 80 km long border in Mizoram, only 7 km long border had been fenced and that too in a very poor condition. One more interesting fact is that there is no fencing along rivers, ponds and in interior regions.[38]

However, erecting fences along the border has not been without its share of problems. The inhospitable terrain, the largely undemarcated border area and consequent border disputes, the non- cooperative attitudes of the various State governments and also that of the Bangladesh Rifles (BDR) are all hurdles in the way of effectively fencing the border.[39] The State governments have not shown much enthusiasm towards the erection of border fences for a number of reasons. The rehabilitation of displaced people due to fencing is a contentious issue between the central and various State governments. The government of Tripura has alleged that the BSF is not adhering to guidelines announced by the Ministry of Home Affairs while constructing the fences. India is also facing stiff resistance from Bangladesh at 265 disputed spots as the security forces of both the countries differ on their perception of the location of the boundary. Bangladesh objects on the ground that the construction of any defensive structure within 150 yards of the international boundary is not permitted under the guidelines agreed to in 1975. On the other hand, India maintains that it is demolition of defensive structures and not construction of fences that forms part of 1975 guidelines. It must be mentioned that the above mentioned contentious parts constitute only 7 percent (297 km) of the

---

2008, also available at http://.www.tribuneindia.com/2008/20080926/jal.htm, (Last Viewed on March 26,2009).

38   Ibid.

39   Supra note 35, also available at http://.www.idsa.in/idsastrategiccomments/ theIndiaBangladesh BorderAProblemareaforTommorrow/Pdas. (Last Modified at June 6, 2011)

4095 km long India- Bangladesh border.[40]

The Indo- Bangladesh border is well on its way to become a major headache for India unless the problems afflicting the border are not addressed urgently. The issues of illegal migration, smuggling, spread of Islamic fundamentalism from across the border etc. need to be effectively tackled. Measures like construction of fences and roads have to be taken undertaken on a war- footing. In addition, it is important to sensitize the border population about the strategic importance of their area and also get them involved in guarding the border.

Difficulty in Identifying Foreign National

Indians of the bordering States and neighbouring countries look alike, speak the same language, wear the same dresses and have similar set of culture and traditions, thus making it difficult to identify a foreign national in the absence of identify cards in the border areas. Connivance of the locals with intruders–for a payment makes the task of detection more difficult.

Likewise at Indo – Nepal border not only the Indian and Nepalese nationals cross the porous border without any restriction, but these days some Pakistani, Bangladeshi, Sri Lankan and even Afghan and Iranian nationals infiltrate into Indian territory, misusing the open border to some extent. Their similar face, attire, posture and behaviour resemble the Napalese and Indian nationals. Some of the Pakistani, Iranian, and Myanmar infiltrators are seeking asylum in mostly western nations through United Nations High Commissioner for Refugees (UNHCR) office in Kathmandu.[41] In one sense, the porous border has helped to initiates rebellion activity in both nations to some extent. So Indo- Nepal open border management system is going to be difficult for the common people of both countries.

Our borders have a variety of problems and issues and need a comprehensive focus for a durable settlement. At many places, the social contours of our borders are mercilessly cut across and divided into various ethnic groups. In time of conflict in neighbouring countries this becomes a

---

40 Ibid.

41 Editorial column, 'The News from the Field' available at http://.www.alertnet.org/ thenews/from the field/219053/121267709215.htm, (last Viewed on May 6, 2009).

source of acute tension. Indo- Pak relations are characterized by existence of a number of bilateral disputes, some of them rooted in historical past such as Kashmir issue, others in current dynamics of bilateral issues viz Baglihar Dam dispute. Pakistan continues to occupy illegally a large area of Kashmir and lays claim over whole State of J&K. Both countries have sections at both ends of the border, which are yet to be settled

Passive and Indifferent Attitude of Border Population

The major problem in combating cross border terrorism is that all border crime takes place in an organised manner. The population residing in the border areas is either dependent on the kingpins or are scared to speak against such criminals. This sometimes happens due to indifferent attitude of the administration where some of them are also a part of the nexus.[42]

One of the main reason for surviving and thriving of terrorists and subversive groups in Kashmir and elsewhere in north east of India is that the people no longer willing to tolerate the inequity, poverty, and corruption in which Sates in these areas have been mired. Disgusted with the governments and despairing of the prospect for peaceful and incremental change within the existing order, the people are looking for an explanation of their personal suffering and societal degradation. The eruption of militancy in Kashmir during late 1980s was not a sudden outburst but the cumulative result of various twists and turns in the State's policies since long. If one wants to understand the growth of militancy in Kashmir, one has to bear in mind that it is both spontaneous as well as the result of some external planning. The denial of basic human needs like genuine decent livelihood, civil liberties and federal autonomy to the people of Kashmir alienated them from the Indian nation and finally crossed over to the side of militancy. Pakistan a traditional rival in the dispute of Kashmir, took advantage of the situation. It not only gave military training to young Kashmiri Muslims but also provided sophisticated weapons. After their return, these young men started an armed struggle in Kashmir.[43]

It is well known that Pakistan has been the main source of arms, ammunition and training for religious groups which operated in the

---

42 N.S Jamwal, 'Management of Land Borders', Starategic Analysis, (July- September, 2002).

43 Mehraj Hajni and Ravinderjeet Kour 'Is Militancy Vanishing in Kashmir?' available at http://.www.ipcs.org/ipcs/kashmirLevel2/universityofkashmir/html., (last Viewed on October 11, 2005).

Punjab in the past and for those which are operating presently in J&K and other parts of India. The training is given by the ISI, either directly or through religious fundamentalist and Pan- Islamic *Jihad* Organisations, in various makeshift camps located in POK, the Northern Areas (Gilgit and Baluchistan) and the North- West Frontier Province. India has a little over 140 million Muslims – the second largest Muslim community in the world after Indonesia. Only a very small section of the community has taken to terrorism due to various grievances and instigation by the ISI and Pakistan's religious, fundamentalist and jihad organisations. The overwhelming majority of Indian Muslims are loyal, law- abiding citizens. They have not allowed their anger against the India government or the Hindus for any reason to drive them into the arms of terrorist organisations. However, terrorist groups always try to bitter the relationship between two communities that is Hindu & Muslims.[44]

Cutting of Barbed Wire by Smugglers, Terrorists

Smugglers, terrorists have invented a very ingenious way of dealing with the security forces who have tried to obstruct their activity – by cutting the barbed wires. Barbed wires spread over a longer distance and passes through to no man's land which may not be under direct observation of security forces. Since a breached wire invites disciplinary action against the respective commanders and troops. Smugglers resort to such acts to force commanders either to connive with them or face the consequences of an inquiry for dereliction of duty.

Nexus between Criminal-Administration and Police

The cross border crimes in the border regions flourish due to the connivance and close nexus of the criminals, police – administration triumvirate. It has been found in certain cases that before the illegal migrants enter India, certain important documents like ration cards, gas connection papers etc., showing them as Indian citizens are all prepared and handed over to them to allow them escape detection on the border. These illegal migrants are then helped to reach any part of this country, including crossing over to fences also. A glaring instance of connivance can be seen from the fact that the cattle smuggled from India to Bangladesh reach the Bangladesh border from places as far as Madhya Pradesh, Uttar Pradesh, Bihar, Orissa, etc., on the basis of fictitious documents and bribing the officials of respective

---

44 Editorial column, 'Indo Pak Border Route of Terrorists', *The Times of India*, October 21, 2008.

checkpoints.[45]

On the other hand India's internal security scenario has grown complex over the years. It has been subjected to cross border terrorism abetted by external power and as many as nine States with 76 districts are affected by naxalite violence in varying degrees. Maintenance of law and order is the responsibility of the State. State police force has been found inadequately trained to deal with situation as such border guarding forces are frequently withdrawn to combat insurgency. They have also been withdrawn many a time to deal with law and order problems. Withdrawal of forces limits their capabilities to guard the borders efficiently. Even the military officers are alleged to have ordered weapons on the basis of how large the kickback will be. There are instances where soldiers and policemen have extorted rather than defended the public. In Kashmir, the line between the police and the criminals is a thin one, and at times may not exist at all.[46]

Change of Profile of Border Areas

Continuous influx of illegal migrants has resulted in a change of profile of the border areas. Mosque and *Madrassas* (training schools) have come up on the border areas, neighbouring countries nationals and their dresses as well as their culture is visible in the border belt an done can see a perceptible difference in the demographic profile compared to as it was 10 years ago.

Likewise people of Nepal have experienced historically from closed to wide open border management system with India since ancient period. Now there is open border system. The terrorists, rebels and criminals have misused present porous border. Meanwhile, Indo- Nepal border is going to be insecure due to threats. Therefore, enforcement of ID card system and fencing the frontier should be the measures to make the border restricted for the terrorists, checked for criminals, controlled for smugglers, stopped for narcotics holders and obstructed for girl traffickers. But it must be regulated for the genuine passengers of Nepal and India; and managed for export and import of merchandise legally, so that people of both the frontiers may feel their life and property safe and secure.

---

45 N.S Jamwal, 'Management of Land Borders', Strategic Analysis, (July- September, 2002).

46 Ibid.

Terrorists in Enclaves

Enclaves pose a problem of a peculiar nature. Since police cannot enter the enclaves, the local heads act as per their whims without attracting any retribution from either country. People from Indian enclaves in Pakistan or Bangladesh have already migrated to India – either due to sale of their land or to escape persecution. Terrorists are taking shelters in these enclaves as these are considers to be the very safe havens for them. In fact, security and border management issues as well as ways to enhance cooperation between the law enforcement agencies have always been prominent issues between India and Bangladesh as five Indian States–Assam, West Bengal, Meghalaya, Mizoram and Tripura share a 4095 km border with Bangladesh. These include a 2979 km land border and 1116 km are river line. So also, issues such as round – the – clock access to two Bangladeshi enclaves on the Indian side, the action taken so far to deport militants and crackdown on rebel training camps are equally important for, India.[47] Enclaves become convenient points for smuggling, avoiding customs and excise duties, importing of contraband, and are a point of entry for illegal aliens. There are 111 Indian enclaves (17158 acres) in Bangladesh and 51 Bangladesh enclaves (7110.02 acres) in India. Historically, enclaves date back to the period of the expansion of the Mughal Empire into northern Bengal in the late seventeenth century and continued till the British established control of the Sate.[48]

Circuitous International Boundary

The international boundary follows a non linear pattern. It passes through villages, fields, houses, rivers and jungles in an uneven manner and at places forms big loops. If one is to follow the proper route along such loops, it is time consuming. The pattern of demarcation is so tedious that people in the border areas find it tempting to trespass and violate the international border as shortcuts.

Relations across the Boundary

Radcliff's scalpel at the time of partition left many people with relations stranded on the other side. It did not matter initially to the people as the borders were virtually porous and they could visit each other freely. Due

---

47 Shibdas Bhattacharjee, 'Indo- Bangladesh Joint Border Management', *The Assam Tribune*, Guwahati, August 12, 2009.

48 N. S Jamwal, 'Border Management: Dilemma of Guarding the India-Bangladesh Border', Strategic Analysis, (January, 2004).

to laxity, they continued to enter into marriage alliances subsequently and nurtured the relations to the extent of settling down, particularly in Assam, Punjab, and J&K. With the tightening of control in the border it became more and more difficult, yet the efforts continue till date to go and meet the relatives across the border.

Limitation to Applicability of Law of the Land

Indulgence in across the border crimes like cattle lifting, kidnapping, crossing over of under trials extremists, trafficking of women and children have become a phenomenon and a way of living because the law of the land ceases to apply after a person crosses over to the other side. Terrorists have entered into an understanding to provide shelter to each other in their respective countries to avoid legal proceedings.

Missing Borders Pillars

Border Pillars show the alignment of the boundary on the ground. There are various types of border pillars like main, minor and subsidiary. These pillars sometimes get stolen or removed by terrorist elements with a view to create tension on the border or nibble ground, as a result boundaries don't get properly demarcated.

There is a very important instance in this regard is that the main reason for the eruption of border disputes between India and Nepal is the ever shifting course of the turbulent Himalayan Rivers, which define the international boundary between the two countries in many areas. These rivers keep changing their courses every now and then, thereby throwing up new territories and submerging old land. Although the riverine boundary is determined on the principle of a fixed boundary, the shifting course of rivers results in adverse possessions. In other words, because the river dissolves old lands and creates new ones, the new lands are "illegally" occupied by people beyond the border. So, what was once Nepalese territory is occupied by Indians and vice versa. This process creates confusion and tensions among people residing in these ever changing border landscapes. The problem is compounded by submergence, destruction and removal of border pillars, a fact also noted by the parliamentarian's team in its June 2009 report.[49]

---

49   Pushpita Das, 'Demarcate the India Nepal Border', available at http://.www.idsa.in/ strategiccomments/ DemarcatetheIndiaNepalBorder/PushpitaDas/html, (Last Viewed on July 18, 2010).

Firing across the Border

There is an intense firing across the International Border at the slightest provocation, causing tension and problem of management. Because of the continuous firing infiltration intrude inside the country, as there is diversion of attention of the troops.[50] Indian and Bangladeshi border guards have often exchanged fire along their porous 4000 km border that runs through rice fields, hills, jungles, marshes and rivers. They accuse each other of targeting civilians on the frontier, which has acquired a reputation for rampant smuggling and illegal migration.[51]

Lack of Development

The produce in the border areas does not find any market on the Indian side for want of communication facilities and the items produced are of a perishable nature. So, the Indians have to perforce resort to sell it in Pakistan or in Bangladesh. But, in case of the Meghalaya border, the boundary lies on the foothills towards Bangladesh while the plains are in India where the vegetables etc., Produced are consumed by Indians. Problems crop up every year during sowing and harvest season when Bangladeshi farmers enter Indian Territory for cultivation, though no Indian farmers ever go to Bangladesh to work on lands under its possession. Some Home Ministry officials feel that it was the indifferent attitude of successive governments since 1975 that had left the issue unresolved for decades now. What is worse nearly 6.5 km of the border is still undemarcated which is beyond the scope of any patrolling or fencing by Indian forces making it one of

---

50 In the year 2006 frequent skirmishes have taken place between the BSF and the BDR. On June 9, 2006, BSF and BDR personnel exchanged fire for over six hours after a Bangladeshi smuggler was shot dead in Nadia district of West Bengal. According to BSF Inspector General Somesh Goyal the Bangladeshi, identified as Mohammad Yousuf, was killed after he attacked an Indian soldier with a knife to evade arrest. Troops of the Bangladesh Rifles (BDR) then opened fire on a BSF patrol, and Indian forces returned fire. The incident took place at the Gede- Namatala frontier, about 140 km north of Kolkata. The deceased was carrying 4 kg of ganja and 50 bottles of cough syrup. Five others accompanying him fled under the Bangladesh smugglers. In another incident of unprovoked firing a BSF constable was killed on June 12 when border guards chasing a gang of Bangladeshi smugglers were fired on by the Bangladesh Rifles in West Bengal's north 24 parganas district. Pursued by the BSF on Indian Territory, the smugglers, numbering five to six, divided into the Ichamati river at Ghojadanga. The BDR then fired on the Indian border guards. Rajendra Kumar Sharma, a constable of 191 BSF battalion died in the incident.

51 "Bangladesh Army Chief in India to boost bilateral defence ties", India Defence reports available at http://.www.india-defence.com/reports-3754, (Last Viewed on October 23, 2009).

the most "porous" and sensitive sections of the country's international border.[52]

Legal Constraints

Some of the legal constraints are also contributing in enhancing the cross border terrorism in India:

Ambiguity of Jurisdiction on the Border

The jurisdiction of border guarding forces differs from border to border. There is no clear cut demarcation regarding the jurisdiction. In some cases, the jurisdiction extends to 5 km and in other cases, it is 15 km and in some States like Meghalaya in the entire State, this results in confusion among the forces.[53]

Lack of Judicial and Law Enforcement Infrastructure

It has been observed in border areas especially in Jammu and Kashmir that the local administration is virtually non- existent. The presence of local police is also grossly inadequate. Often, only a constable may be available at the outpost. This cause complete breakdown of the law enforcement mechanism as in the case of any crime, it takes very long to activate the law enforcement machinery. Lack of this facility with no budgetary provision to feed the arrested Pakistanis results in their being jostled between Border Security Forces and Police Customs. Absence of vehicles with the police, inadequate staff, ambiguous laws and poor road network are also severe constraints for the border guarding forces.

In some of the border areas criminals make use of women and children as carriers in smuggling, as lookouts etc. There is no woman police available on the border as a result of which no woman child can be detained. This is fully exploited by the criminals. The women also take advantage of the fact that strict action is taken against security forces in case of any report against them for ill- treating women. The women also exploit this by leveling false allegations against the security forces that are reluctant to get involved in apprehending any woman or child for fear of being reported against them. The long inquiries, which follow

---

52 Anand Kumar, 'Indo Bangladesh Border Dispute Demands Urgent Attention', available at http://www.southasiaanalysis.org/papers1931.html, (Last Viewed on August 28, 2006).

53 N.S Jamwal, 'Management of Land Borders', Strategic Analysis (July- September, 2002).

after such allegation, are a source of immense stress to the security forces. Most institutions of civil governance in the State, already weakened by inefficiency and corruption, have suffered a complete breakdown in the face of the terrorist onslaught. This includes the States prosecution department and judiciary.

Non-Availability of Witnesses and Evidences

It is very difficult to get any local to testify in the court against any criminal, as a strong bond exists amongst the people in the border areas. Most of the people are involved in some way or the other in one illegal activity to another. This affinity forces them to side with the criminals and extend no help to the security forces.

Moreover, nobody wants to be involved with the police because of the harassment caused by being a court witness. The condition of witnesses, in our country, are best illustrated by the following extract, from a letter written by a Session Judge to the National Police Commission: " The biggest single hurdle which inhibits the citizen from coming forward to help the police is the deplorable conditions prevailing in the courts of law. The lot of witnesses appearing on behalf of the State against a criminal is certainly pitiable."[54]

There is another difficulty and that is the collection of evidence in cases where the search, seizure and arrest in areas where there is no habitation and many a time these have been by security forces. In such a case, the arrested persons' confession to the security forces leading to the recovery of arms and ammunition and explosives is the only thing, which can be brought on record. Even the security force personnel do not come forward for tendering evidence because they keep on moving from place to place for performance of their duties not only within J&K but even outside J&K and sometimes outside India. The security force personnel are reluctant to depose in any case as they feel that they are not attuned for this kind of exercise. In the last 15 years of militancy in J&K, thousands of people have been arrested, lakhs of weapons seized and millions of rounds collected and quintals of explosive material seized. These figures are real eye openers and the fact that not a single case has ended in conviction nor has there been any recording of evidence and even this itself is very

---

54 Joginder Singh, 'OP-ED To counter Simi, involve Muslims in war on terror' available at http://asianage.com/presentation/leftnavigation/opinion/op-ed/tocountersimi, involve-muslims-in-war-on-terror/html, (Last Viewed on September 27, 2008).

disturbing.[55]

Easy Exit across the Border

The terrorist make full use of the porosity of the borders. They are known to cross over after committing a crime and find refuge in sympathizers and relatives till the presence of the law eases on them.

Loopholes in the Legal System

The legal system has several loopholes, which are fully exploited by the terrorists. For example, in case of a claimed seizure the BSF is required to produce the person from whom the contraband has been recovered, before the customs in case the seizure is to be termed as claimed. When this is done the custom officials confiscate the goods and release the criminals, as the offence does not warrant his detention under the Custom Act. In case the man is handed over to the police, the seizure becomes unclaimed. Similarly, in case of illegal border crossing, the intruder is apprehended by the BSF or Army and handed over to the police. The individual is released in time, the same or the next day by the police and pushed back.

Every citizen in India has been guaranteed the freedoms mentioned in the Preamble of our Constitution, they have to be consistent with the unity and integrity of India. The Police are naturally under a lot of pressure, not only to deal and arrest terrorists, but also to collect evidence. Terrorist organisations are closed organisations. They function only on need to know basis. India has antique laws framed in 1863, when there was no problem of terrorism. Confession made to Police, under the law, is not admissible in the courts. The terrorist cannot be expected to admit their guilt and put a hangman's noose themselves. With the heavy court pendency, cases take decades to come to finality. The Indian court system was slow, laborious, and prone to corruption; terrorism trials can take years to complete. Many of India's local police forces were poorly staffed, lacked training, and were ill- equipped to combat terrorism effectively problem faced by us. Unfortunately, now, India does not have even a tough law in place to fight.

Although, there is no as such stringent law against terrorism in the country, though this is the major challenge in front of the country, where there is urgency to eliminate terrorism. Here in our country, the Central

---

55   Editorial column, 'SIMI: Gun and Graves', *PTI – The Press Trust of India Ltd*, September 13, 2008 and also available at http://.www.lawcommissionofindia.nic. in/tada.htm. (Last Viewed on April 6, 2009).

Government is doing the hair splitting. The entire country needs tough laws. The fight against the terrorism is in the domain of the Government, as it has the man power, intelligence agencies, however rudimentary and ineffective, and weaponry.

State police force has been found inadequately trained to deal with situation as such border guarding forces are frequently withdrawn to combat insurgency. They have also been withdrawn many a time to deal with law and order problems. Withdrawal of forces limits their capabilities to guard the borders efficient.

Border Guidelines

There should be proper border guidelines framed for the border guarding forces of all the countries. The aim of these border guidelines was to ensure co- operation between both the border guarding forces over cross border crimes and exchange of information and intelligence at appropriate levels. These guidelines, among other issues, also provide that neither side to have any permanent or temporary border security forces within 150 yards on either side of International Border, and no defensive works of any nature including trenches in the stretch of 150 yards on each side of the boundary. Under this provision, Pakistan objects to the construction of fences within 150 yards from the International Border on the pretext that fencing violates the guidelines.[56] It even objects to construction of roads within this distance on the same pretext.

A major cause of dispute between India and Bangladesh has been the differing interpretation of border guidelines framed in 1975. India maintains that these guidelines are meant for the demolition of defensive structures within 150 yards of No Man's Land.[57] They do not apply to the building of a fence along the border since it is meant to check smuggling and other illegal activities. But the BDR has misinterpreted the guidelines probably with the sole objective of capturing Indian land trapped between the fence and the No Man's Land.

---

56 Anand Kumar, 'Indo-Bangladesh Border Dispute Demand Urgent Attention' South Asia Analysis Group, available at http://saaq.org/common/uploadedFiles/paper1931html, (Last Viewed on October 20, 2010).

57 Ibid.

Collaborative Legal Actions against Terrorism

In reality all the victim States all over the world are fighting for themselves against the menace of terrorism. Moreover, the big nations too don't indulge themselves to fight for the problems of small nations. This lacuna is still subsisting in actual.

In view of above- mentioned points, all the governments of India's neighbouring countries must jointly come to an agreement to make the border safe and secure. Blaming each other on the issue of peace and security must be stopped. For this, the border must be restricted for the terrorists, controlled for smugglers, checked for the criminals, obstructed for girl's traffickers, and stopped for narcotic holders. However, it must be regulated for the genuine passengers of neighbouring country and India with the efficient management for legal export and import of merchandise. At the same time, special arrangement must be made for the inhabitants living in 5 km of either side of the frontier to cross the border at International Borders many times a day, without feeling insecure. Insecure international Border could be made secure, to a large extent, with the political will and commitment from both sides. Security should be a key dimension of border management among neighbouring countries and India.

Conclusion

There is a requirement of a will to win the war over terrorism backed up by strict enforcement of existing laws at national and international level. Any system as it marches ahead reveals certain lacunae and loopholes, which in the instant case affords the terrorists and advantage and ultimately in getting away rather mildly. There should be parity in the norms to be adopted by different countries at the international level when it comes to protect the national interest. Such measures should be undertaken which include special patterns of cooperation between like- minded governments, sanctions against States that sponsor or support terrorism in other nation's territory and intervene with its peace and harmony and there should be a fuller application of international legal norms. With regard to international law, greater respect must be accorded to the principle of "extradite or prosecute", Sates must respect the definition of aggression approved by the General Assembly in 1974 and terrorist must come to be regarded by all States as common enemies of humanity. Taken together such measures could severely limit the likelihood of cross border terrorism.

India ranks among the world's most terrorism- affected countries in the US State department's annual report on terrorism released on April 30, 2009. The report said, India's effort to counter menace "remain hampered by its outdated and overburdened law enforcement and legal system. The report which highlighted the 26/11 Mumbai carnage[58] and seven other major terror strikes across India in 2008, noted, "None of the perpetrators of these attacks have yet been prosecuted." Ranking India as the world's most terrorism affected country, the report said, "India continues to be the focus of numerous attacks from both extremely- bases terrorist organisations and internationally based separatist or terrorist entities". While calling the Indian counter- terrorism outmoded and legal system overburdened, the report took note of the post- Mumbai pieces of legislation in Parliament to restructure the counter terrorism laws and the proposed National Investigative Agency to create national level capability to probe and prosecute acts of terrorism.[59]

There are few which poses a serious challenge to the national security of the nations unless immediate measures for border areas are taken without peaceful borders with its neighbours. The problems involved are so complex that they defy easy solutions. In this situation, it would be advisable if India starts by first solving the border issue of illegal migration and terror camps in Bangladesh as well as other bordering nations with India. Problems on the Indo-Bangladesh border have persisted also because it figures very low on the priority list of the Indian government. In view of above- mentioned points, all the governments must jointly come to an agreement to make the borders safe and secure. Blaming each other on the issue of peace and security must be stopped. For this, the border must be restricted for the terrorists, controlled for smugglers, checked for the criminals, obstructed for girl traffickers, and stopped for narcotic holders.

India can hardly play its legitimate role in global affairs at this time of seminal global change. Since borders are with neighbours and neighbours are people, one has to take into consideration the people and the State when talks about borders and problems related to them. Due to the proclivity of India's neighbours to exploit India's nation- building difficulties, the

---

58 ibid.

59 Editorial column, 'India- Most Terrorism Afflicted Country'. available at http:///:www. News.indiamart.com/news-analysis/IndiaMostTerrorismAfflictedCountry/ html, (Last viewed on September 18, 2009) And also available at http://www.state. gov/s/crt/2008/122434.htm, (Last viewed on November 18, 2009).

country's internal security challenges are inextricably linked with border management.[60] The challenge of coping with long- standing territorial and boundary disputes with China and Pakistan, combined with porous borders along some of the most difficult terrain in the world, has made effective and efficient border management a national priority.

The national borders cannot be protected by guns alone; 'hot & live' borders drain the economy and fuel threat perception. India must conceptualise national borders of friendships and friendly linkages. We are handicapped because of inadequate knowledge and understanding of our neighbour's threat perception, their strategic behavior and about the people living on the borders on either side. For future proper management and operational planning regarding the borders, information and documentation should be systematically developed. The fight against terrorism should be in the prime most things in the policy of the Government, as it has the man power, intelligence agencies. It is the conservative policy of the government not to arm the citizens. Not one percent crime is committed with licensed weapons. Indeed, the criminals and terrorists do not need any license to bear arms and kill the people. It is the innocent, unarmed people who have to bear the burnt. Licensing of the weapons should be liberalized, so that if the government is not able to protect the people, the people themselves can do so. Private security agencies should be involved in a big way and the weapons licensed to them to protect private and even government establishments. The government should stop giving the impression of being soft on terrorists.

---

60 Brig. Gurmeet Kanwal, 'India's Borders', Indian Defence Review, Vol. XXIII, available at http://www.indiandefencereview.com/2008/10/indias-borders. html, (Last viewed on April 17, 2010).

Chapter IV

Cross Border Terrorism In India: International And National Legal Perspective

Undoubtedly, terrorism is a complex problem and its origin is diverse. It is resorted as willful choice by organisation for political and strategic reasons. Those who practice it assume collective rationality. It is selected as a course of action from a range of perceived alternatives. It is a policy of violence designed to promote desired outcomes by instilling fear in the public at large. The key element is public intimidation. That is what distinguishes it from other form of violence. In customary violence the victim is personally targeted but in terrorism the victims are incidental whereas, terrorists intended objectives are used simply as a way to provoke social conditions designed to further their broader aims.

Due to globalization, the reach and speed of communication, reduced travel barriers, and increasing environmental interdependency, the political and the personal are moving towards convergence. We are living in a world where rapidly evolving international conflicts have the overwhelm safety and security everywhere. Conflicts in Afghanistan, Sudan, Brazil, and Yemen can no longer be ignored, as they touch our lives in increasingly significant ways.[1] Nearer home the Liberation Tigers of Tamil Eelam (LTTE) in Srilanka and various organisations in Pakistan have gained prominence. The situation in Kashmir is well known to everyone where the number of incidents of violence is peaked with highest rate of casualties. The terrorist collect huge sums in the name of religion and utilize it for creating political instability. In India the naxalities in Andhra Pradesh and Bihar carry out terrorist activities everyday indulge in mass killings.[2]

---

1   Kenneth Cloke, "Mediating Evil, War and Terrorism the Politics of Conflict", *Settle it Now! Dispute Resolution Journal* available at http://.www.settleitnow. org, (Last Viewed on April 11, 2009).

2   Editorial column, 'What We Talk about Law When We Talk about Law', *The Indian*

Terrorism is thus a disease, an ailment caused due to variety of reasons which have been endeavored to be eradicated from time to time by enacting laws to curb and efface it. Recent, Ahmedabad, Delhi and Mumbai bombings resulting in horrible killings have understandably caused indignation at the almost total failure of intelligence machinery. Those attacks have revived the debate on terror and the state's inability to deal with it.

Cross border terrorism has been the most powerful hazard to international security, and terrorism driven by religious extremism, is even double so. Plural and open democracies are the target of the very root of tolerance, mainstay of civil society in a free world. India has been witnessing terrorist violence since 1980, initially in Punjab, and since, 1989, in J&K and other parts of North East and North West of India. India is in favour of a collective international policy to combat the reinsurance of international terrorism. Time and again, India has raised its voice at the UN and other international Forums to draw world community's attention towards this burning issue. India strongly advocates that cross border terrorism should be seen along with other international crimes like drug trafficking, money laundering and trafficking in arms and personal, and should be accorded top priority during the next few years.

However, it is clear that the fight against terror should not be confused with the necessity of appropriate and effective legislation to deal with terrorists. The harshest of laws are not an impediment in the way of terrorist organisations in spreading terror. Terrorism postulates that a terrorist is willing to sacrifice his life for whatever cause he espouses, since his arm is not to avenge a personal grouse through violent means, but to terrorise the community at large, to have it pay attention to his perceived mission. No laws, no matter how harsh, can stand in his way. The most powerful nation in the world with the most modern technologies at its command cannot stop terrorist activity in Iraq or prevent American soldiers becoming victims of such attacks.[3]

India has been among the major victims of terrorism – mostly cross border state sponsored Terrorism -for over two decades. Despite the intolerably high cost in terms of human lives, people and material, India

Express, September 25, 2008.

3   Dr. Surat Singh (2007), *Law Relating to Prevention of Terrorism*, Delhi and also available at http://.in.news.yahoo.com/htm, (Last viewed on March, 30, 2009).

has steadfastly pursued a counter strategy which gives primacy to dialogue, democratic political processes and the rule of law. Armed counter actions are based on the doctrine of "minimum use of force" within the framework of the Constitution which guarantees human rights.[4] As it is mandatory to give complete protection to the human rights of each and everyone within the territory otherwise this would also turn out to be one of the main cause of eruption of terrorism when somebody's human rights have been infringed.

International Law And Terrorism

However, all the forms of terrorism are criminal and unjustifiable and therefore it has to be curbed. In the past, a number of attempts have been made to control international terrorism within and outside the League of Nations and UN. The question of combating terrorism at international level has been constantly on the agenda of the international law and the international institutions especially UN even prior to the Second World War. After the assassination of King Alexander I of Yugoslavia and the Prime Minister Louis Barthou of France on October 9, 1934, the Council of the League of Nations on December 10, 1934 unanimously passed a resolution to institute a Committee of Experts with a view to draft a tentative international convention to curb any scheming or offences in pursuant of 'political terrorism'. Later on, an international conference was convened in Geneva which met from November 1 to 16, 1937. The Conference examined and adopted two conventions: The Convention for the Prevention and Punishment of Terrorism and the Convention for the Creation of an International Criminal Court.[5] The Conventions did not come into force for want of requisite ratifications. Subsequently many more conventions have been concluded for the suppression of specific forms of international terrorism, after the establishment of UN. As terrorism is no doubt an old and dynamic concept as its roots and implications are subsisting in the society since ages. Therefore time and again effective efforts have been undertaken as the steps to curb this menace by the nations as such. Hereby, a review of these efforts has been made under the following headings:-

---

4   D.K Patahk, 'Country Report: India' available at http://www.unafei.or.jp/html, (Last Viewed on March 23, 2010).

5   The first Convention received only one ratification that of India on January 1, 1941. the Convention did not enter into force.

United Nations and Terrorism

However, in front of one of the substantial and fundamental international organisation UN, terrorism is a burning as well as debating issue which is of great concern. The problem of terrorism in general, has been under consideration of the General Assembly since 1972. On September 23, 1972, the Assembly recommended the following item to be included in the agenda and brought before the Sixth Committee.[6]

Measures to prevent international terrorism which endangers or takes innocent human lives or jeopardizes fundamental freedoms and study of the underlying causes of those forms of terrorism and acts of violence which lie in misery, frustration, grievance and despair and which cause some people to sacrifice human lives, including their own, in an attempt to effect radical changes.

In the deliberations of the Sixth Committee divergent views were taken by the representatives of different States. On its recommendation the General Assembly on December 18, 1972 adopted a resolution[7] wherein it decided to establish an Ad Hoc Committee on international terrorism of 35 members. The Committee held its first session in 1973 without achieving any positive results. However, the Committee submitted its report to the Assembly. The latter was unable to consider the item for want of time until the thirty first session held in 1976. In 1976, the Assembly adopted a resolution wherein it invited the Ad Hoc Committee to continue its work in accordance with the mandate originally entrusted to it. By the same resolution, the Assembly also invited States to submit their observations as soon as possible to the Secretary General so as to enable the Committee to perform its mandate more efficiently, and it requested him to transmit to other Committee and analytical study of those observations. The Ad Hoc Committee met in 1977 and submitted a report to the Assembly without any further progress. In 1979 session, the Ad Hoc Committee worked out general recommendations relating to practical measures of international terrorism. These recommendations reflected a common view of fundamental importance. On the recommendations of the Ad Hoc Committee, the General Assembly on December 17, 1979 adopted

---

6   Y. Sverdlov(1984), *Terrorism and International Law*, USSR and also available at http://leninist.biz/htm, (Last Viewed on October 18, 2009).

7   General Assembly Resolution 3034 (XXVII), December 18, 1972.

a resolution[8] wherein the act of terrorism was condemned and it urged all States, unilaterally and in co- operation with other States as well as relevant UN Organs to contribute to the progressive elimination of the causes underlying that kind of terrorism.[9]

By the resolution, the Assembly called upon all the States to fulfill their obligations under international law to refrain from organizing, instigating, assisting or participating in acts of civil strife or terrorist acts in another state or acquiescing in organised activities within its territory directed towards the commission of such acts.[10] Since 1979, no further progress has been made in the following years excepting the endorsement of the resolution adopted in 1979.[11]

It was only in the year 1994, a declaration on Measures to Eliminate International Terrorism[12] was adopted by the Assembly which stated that terrorism includes criminal acts intended or calculated to provoke a state of terror in the general public, a group of persons or particular persons for political purposes. The Declaration further stated that such acts are in any circumstances unjustifiable whatever the consideration of a political, philosophical, ideological, racial, ethnic, religious, or other nature that may be invoked to justify them. In 1996 the Supplementary Declaration[13] was adopted which condemned all acts and practices of terrorism as criminal and unjustifiable whenever and whosoever committed and urged all States to take measures at the national and international levels to eliminate international terrorism.[14]

Since the present multilateral conventions on international terrorism do not cover all means and a method used for commission of terrorist's acts, India proposed at the 51st General Assembly the adoption of a comprehensive convention on international terrorism. In resolution 54/110, the Assembly mandated the Ad Hoc Committee on International Terrorism,

---

8   General Assembly Resolution 34/145, December 17, 1979

9   Ibid.

10   Amos Yoder. "UN Resolutions against International Terrorism", *Studies in Conflict & Terrorism*, (1983).

11   General Assembly Resolution 38/130.

12   General Assembly Resolution 49/60 of December 9, 1994.

13   General Assembly Resolution 51/20 of December 17, 1996.

14 Editorial column, 'The UN Response', UN Chronicles, Vol.IIIVII, 2001, p.3 available at http://.www.un.org, (Last viewed on April 18, 2010).

established on 17 December 1996, to elaborate the Convention. India then submitted a revised draft text. Similar to the provisions of the International Convention for the Suppression of the Financing of Terrorism, the draft distinguishes between terrorist and non-terrorist crimes, when they are committed to intimidate a population or to compel a Government or an international organisation to certain actions.[15] It considers as criminal and any act causing death or serious bodily injury to any person, or causing serious damage to public or private property, a place of public use, a public transportation system or an infrastructure facility. States parties are required to establish these offences as criminal offences punishable by appropriate penalties, taking into account their grave nature. A State is required to establish jurisdiction over these offences when committed in its territory, on board its ships or aircraft, or by its nationals or habitual residents in its territory, and also when an act committed outside its territory results in an offence within its territory. States are not required to adopt legislation to ensure that the offences are not justifiable by any ideological, religious or other considerations, nor in extradition proceedings give grounds to perpetrators to claim that their acts were politically motivated. States are also obliged to extend mutual legal assistance and required to prohibit and prevent training camps and financing of those offences, deny asylum to those connected with terrorist activities, and extradite or prosecute them if found in their territory. Many provisions of the draft were generally acceptable to delegations, and it was hoped that the Convention can be finalized at the session of the General Assembly, providing an effective instrument for international cooperation against international terrorism.[16] Unfortunately the draft did not enter into force.

The Ad hoc Committee in the year 2002 restarted negotiations on a comprehensive international treaty on terrorism. The Committee began deliberation on difficult topics to tackle terrorism including those dealing with a definition of terrorism and its relation to liberation movements, possible exemptions to the scope of the treaty, in particular regarding the activities of the armed forces, and how to advance the level and types of international cooperation to combat terrorism. The Ad hoc Committee in its seventh session held in April 2003 made a recommendation that the Assembly's Legal Committee consider the setting up of a working group to continue the elaboration of two draft conventions on terrorism – a

15 Ibid.
16 Ibid.

comprehensive convention on international terrorism and an international convention for the suppression of acts of nuclear terrorism.

How far the Assembly would succeed in curbing international terrorism is a question which is difficult to answer in affirmative. It has been considering the topic since 1972 without any success. Divergent views taken by the States before the Ad hoc Committee shows that unless and until States come close on certain broad issues, general recommendation would be of little use. The imminent and indispensable task in suppressing the act of terrorism is therefore to achieve international co-operation. Measures to combat terrorism on international level would be grim as long as the attitude of the States is not changed.

Role of Security Council

The fundamental organ of UN, Security Council also became active to curb the terrorism after the terrorists acts that took place in New York, Washington and Pennsylvania on September 11, 2001. The Council condemned unequivocally the attack by adopting resolution 1368 on September 12, 2001[17] and called on all States to work together urgently to bring the perpetrators to justice.[18] On 28 September, the Security Council unanimously adopted resolution 1373 (2001), declaring that terrorists' acts, methods, and practices of terrorism, as well as their financing, planning and incitement are "contrary to the purposes and principles of the UN".[19] The Council noted with concern the close connection between international terrorism and transnational organised crime, illicit drugs, money laundering and illegal movement of nuclear, chemical, biological and other deadly materials. It emphasized the need to enhance the coordination of efforts to strengthen a global response to combat threats to international peace and security caused by terrorist acts, and expressed its

---

17 Security Council Resolution 1373/2001, dated September 28, 2001. earlier the Security Council had adopted Resolution 1269 (1999) on the initiative of Russia, the first comprehensive anti-terrorist resolution on a global scale in the history. The resolution laid the groundwork for the establishment of the counter-terrorist coalition, articulated its key principles and defined the areas for collective efforts. Before that, the Council had considered some specific cases related to terrorism as in the case of sanctions against Taliban.

18 Security Council unanimously adopts wide-ranging anti-terrorism resolutions calls for suppressing financing, improving international cooperation resolution 1373, Security Council SC/7158 4385th Meeting (Night) 28 September 2001, available at http://. www.geocities.com, (Last Viewed on April 16, 2009).

19 Ibid.

determination to take all necessary steps to fully implement this resolution.

Acting under Chapter VII of the UN Charter, which makes its provisions mandatory on all States immediately, the Council laid out wide-ranging strategies to combat international terrorism, and established a Committee, consisting of all Council members, to monitor implementation of the resolution. It called upon all States to report within 90 days on actions they had taken to that end. The resolution requires all States to prevent and suppress the financing of terrorism, as well as criminalise the willful provision or collection of funds for such acts. The financial assets of those who commit, attempt to commit or facilitate terrorist acts should also be frozen. The Council decided States should prohibit their nationals or people in their territories from making funds or services available to those involved in terrorism, refrain from providing support to people involved in terrorism, take steps to prevent terrorist acts, and deny safe haven to those who commit or support terrorist acts or provide safe havens.[20]

States are also required to prevent terrorists from using their territories for those purposes against other countries, bring to justice anyone who has participated in terrorism, and ensure that terrorist acts are established as serious criminal offences in domestic laws and are punishable accordingly. States should further assist one another with criminal investigations or proceedings relating to the financing or support of terrorist acts, and prevent the movement of terrorists or their groups by effective border controls and regulation of identity and travel documents. The Council called on all States to intensify and accelerate the exchange of information regarding terrorist actions or movements, forged or falsified documents, traffic in arms and sensitive material, use of communications technologies by terrorist groups, and the threat posed by the possession of weapons of mass destruction. States should also become parties to the relevant conventions and protocols to combat terrorism.

The Council called on States to ensure that before granting refugee status, in conformity with international law, including international standards of human rights, asylum seekers had not taken part in terrorist acts and that refugee status would not be abused by terrorists. Claims of political motivation, it said, should not be recognized as grounds for refusing requests for the extradition of alleged terrorists.

---

20 Supra note 8.

The Security Council by the same resolution also decided to establish a Committee of the Security Council consisting of all the members of the Council. The mandate of the committee is to monitor implementation of the resolution with the assistance of appropriate expertise. The Council called upon all States to report to the Committee, no later than 90 days from the date of the adoption the resolution and thereafter according to a time table to be proposed by the Committee, on the steps they have taken to implement it. The Council directed the committee to delineate its tasks, submit a work programmed within 30 days of the adoption of the resolution.[21]

The main thrust of the resolution is on the financing of terrorist operations and to stop providing safe havens to anyone who supports terrorists or their organisations. The resolution invoked Chapter VII of the UN Charter which makes it mandatory for all the members.[22] However, the resolution does not provide for any action against those States which violate the provisions of the resolution. Further, the resolution does not define terrorism which is an important element as some of the States are seeking to differentiate between terrorism and freedom struggle (or to say terrorists and freedom fighters). Thus it is difficult to draw the boundaries between the legitimate and illegitimate, use of terror and between the right way to fight and wrong way to fight. It is also to be noted that resolution uses the terms 'terrorist groups' but the Council has not identified them and therefore States might feel difficulty in implementing the resolution.

These points go to conclude that it is premature to say as to the implementation of the resolution by the States. However, the Committee of the Security Council known as Counter-Terrorism-Committee (CTC) established by the resolution has received reports from a number of countries on the steps they have taken from implementing anti–terrorism measures as required therein.[23] The three countries – Sao Tome and Principe Swaziland and the Vanuatu have not submitted even a preliminary report by the end of March 2003 and 51 States were late in submitting a follow–up report. The Security Council called on them urgently to do so as required by its resolution 1373.[24] Submission of reports by such a large number of States is indeed a demonstration of 'excellent cooperation' by

---

21 H.O. Aggarwal (2010), *International Law and Human Rights*, Allahabad.

22 S.K Kapoor (2009), *International Law,* Allahabad.

23 Alex Conte (2010), *Human Rights in the Prevention and Punishment of Terrorism*, USA.

24 "International developments", *Commonwealth Law Bulletin*, Vol. XXVIII, 2002

the states in the implementation of the resolution.

Member States through the General Assembly have been increasingly coordinating their counter-terrorism efforts and continuing their legal norm-setting work. The Security Council has also been active in countering terrorism through resolutions and by establishing several subsidiary bodies. At the same time a number of programmes, offices and agencies of the UN system have been engaged in specific activities against terrorism; further assisting Member States in their counter-terrorism efforts.[25]

To consolidate and enhance these activities, Member States in September 2006, embarked upon a new phase in their counter-terrorism efforts by agreeing on a **global strategy to counter terrorism**.[26] The Strategy marks the first time that all Member States of the UN have agreed to a common strategic and operational framework to fight terrorism.

The Strategy forms a basis for a concrete plan of action: to address the conditions conducive to the spread of terrorism; to prevent and combat terrorism; to take measures to build state capacity to fight terrorism; to strengthen the role of the UN in combating terrorism; and to ensure the respect of human rights while countering terrorism. The Strategy builds on the unique consensus achieved by world leaders at their 2005 September Summit to condemn terrorism in all its forms and manifestations.[27]

The UN Global Counter-Terrorism Strategy adopted by Member States on 8 September 2006, serves as a common platform, bringing the efforts of the UN system entities that work on counter-terrorism related issues into a common, coherent and more focused framework. The Strategy gives support to the practical work of the UN Counter-Terrorism Implementation Task Force (CTITF), established by the Secretary-General in July 2005 to ensure overall coordination and coherence in the counter-terrorism efforts of the UN system. Member States expressed support and appreciation for the work of the Task Force when they met to examine progress in the implementation of the Strategy in September 2008. In June 2009, the Secretary-General made initial arrangements to institutionalize the Task Force by establishing a CTITF-Secretariat in the Department of Political Affairs (DPA). CTITF aims to catalyze and mobilize counter-

---

25 "Hurriyat's Worth?" Azad Kashmir, available at http://.www.kashmirmedia. wordpress.com, (Last Viewed on November 11, 2009).

26 Ibid.

27 Ibid

terrorism efforts of various UN system entities to assist Member States in implementing the Strategy.[28]

However, in the strategy there are certain agendas and proposed targets which are required to be achieved by all the members of the international communities. Following is the full text of the Resolution and the Plan of Action:

- Measures to address the conditions conducive to the spread of terrorism

- Measures to prevent and combat terrorism

- Measures to build States' capacity to prevent and combat terrorism and to strengthen the role of the UN system in this regard

- Measures to ensure respect for human rights for all and the rule of law as the fundamental basis of the fight against terrorism

The General Assembly held its first review of the implementation of the Strategy on 4-5 September 2008, and adopted a **resolution** reaffirming its commitment to the Strategy and its implementation. As one of the inputs to this process, the Secretary-General has compiled a **report** on activities of the UN system in implementing the Strategy.[29]

On 9 September 2008, the Secretary General convened the first ever global Symposium on Supporting Victims of Terrorism. A report summarizing the key themes and recommendations of the Symposium and a video summary have been produced and were released at a discussion with Victims, Member States, and NGOs on 18 March 2009. In June 2009, the Secretary-General made initial arrangements to institutionalize the Task Force by establishing a CTITF-Secretariat in the Department of Political Affairs (DPA).[30] CTITF aims to catalyze and mobilize counter-terrorism efforts of various UN system entities to assist Member States in implementing the Strategy.

---

28 M.K Teng 'Kashmiri Pandits Virtual Homeland of Kashmiri Pandits Panun', available at http://ikashmir.org, (Last Viewed on November 22, 2002).

29 Supra note 8.

30 Supra note 21.

International Conventions and Terrorism

Several conventions have come into force from time to time, to effectively face the challenges posed by ever increasing international act of terrorism, jeopardising the human life, fundamental freedoms and property across the globe. A wide range of subjects are being covered by these conventions, which are withering directly or indirectly related to counter the terrorism at international level. The resolutions of the General Assembly, the UN Charter itself and several covenants on Human Rights promising to protect and secure the civil, political, economic and cultural rights of the people of the world. The Genocide Conventions etc., are also there but a few which have shown a great concern and the anxiety to curb international terrorism.

Some of the international conventions[31] which embody the international law and principles governing the checking of international terrorism, however, need a special mention in this regard:

A. Convention on the Prevention and Punishment of Terrorism, 1937

This convention as well as, incidentally, other documents of a similar character, had been worked out in view of the events which the international community could not pass over. The convention, which is the result of the efforts of the League of Nations, consists of a preamble and 29 Articles and emphasizes that the convention is designed to make more effective the prevention and punishment of terrorism of an international character. The important provisions of the convention include, duty of every state to refrain from any acts designed to encourage terrorist activities developed against another state to make municipal legislations fixing liability for such acts, to conclude extradition arrangements.

Further, the convention also reaffirms the principle of international law in virtue of which it is the duty of every state to refrain from any act designed to encourage terrorist activities directed against another state.

B. Convention on Prevention of Punishment of Crimes against Internationally Protected Persons including Diplomatic agents, 1973

The General Assembly on December 13, 1973 adopted the convention on the prevention land punishment of crimes against internationally protected

---

31 H.O. Aggarwal (2010), *International Law and Human Rights*, Allahabad

persons, including diplomatic agents. The convention came into force on February 20, 1977. As on September 17, 2001, the convention had 107 states parties. The convention defines an internationally protected person as a Head of State, minister of foreign affairs, representative or official of a State or an international organisation that is entitled to special protection from attack under international law. The main object of the adoption of the convention was to render inescapable the punishment of the crimes committed against persons entitled to protection.[32]

The convention required each party to criminalize and make punishable by appropriate penalties, which take into account their grave nature. The international murder, kidnapping, or other attack upon the person or liberty of an internationally protected persons: a violent attack upon the official premises, the private accommodations, or the means of transport of such person, threat or attempt to commit such an attack and an act constituting participation as an accomplice.

Although the **'Principle of Inviolability'** of the diplomatic and diplomatic missions, the principle of protection of consular officers and premises and the inviolability of the representatives of the sending States and that of the members of the diplomatic staff of a special mission as well as the premises of that mission is envisaged by the provisions of adopted to specify the range of persons and objects, the commission of an act of violence against whom, or threat of such an act or attempt at committing one, or acting an accomplice in any such act.

The important provisions of the convention include, an elaborate definition of the term internationally protected person, the State parties to make certain offences punishable under laws such as murder or kidnapping or other attempts on the person or liberty of an internationally protected person, the State parties to take measures to establish jurisdiction over the rimes mentioned in the convention, ensure the presence of the offender for the purpose of prosecution or extradition.

C. The International Convention against the taking of Hostages, 1979

A review of the substance of terrorist acts falling within the scope of international law indicates that in a number of instances the commission of

---

32 South African Law Commission Project 105, Review of Security Legislation (Terrorism: Section 54 of the Internal Security Act, 1982, August 2002, available at http://wwwserver.law.wits.ac.za, (Last viewed on August 10, 2002).

such offences involves the taking of hostages. Through international law already have some perceptions in force to ban hostages taking in specified circumstances. With a view to have a uniform international convention against the taking of hostages, under the auspices of UN, this convention has been concluded on December 7, 1979. As on September 17, 2001, the convention had 96 State parties.[33]

The preamble of the convention clearly laid down that the taking of hostages is an offence of grave concern to the international community and that it is urgently necessary to develop international co- operation between states in devising and adopting effective measures for the prevention, prosecution and punishment of all acts of taking of hostages and manifestation of international terrorist. The convention provides that any person who seizes or detains and threatens to kill, to injure or to continue to detain another person in order to compel a their party, namely, a State, an international inter- governmental organisation, a natural or judicial person, or a group of persons, to do or obtain from doing any act as an explicitly or implicit condition for the release of the hostage commits the offence of taking of hostages within the meaning of this convention.

The convention under Article 8 stipulated that the State party in the territory of which the alleged offender is found shall, if it does not extradite him, be obliged to summit the case to its competent authorities for the purpose of prosecution, through proceedings in accordance with the laws of that State. This is, therefore, in line with one of the major principles of the convention machinery assuming inescapable punishment of the crimes committed 'extradition or prosecution'.

The convention makes it imperative for the signatory States to prosecute under criminal law or extradite and person committing, an act of hostage taking and also take appropriate measures of punishment, thus some progress towards resolving the question of hostage taking has been made through international law.

D. Convention to Ensure the Safety and Security of the UN and Associated Personnel, 1994

The General Assembly on December 9, 1994 adopted a convention the safety of UN and associated personnel.[34] The convention consisting of 29

---

33 Supra note 24.

34 Editorial column, 'The UN Response', UN Chronicles, Vol.IIIVII, 2001, p.3 available

Articles covers UN personnel engaged or deployed by the Secretary-General as members of a military police or civilian component of an operation, as well as officials and experts on missions, associated personnel are defined as those assigned by a government or an international organisation to carry operation.

The convention obliges States to establish jurisdiction over crimes including murder, kidnapping or threat of attack against UN and associated personnel. It defines the duties of States to ensure the safety and security of such personnel and to release or return those captured or detained. The convention calls on host States and the UN to quickly conclude arrangements on the States of the UN operation and personnel.[35]

The convention also addresses such issues as prosecution or extradition of alleged offenders. The convention came into force on January 15, 1999. As on September 8, 2003, the convention had 66 States parties.[36]

E. International Convention for the Suppression of Terrorism Bombings, 1997

The General assembly on December 15, 1997 adopted an international convention for the suppression of terrorist bombings. The convention consists of 24 articles, as on convention has 26 States parties.

This is yet another convention added to the armoires of international law, for the suppression of terrorism bombings. In recent times, the world has witnessed the increasingly wide spread terrorist attacks by means of explosives or other lethal devices, in crucial areas of States, targeting innocent civilians and property. Accordingly responding to the need for strengthening the hands of international law to curb the terrorist bombings, at the initiation of UN General Assembly, the convention has come into existence.

The important provisions of the convention include, definition of the offence of terrorist bombings, making of domestic laws to punish such crimes, taking up of measures to establish jurisdiction to try and punish the offenders or otherwise, take steps to secure the presence of the offenders or extradite for facing the trial.

---

at http://.www.un.org, (Last viewed on April 18, 2010).

35 'Convention on Safety of UN personnel, Terrorism Declaration adopted. (Report on the UN General Assembly), UN Chronicle, March 1995.

36 Ibid.

The convention defines a terrorist bomber under article 2 as a person who unlawfully and internationally delivers, places, discharges or detonates explosive or other lethal devices in, into or against a place of public use, a state or government facility, a public transportation system or an infrastructure facility: (a) with the intent to cause death or serious bodily injury; or (b) with the intent to cause extensive destruction of such place, facility or system, where such destruction results in or is likely to result in major economic loss.[37]

An attempt to commit the above offence shall also be treated as an offence under the convention. Further, any person who participates as an accomplice in an offence or any person who organises or directs other to commit an offence shall also be considered to have committed an offence is committed within a single state, i.e., where the alleged offender is found in the territory of that State and the alleged offender is found in the territory of that State and no other State has a basis to exercise jurisdiction.

The convention provides under Article 8 that states shall either prosecute or extradite those accused of terrorist bombings within their territory and also calls on state to adopt further measures to present terrorism and strengthen international cooperation in combating such crimes. Article 9 of the convention lays down that the offence of terrorist bombings shall be deemed to be included as extraditable offences State parties before the entry into force of this convention. Further, State parties undertake to include such offences as extraditable offences in every extradition treaty to be subsequently concluded between them.

F. Convention for the Suppression of Financing of Terrorism, 1999

The General Assembly on December 9, 1999 adopted the convention for the suppression of the financing of terrorism which was opened for signature on January 10, 2000. The convention provides that it is a crime for anyone to provide or collect funds to be used to carry out acts that are considered as a terrorist activities, as defined by existing treaties. The term 'Funds' has been defined under article 1 as assets of every kind, whether tangible or intangible, movable or immovable, however acquired,

---

37 The Rule of Law in Countering Terrorism", Paper presented at Advisory Council of Jurists Asia Pacific Forum of National Human Rights Institutions, August 2003 available at http://.www.Asiapacificforum.net, (Last Viewed on September 10, 2003).

and legal documents or instruments in any form, including electronic or digital, evidencing title to, or interest in, such assets, concluding, but not limited to, bank credits, travelers cheques, bank cheques, money orders, shows, securities, bonds, drafts, litters of credit.

Any other act intended to kill or harm civilians in order to intimidate them or a government or international organisation would fall under the treaty's jurisdiction. The treaty also compels countries to confiscate funds found to be intended for use in terrorist activities and to investigate information that a person who has or is alleged to have committed such a crime is in its territory. The convention came into force on April 10, 2002 after it received the required 22 ratifications.[38]

It is to be noted that above conventions and a few other international and regional conventions have not been able to suppress the acts of terrorism. Mainly because these conventions whether international and regional conventions have not been ratified by most of the States of the world. For instance the convention on the prevention and punishment of crimes against internationally protected persons including diplomatic agents has been ratified only by 107 States by September 2001.[39] It is submitted that one of the most effective ways in which the substantial progress could be achieved for curbing international terrorism lies in the universal adherence to these conventions by all or most of the States.

Human Rights and Terrorism

Terrorism brings suffering and miseries to human beings. It being immoral and inhuman act puts under threat the rights and freedoms of innocent people. It, therefore, abuses the fundamental human rights of the victims, particularly, the right to life, the right to physical integrity and the right to personal freedom. The increasing number of innocent persons including women, children and the elderly have been killed, massacred or maimed by terrorists in indiscriminate and random acts of violence and terror which in no case can be justified. It has put a question mark on the most essential and basic human right of the people, i.e. right to life. The General Assembly has repeatedly expressed its deep concern about the world wide escalation of acts of terrorism in all its forms, which endanger or

---

38 This Additional Protocol supplements the SAARC Regional Convention on Suppression of Terrorism, done at Kathmandu, November 04, 1987, available at http://.mea.gov. in, (Last Viewed on April 17, 2009).

39 Ibid.

take innocent human lives, jeopardize fundamental freedom and security impair the dignity of human beings.[40]

Terrorist acts and methods, on the one, do provoke or give an excuse for serious violations of human rights and fundamental freedoms by the government which feel threatened by terrorism, and on the other hand, it has put into a difficult situation in maintaining and safeguarding the basic rights of the individuals in accordance with the relevant international human rights instruments. The above account shows that there is inescapable link between terrorism and human rights violations. Terrorism is clear threat to the concept of human rights and underlines the creation of the UN and to the life and dignity of the individuals.[41]

It is unfortunate that the concept of human rights with reference to terrorism has not been taken up seriously by the human rights bodies though the problem of international terrorism in general has been under consideration eliminate international terrorism which endangers and jeopardizes fundamental freedoms, and study of the underlying causes of those forms of terrorism and acts of violence which lie in misery, frustration, grievance and despair and which cause some people to sacrifice human lives, including their own, in an attempt to take radical changes. It was only in the year 1993 following the Vienna World Conference on Human Rights, the General Assembly, on the recommendation of the Third Committee started to adopt resolutions on Human Rights and Terrorism.[42]

The resolution on Human Rights and Terrorism adopted by the general Assembly since 1993 stated that terrorism creates an environment that destroys the freedom from fear of the people.[43] They condemned all acts, methods and practices of terrorism, as activities aimed at the destruction of human rights, fundamental freedoms and democracy. They also refer that terrorism constituted gross violations of human rights perpetrated by terrorist groups.

Killing innocent people destroying property and fostering an atmosphere of alarm and terror amount not merely to a violation of the rights of the victims, but it also poses threat to the society and to the State.

---

40 J.N.Sexena (1998), *International Terrorism: State Terror and Human Rights*, p.46.

41 Id.

42 Kalliopi K. Koufa, 'Terrorism and Human Rights' paper available at http://.www. unhchr.ch, (Last Viewed on August 11, 2009).

43 Ibid.

The authorities of the State which is responsible for bringing the terrorist violence to an end are entitled to respond with counter terrorist measures and may not be constraint by the normal limits of official measures for the prevention of ordinary crimes. In such cases, no doubt, there will be repression and violation of human rights of the terrorists but such acts shall be justifiable as they are taken in the larger interest of the society and the State. Terrorism is an assault against the society and the institutions which protect the liberty and society of the citizens. It has to be curbed in order to maintain peaceful international relations and cooperation.

Punishment to the terrorists is not a new proposition. UN has managed to adopt a number of Conventions with specific cases of terrorism such as aircraft hijacking, taking of hostages, prevention and punishment of crimes against internationally protected persons. They all are anti- terrorist's conventions and they provide either for extradition or for the prosecution so that terrorists may not go unpunished. Further, a few regional conventions are also anti- terrorists in the sense that they provide the application of the extradition or prosecution principle which is known by the maxim **Aut Dedre Aut Judicare.** This derogation to human rights is permissible if they are proportionate to the danger that those events represent.

International Criminal Court and Terrorism

By March 20, 2002, a total of 55 countries has ratified the treaty of setting up the new such court, which will have the power to try people accused of violating international humanitarian law.

The existing International Court of Justice (ICJ) in The Hague deals only with States, not with individuals. Just five more ratifications were needed before the International Criminal Court (ICC) comes into force. If the threshold of 60 countries would reached, the Rome Statute, setting up the ICC, would come into effect on July1, 2002.[44] Since the statute does not operate retrospectively, that data will mark the start of the court's jurisdiction over genocide, crimes against humanity, and war crimes. If the US had not campaigned so hard against the ICC, it is possible that the treaty could have been ratified in time to try any captured terrorist accused

---

44 Joshua Rozenberg, 'Vision of Global Crime Court Sees Light of Day at Last - Global Policy Forum - International Justice', available at http://www.globalpolicy.org, (Last Viewed on March 21, 2002).

of attacks on September 11, 2001.[45]

However, individuals who commit war crimes and other grave offences after the statute comes into effect will be at risk of prosecution, even though the court's prosecutor and judges will not be elected before next year.

Law Applied by the Court[46]

Article 21 of the statute lays down the law which shall be applied by the court. It is mentioned that the application and interpretation of law must be consistent with internationally recognized human rights and be without any adverse distinction founded on grounds such as gender, age, race, colour, language, religion or belief, political or other opinion, national ethnic or social origin, wealth, birth or other status.

The court while deciding a case shall apply the general principles of criminal law. Article 33 of the statute says that the fact that a crime within the jurisdiction of the court has been committed by a person pursuant to an order of a government or of a superior, whether military or civilian, shall not relieve that person of criminal responsibility unless

- The person was under a legal obligation to obey orders of the government or the superior in question

- The person did not know that the order was unlawful

- The order was not manifestly unlawful

The statute also lays down that orders to commit genocide or crimes against humanity are manifestly unlawful. The fight against terrorism in 21 century will be a complicated task. Hence, a concrete action is required to combat terrorism. Unity of efforts requires ways to integrate the actions of various responsible agencies- national as well as international. For waging a successful war against terrorism, an international political will coupled with cooperation and coordination among the states is required.

---

45 Ibid.

46 See, UN Juridical Year Book 2009, available at http://untreaty.un.org/cod/pdf, (Last Viewed on April 11, 2010).

United Kingdom (UK)- Anti- Terrorism Laws [47]

The UK has a long history of exposure to terrorism coming from within, in the 1970's the skinhead movement began among the working-class youths as a countermovement to the hippies; it also engaged in violent acts and racial harassments against the Asians and Blacks.

Thus, it is normal for this state to have terrorism laws existing in its legislature long before the September 11, 2001 attacks on the US. The difference is that after these attacks which coincided with the rise of radical Muslims in European countries generally, more attention has been given to national terrorism, security and asylum laws and acts. In the years following the September 11th attacks, a large number of Muslims have been arrested and detained; and most of the time released without being charged. Some European governments have passed laws with the intention of tightening security and seeking more protection, however, these laws are greatly affecting one's personal life, liberty, and in many cases future.

The rise of radical Muslims in the UK and other European States could be the consequence of a number of reasons both national and international such as the military presence of these countries in the Middle East under the banner of the war on terror, and/or the discrimination faced by the Muslim minorities on national levels, and segregation from the dominant society. Radicalism could also be due to "public provocation" acts such as the recurring publication of the "Danish cartoons" of Prophet Mohammed (PBUH) under the notion of defence of freedom of expression, while knowing that laws criminalizing holocaust denial and incitement show that there could be limits to freedom of expression in Western societies.

After worldwide criticism, the British Government has passed the Terrorism Act, 2000. Britain had been fast turning into a haven for terrorist groups and organisations that used the loopholes in the country's law to carry on their operation unhindered. The UK's Home Office states that the Terrorism Act 2000 is the primary piece of counter-terrorism legislation and contains the most vital counter-terrorism measures. This act aims at tackling international terrorism and has replaced previous anti-terrorism temporary legislation that specifically dealt with Northern Ireland.[48] The salient features of this Act are as follows:

---

47 'Terrorism Laws in UK', available at http://www.Magnacartaplus.org./bills/
    terrorism/index, (Last Viewed on December 17, 2009).

48 Ibid.

- The definition of terrorism is drawn very widely. It includes actions that cause serious damage to property, interfere with or seriously disrupt electronic systems or endanger public health. It matters not which governments are being influenced or where the actions take place. Thus direct action groups, supporting struggles against repressive regimes, or even unions on strike in the health sector could be classed as terrorist, with all that implies, under this bill.

- The home secretary can prescribe organisations he believes are concerned with "terrorism". Once proscribed membership of, professed membership of and support for an organisation becomes an offence punishable by 10 years in prison. Both the wide definition of terrorism and the vagueness of the grounds for proscription could lead to this being abused to shut down legitimate protest organisations. It is also there that proscription occurs without a case being proved in court.

- Powers to arrest and search without a warrant are granted where police suspect someone to be a terrorist.

- Powers to stop and question anyone in Northern Ireland is granted with respect to a "recent" explosion or incident that endangered life or to anyone killed or injured in recent explosion or incident endangering life. Failure to stop and answer the questions to the best of your knowledge and ability would result in a fine.

- The burden of proof is reversed for several offences, so that the defendant has to prove his or her innocence, rather than the prosecution proving guilt.

- Collecting or possessing information likely to be useful to terrorists is made an offence.

- Possession of an article in circumstances which arouse suspicion that it is for terrorist purposes is made an offence.

- Wearing clothing in public that arouses suspicion that you may be a supporter or member of a proscribed organisation, such as the IRA, is made an offence. You could be banged up simply for wearing clothes that made the authorities suspicious of you!

- Failing to inform the police of any suspicions or knowledge you have that someone might be engaging in terrorist activities is made an offence. Investigative journalists look out!

- Scheduled offences in Northern Ireland will be tried without a jury, but the court will still have the same powers as a crown court in such a case.

- Arranging a meeting which will be addressed by someone belonging to or professing to belong to a proscribed organisation will become an offence. A meeting is defined as a meeting of three (3) or more people.

In response to the September 11 attacks, Britain passed the **Anti-terrorism, Crime and Security Act 2001**; which gives more powers to the police to investigate terrorist acts and other "serious" crimes. However, following the 7th of July London bombings the **Prevention of Terrorism Act 2005**, also known as the Control Order Act, were introduced. The 2005 Act, permitted control orders to be imposed on suspects of terrorism (UK nationals or not, and whatever the nature of the terrorist activity). Breach of such order without valid justification is considered a criminal offence and meets a sentence of up to 5 years. In 2006, a more "controversial" legislation was passed by the government. **Terrorism Act 2006,** created a number of new offences which once brought to force would be considered a criminal offence to commit. Such offences cover Acts Preparatory to Terrorism, Encouragement to Terrorism, Dissemination of Terrorist Publications, and Terrorist Training Offences. The 2006 Act, also amends existing legislation–particularly the 2000 Act,- as it introduced warrants to enable the police to search any property owned or controlled by a terrorist suspect, extended terrorism stop-and-search powers to cover bays and estuaries, extended police powers to detain suspects after arrest for up to 28 days (though periods of more than two days must be approved by a judicial authority), improved search powers at ports, increased flexibility of the proscription regime, including the power to proscribe groups that glorify terrorism. The Terrorism Act 2006 came in after the 7 July London suicide bombings. It was the source for the Commons row over 90 day's detention, with MPs finally settling on 28 days. It also introduced offences including preparing a terrorist act and glorification of terrorism.

United States (US)- Anti- Terrorism Laws[49]

Since its passage following the September 11, 2001, attacks, the Patriot Act has played a key part and often the leading role in a number of successful operations to protect innocent Americans from the deadly plans of terrorists dedicated to destroy America and our way of life. While the results have been important, in passing The Patriot Act, Congress provided for only modest, incremental changes in the law. Congress simply took existing legal principles and retrofitted them to preserve the lives and liberty of the American people from the challenges posed by a global terrorist network. Congress passed the **US Patriot Act** in response to the terrorist's attacks of September 11, 2001. The Act gives federal officials greater authority to track and intercept communications, both for law enforcement and foreign intelligence gathering purposes.

Undoubtedly, the US Patriot Act contains a number of immigration provisions that will improve our ability to identify and either exclude or prosecute aliens with terrorist ties. It is equally clear, however, that this new law represents only a first step in the immigration-policy reforms that are necessary to combat terrorism effectively and to protect Americans from future terrorist attacks

It seeks to further close borders to foreign terrorists and to detain and remove those within U.S borders. It creates new crimes, new penalties, and new procedural efficiencies for use against domestic and international terrorists. Although it is not without safeguards, critics contend some of its provisions go too far. The so-called Patriot Act in the US is applicable to non- citizens as far as definition is concerned and the American Civil Liberties Union is opposing it and this Act is likely to be challenged in the courts.

The US House of Representatives passed the Anti- Terrorism Bill on October 24, 2001, with a vote of 357 to 66. The Senate adopted the legislation very next day with 98 to 1 vote. The act provides expanded powers to the federal government to fight terrorism in the wake of September 11 attack on US. The House approves the measures that gives federal law enforcement agencies broader wiretap powers as well as rights to keep suspect immigrants in detention.[50]

---

49 Siddharth, 'Anti – Terrorism Laws in India and The Need of POTA', available at http://www.legalserviceindia.com/articles/html, (Last Viewed on April 20, 2011).

50 Editorial Column, 'Anti – Terrorism Laws – UN', Civil Services Chronicle, (November,

On September 24, 2001 US released a list of Foreign Terrorist Organisations (FTO) and vowed to wage a war against them. It froze their assets to starve them financially. It also allowed blocking US assets of foreign banks who refuse to freeze terrorist assets abroad.

Pakistan Anti Terrorism Laws[51]

In 2002, ordinance was issued for the inclusion of military officers in the panel of judges to try terrorist offences. This not only undermines the independence of the judiciary but makes the anti-terror law in the country even more draconian Described as necessary that appropriate administrative and judicial measures be adopted to fight a spate of terrorist activities and commission of heinous offences in Pakistan these anti-terrorism laws opened the door to grave violations of human rights including the right to life, the prohibition of torture, the right to liberty and security and the right to fair trial. Inter alias, they provide for the creation of anti terrorist courts and give wide powers of arrest and interrogation to the police and army. Amnesty International has criticized the legislation in its report,

It is important to note that the existing legal and judicial system is already equipped to deal with offences referred to in the act. The problem then seems to be a lack of implementation, not a lack of laws. However, in an attempt to hide this inefficiency, Pakistan adopted the anti-terrorist acts which provide speedy trial without necessary guarantees for the accused, unfair trials and license to kill etc.

The right to shoot and kill 1997 Anti-Terrorism Act Under Section 5(2)(1): an officer of the police, armed forces and civil armed forces may: (i) after giving prior warning use such force as may be deemed necessary or appropriate, bearing in mind all the facts and circumstances of the situation, against any person who is committing, or in all probability is likely to commit a terrorist act or a scheduled offence, and it shall be lawful for any such officer, or any superior officer, to fire, or order the firing upon any person or persons against whom he is authorized to use force in terms hereof The enactment of broad provisions empowering summary executions is not the way a modern civilized state ought to act. Rather the government should set strict limits to the circumstances in which firearms could be used to prevent arbitrary killing by the security forces. The broad

---

2001).

51 Siddharth, 'Anti–Terrorism Laws in India and The Need of POTA', available at http:// www.legalserviceindia.com/articles/html, (Last Viewed on April 20, 2011).

powers given to the police and consequently, to the military and civil armed forces contravene major international standards of human rights.

Indemnity for acts done in good faith: Section 39 of the act says: No suit, prosecution or other legal proceedings shall lie against any person in respect of anything which is in good faith done or intended to be done under this act. This is tantamount to providing impunity to the security forces for abuses, including extra judicial killings. To explicitly place any acts of police or other law enforcement personnel, including possibly random resort to lethal force, outside scrutiny and accountability may give law enforcement personnel the impression that they may commit such acts with impunity if only they can claim to have done them in good faith. It breaches a basic requirement of the rule of law, namely its equal and exception less application to everyone. **Confessions to police made admissible in court: The provision in the act in section 26 which says**: The special court may, for admission of the confession in evidence, require the police officer to produce a video tape together with the devices used for recording the confession.

Article 14(2) of the Constitution of Pakistan prohibits the use of torture, though only in the limited context of extraction of confessions: No person shall be subjected to torture for the purpose of extracting evidence. However, Pakistani law enforcement officials, to extract confessions from the accused, routinely use torture. Lending greater legal weight to confessions and putting pressure on police to speedily resolve crime may indirectly contribute to the continued and perhaps increased use of torture. **The right to be tried in a public place without prejudice to the defendant: Section 15 of the 1997 Anti-Terrorism Act states,**

The government may direct that for the trial of a particular case, the court shall sit at such place including the place of occurrence as it may specify. This is intended to expose the defendant to public expressions of outrage, anger or even violence for his deeds, to humiliate him and to deter others by the specter of public exposure; it does not appear to serve the purpose of helping the judiciary establish the truth and do justice in a detached circumspect manner and in calm circumstances.

The right to be presumed innocent: The act lays down that only special courts may grant bail to people tried for offences under the act but they may not release a defendant on bail if there are reasonable grounds for believing that he has been guilty of the offence with which he has been charged and unless the prosecution has been given an opportunity to show cause why he should not be released. This gives the prosecution the right to veto to deny bail.

The right to appeal: Section 31 of the act reads: A judgment or order passed, or sentence awarded, by a special court, subject to the result of an appeal under this act shall be final and shall not be called in question by any court. The possibility of the defendant to appeal to a court in the regular judicial system, either to the provincial high court or the Supreme Court of Pakistan is therefore excluded. People convicted and sentenced by the special courts are clearly disadvantaged in so far as their legal remedies are restricted: they have only one possibility of appeal, whereas people convicted by regular courts may also appeal to the Supreme Court. This provision violates the principle of equality before law laid down in the Constitution of Pakistan. It is one of the fundamental principles of international human rights law. Moreover, the right to appeal is restricted in so far as it is subject to severe time limitations. The defendant may not in seven days be able to present an adequate appeal while the prosecution has 15 days for the appeal.

Moreover, the right to appeal of those facing the death penalty also appears to be seriously infringed under the act. Death penalty: **Under Section 7(1) of the 1999 Amended Anti-terrorism Act, for terrorist acts resulting in death, courts have to mandatory impose the death penalty.** This does not give any discretion to the judiciary. Section 22 of the 1997 Anti Terrorism Act, The government may specify the manner, mode and place of execution of any sentence passed under this act, having regard to the deterrent effect which such execution is likely to have?. Section 22 opens the possibility for public executions of the death.

Role of South Asian Association for Regional Cooperation (SAARC) to Combat Terrorism[52]

The SAARC was established in 1985 with India, Srilanka, Maldives, Bhutan, Bangladesh, Nepal and Pakistan, as its seven members. It is for the first time in its 22-year-old history that the association that groups Bangladesh, Bhutan, India, Maldives, Nepal, Pakistan and Sri Lanka has expanded its membership. The 13th SAARC Summit in Dhaka in November 2005 had approved Afghanistan's request for membership. The

---

52 Abdul Ruff Colachal, 'Leave Terrorism Plank', available at http://drdivas.wordpress. com/2008/html, (Last Viewed on March 24, 2010).

issue of combating terrorism has been on the active agenda in the SAARC summit since its inception.

The two days meeting of the Foreign ministers of SAARC meeting at Dhaka in the second week of August 1986 condemned terrorism and called for concrete steps to fight it. But the summit of the SAARC which was concluded on November 19, 1986 in New Delhi failed to define terrorism. Thus one of the most formidable problems facing the legal control of terrorism is the precise definition of terrorism.[53]

On November 4, 1987, the member States of the SAARC adopted SAARC Regional Convention on Suppression of Terrorism. Article 1 of the provision provides that subject to the overall requirements of the law of extradition, conduct constituting any of the law of extradition, conduct constituting any of the following offences, according to other law of the contracting States shall be regarded as terrorist and for the purpose of extradition shall not be regarded as a political offence or as an offence connected with a political offence or as an offence inspired by political motives:

- An offence within the scope of the convention of the suppressing of Unlawful Seizure of Aircraft, signed at Hague on December 16, 1970.

- An offence within the scope of the convention for the suppression of unlawful acts against the safety of civil aviation, signed at Montreal on September 23, 1971.

- An offence within the scope of the convention on the prevention and punishment of crimes against internationally protected persons, including diplomatic agents, signed at New York on December 14, 1973.

- An offence within the scope of any convention to which the SAARC member States concerned are parties and which obliges the parties to prosecute or grant extradition.

- Murder, manslaughter, assault causing bodily harm, kidnapping, hostage taking and offences relating to firearms, weapons,

---

53 Brig. N.B.Grant (Retd.), 'Terrorism in Search of a Definition', *Indian Express*, November 25, 2006.

explosives and dangerous substances when used as a means to perpetrate indiscriminate violence involving death or serious bodily injury to persons or serious damage to property.

- An attempt or conspiracy to commit an offence described in sub-paragraphs, aiding, abetting or counseling. The commission of such an offence or participating as an accomplice in the offences so described.

Article III of the convention provides that the provisions of all extradition treaties and arrangements applicable between contracting States are hereby amended as between contracting States to the extent that they are incompatible with this convention. Article IV, however gives very wide power and discretion to the contracting States with regard to extradition. It provides that contracting States shall not be obliged to extradite, if it appears to the requested State that by reason of the trivial nature of the case or by the reason of the request for the surrender or return of a fugitive offender not being made in good faith or in the interests of the justice or any other reason it is unjust or inexpedient remarked. "The law of extradition has obstructed international reaction against terrorism though all States agree that terrorism should be effectively suppressed."

With a view to give effect to SAARC Regional Convention on Suppression of Terrorism, on April 26, 1996, the Parliament enacted the SAARC convention (Suppression of Terrorism), 1993. Reference may also be made to the Delhi declaration adopted by the Eight summit of SAARC held at New Delhi on May 2-4, 1995. Though this declaration the Heads of the State or Government expressed serious concern on the spread of terrorism in and outside the region and reiterated their unequivocal condemnation of all acts, methods and practices of terrorism as criminal. They deplored all such acts for their impact on life, poverty, socio- economic development and political stability as well as on regional and international peace and cooperation. They once against emphasized that highest priority should be according to the enactment of enabling legislation at the national level to give effect to the SAARC Regional Convention on Suppression of Terrorism.[54]

The 11 SAARC summit held at Kathmandu decided that setting aside, mutual differences the members emphasized on implementing the

---

54 S.K. Kapoor(2009), *International Law,* p.747..

UN Security Council and anti- terrorism resolution 1373 in totally. The SAARC declaration emphasized the need for international cooperation to combat terrorism. It asserted that terrorism violates fundamental values of the UN and the SAARC Charter and constitutes one of the most serious threats to international peace and security in the 21 century. The member States unanimously agreed that regional cooperation which includes police- networking could go a long way in rooting out this scourge which afflicts almost all members (Apart from Pakistan and Bangladesh all the members implemented domestic legislations against terrorism).[55]

The 15 SAARC Summit in Colombo throws some light on the issues and challenges facing the forum and offers some suggestions to improve the functioning of the SAARC in order to curb terrorism. Eight SAARC nations, namely Sri Lanka, Pakistan, Nepal, Afghanistan, Bhutan, India and Maldives met in Colombo on 2-3 August, 2009 essentially to discuss issues including trade imbalance, poverty, food crisis, price-rise, climate change and terrorism. Rising tensions in Kashmir, deadly bombs blistering through Indian cities with Indian media-cum-intelligence speculation that Muslim "militants" are behind the series of blasts, issues of nuclear power and prestige, these, rather than poverty alleviation of a third of the world's population who call this region their home, will most likely dominate the talks even as the summit winds down today. Its non cooperation is best reflected by the fact that intra-regional trade of SAARC is still said to be only approximately 5.5% of the total trade of the member countries. In negotiations it is more a focus on the differences rather than the similarities that hold sway.

While discussing "terrorism" the leaders always skip the major component of terrorism, the state terrorism. Unfortunately, the issue of so-called "terrorism" has been haunting the SAARC, rather than any joint economic enterprises. India, the major player in the region with its new economic muscle got out of the public sector sales, has been using the SAARC to strengthen its hold over Kashmir and to warn the freedom seeking Kashmiris and hence "terrorism" has remained the focus of its addresses. That seems to be the crux of the weakening scenario in the South Asian region. Invariably acts of terrorism take place on thieve of international summits and SAARC is no exception. That India remains focused on anti-Pakistanism and anti-Kashmiris is not news for the world.

---

55   Editorial Column, 'Role of South Asian Association of Regional Cooperation to Combat Terrorism', Civil Services Chronicle, (March 2002), p.35.

It is because India occupies its neighbor Kashmir that terrorism is sustained and promoted by New Delhi to gain sympathy form the US-led West. India also is always talking about combating the menace of "terrorism" but the facts are not unknown to SAARC.

Terrorism in Kashmir is the creation of New Delhi strategists to suppress the freedom movement and secret grave-yards characterize Indian democracy and neo-Gandhian approach to settle crises. New Delhi believes it should control the Kashmiris seeking their sovereignty back from occupier India with an iron hand which India has successfully done so far. India slams Pakistan as a routine matter to evade any serious business in SAARC.

Violence has always been on the top of the agenda of SAARC summits. A declaration was made in 1987 at the Kathmandu summit due to the increase in sectarian violence in Sri Lanka and the rise of militancy in J&K. The myriad problems of SAARC countries cannot be solved through a one-off resolution on terrorism. Security, prosperity and economic integration can only be achieved by the strength of equality, unity, fraternity and soft borders. Due to these opposing forces, SAARC has failed to achieve its objectives of integrating the region as an economic, social, cultural and scientific entity. This is highly evident when it comes to the free movement of peoples across the region. There are visa restrictions, mostly for visitors traveling from Sri Lanka, Pakistan and Bangladesh to India.

It is been generally noticed by the Heads of State or Government that terrorism violates the fundamental values of the SAARC Charter and the UN, and constitutes one of the most critical threats to international peace and security. The Heads of State or Government expressed their satisfaction at the ratification of the Additional Protocol to the SAARC Convention on Suppression of Terrorism by all Member States and called for putting in place effective mechanisms for its implementation. They strongly condemned terrorist violence in all its forms and manifestations, agreed that terrorism is a challenge to all States and a threat to all of humanity, and cannot be justified on any grounds. They underlined that there should be no double standards in the fight against terrorism. In view of the continuing and recent terrorist attacks in the region and their impact on security, economic stability and social development, they expressed their determination to unite in their efforts in preventing and combating terrorism. They also noted the UN Security Council resolution 1373

(2001) in this regard.

However, the Heads of the States called for early and effective implementation of the Additional Protocol to the SAARC Convention on Suppression of Terrorism. They underscored the need for an early conclusion of a Comprehensive Convention on International Terrorism. They also agreed that Member States would strengthen their cooperation in such important areas as exchange of information, coordination and cooperation among their   relevant agencies. They decided that SAARC Interior/Home Ministers would meet annually preceded by a meeting of the Interior/Home Secretaries. The Heads of State or Government directed that concrete measures be taken to enforce the provisions of the Regional Convention on Narcotic Drugs and Psychotropic Substances through an appropriate regional mechanism.

Role of ASEAN Regional Forum (ARF) to Combat Terrorism[56]

The ASEAN Regional Forum (ARF) was established in 1994, with the intent to "foster constructive dialogue and consultation on political and security issues of common interest and concern" and to "make significant contributions to efforts towards confidence-building and preventive diplomacy in the Asia-Pacific region" which operates on the principles of non-intervention, informal dialogue, and non-binding confidence building measures. There are 10 ASEAN members, in addition to that there are extra additional members among them India is one of an active member. The 10 ASEAN members – Brunei Darussalam; Cambodia; Indonesia; Lao Peoples Democratic Republic; Malaysia; Myanmar; Philippines; Singapore; Thailand; and Vietnam. Non ASEAN members – Australia; Bangladesh; Canada; the People's Republic of China; the European Union; India; Japan; North Korea; South Korea; Mongolia; New Zealand; Pakistan; Papua New Guinea; Russia; East Timor; and the United States

In their counterterrorism mandate which was set forth at the 2002 ASEAN Regional Forum, where Senior Officials provided recommendations on the future direction of the ARF. Recommendations included plans to strengthen measures to combat terrorism including: the enhancement intelligence-sharing, police cooperation, and financial measures against terrorism, the establishment of an Inter-Session Group on Counter-Terrorism and Transnational Crimes (ISM on CTTC), and the

---

56 'The ASEAN Regional Forum: A Concept Paper', available at http://www.globalct. org/resources/htm, (Last Viewed on June 11, 2011).

enhanced role of the ARF Chair. The majority of the ARF's regular work on counterterrorism takes place under the auspices of the In ISM on CTTC and the Inter-Session Group on Confidence Building Measures. Topic specific seminars and workshops have also been held where ARF participants meet, share best practices, discuss cooperative counterterrorism efforts and provide recommendations for the meetings of senior officials and foreign ministers.

In July 2007, operating rules were established for the creation of "Friends of the ARF Chair," an ad hoc group designed for quick reaction to emergencies. The group will consist of the current ARF Chair along with three foreign ministers to be chosen by all ARF participants based on the issue at hand.

In addition to the official dialogue process, the ARF also includes a "Track II" process, which seeks to incorporate contributions from non-governmental experts primarily from the ASEAN Institutes of Strategic and International Studies and the Council on Security Cooperation in the Asia-Pacific.

In 2004, ASEAN established the small ARF Unit, which is located within the ASEAN secretariat. The ARF Unit works to increase interaction with regional and international organisations. Aside from the ARF Unit, ARF counterterrorism responsibilities primarily fall on the individual foreign ministers at the ISMCTTC. The ARF Unit does not have a mandate to monitor compliance of the voluntary commitments made by ARF countries on a number of counterterrorism-related matters.

Achievements of ASEAN Regional Forum (ARF)

Since its formation in 1994, the development of ARF has been deliberate and incremental. As conceived in the 1995 ARF Concept Paper, ARF has proceeded from the promotion of confidence-building measures, to the development of preventive diplomacy mechanisms, and ultimately to conflict resolution.

ARF leaders have issued non-binding statements since 2001 related to counterterrorism on a range of issues, including the financing of terrorism; border security; piracy and maritime security; transportation security; non-proliferation; and information sharing, intelligence exchange and document security. In these statements, ARF participants have, among other things, have agreed to improve border security by adopting measures proposed by ICAO, the IMO, and the WCO. This includes a commitment to implement ICAO standards for Machine Readable Travel Documents. It also issued a statement supporting national implementation of UN Security Council Resolution 1540, which focuses on taking steps at the national level to prevent weapons of mass destruction and their means of delivery from getting into the hands of terrorists and other non-state actors.

Until recently, the ARF focused primarily on short-term preventative measures against terrorism, such as maritime security. Through nonbinding consensus statements, workshops, and seminars, ARF has aimed to prevent terrorist attacks at ports and on ships in the highly trafficked waters of the region. The establishment of the "Friends of the ARF Chair" quick-action group has the potential to act more swiftly and decisively in implementing the UN Strategy. To date, however, the ARF's counterterrorism contributions have been limited by its weak institutional capacity and strict adherence to ASEAN principles of non-interference.

The 2007 ISM on CTTC focused on addressing the "conditions conducive to the spread of terrorism," which involves a "sustainable strategy to win the hearts and minds of the people." ARF participants reiterated the importance of "nation-building measures such as the provision of basic economic and social services, the importance of good governance and institution-building, the necessity of achieving national political consensus through reconciliation and negotiation, and the importance of national will." The participants officially endorsed the UN's "Alliance of Civilizations" Initiative as well as the UN Global Strategy Counter-Terrorism Strategy. To this end, the ARF convened a "Special Informal Session on Inter-Civilisational Dialogue," and has actively promoted initiatives aimed at facilitating Inter-Civilizational Dialogue in the region, such as the Asia-Pacific Inter-Faith Regional Dialogue.[57]

On the future direction of the ISM on CTTC, the participants in the 2007 meeting suggested that ARF efforts to counter terrorism and combat transnational crime continue to encompass concrete cooperation such as information sharing among civilian and military agencies, capacity building, and practical cooperation in areas such as anti-money laundering and maritime security.

It is unfortunate that terrorism is being committed by the State for achieving their own ends in spite of its prohibition. It is so mainly

---

57 Ibid.

because International Law regarding the implementation and enforcement of its rules is not as strong as it should be. Weaknesses have resulted in committing the terrorism by states especially by those which are enormous and powerful. It has become a part of the system and as a weapon of warfare used by a government against another government. If States are at all serious to curb terrorism, they themselves have to realize that the immoral and inhuman act of terrorism brings sufferings and miseries to human beings. Its elimination therefore depends primarily upon the political will of the Sates.

Legal Regime In India To Curb Terrorism

After the discussion on the international efforts to curb the menace of terrorism, it is also pertinent to have a mention of Indian efforts in this regard. International measures alone are not capable in combating the acts of terrorism unless States themselves are not enthusiastic in suppressing it. The General Assembly on realizing the importance of the role of the States in this regard has called on States to take 'appropriate measures' at the national level and to cooperate with each other to eliminate terrorism. To deal with the problems of terrorism India has taken several initiatives at various levels.

At the International Level

All too often we are reminded that terrorism continues to inflict pain and suffering on people's lives all over the world. Almost no week goes by without an act of terrorism taking place somewhere in the world, indiscriminately affecting innocent people who just happened to be in the wrong place at the wrong time. Countering this scourge is in the interest of all nations and the issue has been on the agenda of the UN for decades.

Therefore, being as an active member of UN, right from its inception, India supports a strengthened and revitalizes UN with its various organs functioning within their mandates in accordance with the UN Charter. India supports an enhanced role for the UN in development and development cooperation dialogue. India firmly believes that development should be central to UN's agenda and be pursued in its own right. It is an indispensable prerequisite to the maintenance of international peace and security. India has actively participated in all reforms and restructuring exercises that could enhance the capacity of the UN in the fulfillment of its primary tasks.[58]

- India has been supportive of all efforts, particularly in the UN to combat terrorism and has played a leading role in shaping international opinion and urging the international community to prioritize the fight against terror. Its consistent and basic stand before the international community has been that-

- There could be no justification for terrorism on any grounds: religious, political, ideological or any other.

- The fight against terrorism must be given the highest priority

- To be effective, the fight against terrorism has to be long term, comprehensive and sustained.

- Strengthening of international cooperation is vital to ensure that action is not restricted simply to the perpetrators but also encompassed States, which sponsor, support, or provide safe haven to terrorists.

- Ad hoc and selective actions have limited chances of success and compartmentalization of actions in terms of regions, religions or organisations is bound to be counterproductive

Multi-Lateral Arrangements and Agreements[59]

- It welcomed UN Security Council Resolution 1373 and is fully committed to implement it. It has submitted its national report on measures taken to implement UN Security Council Resolution 1373 in December 2001 and also submitted a supplementary report on specific queries by the Counter Terrorism Committee under the Security Council.

- It is signatory to all the thirteen UN Sectoral Conventions on Terrorism. It has been supportive of all measures within the UN General Assembly, the sixth Committee and the UN Security

---

58 'UN Reforms process', available at http://.www.meadev.nic.in/un/reform.htm, (Last Viewed on December 9, 2009).

59 D.K Pathak, "Country report: India", available at http://www.unafei.or.ip/english/ pdf, (Last Viewed on March 23, 2010).

Council. It has supported UN Security Council Resolution 1269 and 1368, which clearly identify terrorism as a threat to international peace and security. In addition, India has supported and fully implemented Resolutions 1267, 1333 and 1363 relating to terrorism by the Taliban Regime in Afghanistan.

• It has piloted the comprehensive Convention on International Terrorism (CCIT) in the UN with the objective of providing a comprehensive legal framework to combat terrorism

Regional Arrangements[60]

• At the regional level, India is a party to the SAARC Regional Convention on Suppression of Terrorism 1987 and has enacted the enabling legislation in the form of the SAARC Conventions (Suppression of Terrorism Act) 1993.

• The ASEAN Regional Forum (ARF) was set up in 1994 as a regional security dialogue platform with ten ASEAN countries of which India is also a member.

Bilateral Arrangements

India has entered into three types of bilateral treaties to combat international terrorism

1. Agreements to combat terrorism and organised crimes, drug related offences, etc. Such agreements are essentially framework agreements to facilitate the exchange of operational information and development of joint programmes to counter organised crimes and terrorism

2. Extradition Treaties to facilitate transfer of fugitive offenders and suspected terrorists. Such treaties have been signed with seventeen countries, signed but not exchanged with eight countries in addition to extradition arrangements with eleven countries.

3. Bilateral Treaties on Mutual Legal Assistance (MLATs) in criminal matters to facilitate investigation, collection of evidence, transport of witnesses, location and action against proceeds of crime, etc. Such MLATs have been signed with ten countries in addition to

---

60 Ibid. Dr54

those signed but not exchanged with nine countries.

General Agreements

In order to combat growing cross border terrorist activities and insurgency problems, the armies of India and Bangladesh will jointly conduct a counter terrorism exercise in the northeastern state of Assam. The training would be held from Feb 22 to Mar 7, 2009 at Jorhat[61] in Assam. The joint exercise would be held as part of confidence building measures between both the neighbouring nations threatened by terrorism. Five officers and 15 other personnel from Bangladesh will be taking part in the exercise and will train with the special para-commandos of the Indian Army. The exercise by Indian and Bangladeshi Special Forces will comprise of airborne operations. The modalities of the combat maneuvers were finalised during a military conference held in Kolkata December 2008.

India has been training and also conducting counter terrorism exercises with various countries in Mizoram. With India keen on securing Bangladesh's firm cooperation in fighting anti-Indian terror and insurgent outfits operating from its soil, the armies from the two countries will come together to hold their first-ever counter terrorism exercise. The Indian army and the security forces have been fighting the ULFA cadres in the state.[62]

Even Indian and Chinese army personnel celebrated as they pulled the curtains down on their nine-day joint anti-terrorism exercise in Belgaum, Karnataka. The joint drill, named "Hand in Hand 2008", was held here from December 6 to 14, 2008, and was a continuation of the ongoing military cooperation between both countries as part of the Annual Defence Dialogue (ADD) initiated in 2006.

Chinese troops from the 1st Company of the Infantry Battalion of the Chengdu Military Area Command and troops from India's 8 Maratha Light Infantry Battalion participated in the exercise. Both Indian and Chinese officials said such exercises help enhance military to military cooperation. The experience has been fantastic. Indian troops have got much more experience as far as counter-terrorism is concerned, than the PLA troops, since 1950s, India is fighting terrorism. Contingents of both

---

61 Jorhat is located on the fringes of dense forests and riverine plains of Assam, India.

62 'Bangladesh, India to Conduct Joint Military Training Exercise in Assam', available at http://www.india-defence.com, (Last Viewed on January 14, 2009).

countries trained in joint tactical manoeuvres and drills, interoperability training and joint command post procedures. A joint directing panel of Indian and Chinese army officials supervised the training and manoeuvres. The first-ever joint army exercises between both countries were held in Kunming, China, in 2007.[63]

This drill is aimed to enhance mutual understanding and trust and strengthen bilateral exchanges in the field of anti-terrorism and promote the development of the bilateral strategic partnership. The aim of this programme is also to safeguard regional stability and security.

Legal Policies of India For Rapprochment Processs

There is also a requirement to look into India's legal policies with its neighbouring countries in order to curb the scourge of terrorism. As this revision of legal policies is a kind of indicator which indicates about where all these nations are standing and what more is required by India and its neighbouring countries towards merging the diverse positions.

India and Pakistan

India and Pakistan have fought four wars over Kashmir and have held several rounds talks to resolve this old issue, but without any tangible success. The only progress thus far has been that India has agreed to discuss the issue as a part of the composite dialogue process and Pakistan has shown willingness to explore options other than the UN resolutions on Kashmir. Although both India and Pakistan appear trying to breakaway from the past and think afresh on Kashmir, yet both fail to bring about any significant policy swifts. For Pakistan, it still is the 'problem of Kashmir', i.e Kashmir a 'disputed territory' and an 'unfinished agenda' of partition; for India, it is the 'problem in Kashmir; suggesting that the accession of Kashmir to India is final and complete and the challenge now remains of addressing cross-border terrorism, and development and grievances of the people of Kashmir.

The thaw and improvement in relations could lead to atleast re-establishment of a balanced relationship between the two countries is closely linked to the resolution of the Kashmir issue. Various policies and steps are taken by India and Pakistan which fathoms the prospects of a rapprochement on Kashmir and combating cross border terrorism.[64]

---

63 Ibid

64 Ashutosh Mishra, 'The Problem of Kashmir and the Problem in Kashmir: Divergence

A. Establishment of Bilateralism

For the first time in Shimla Agreement, 1972, between India and Pakistan, bilateralism was considered as the basis for all Indo- Pakistan negotiations purposes to govern the relations between the two countries. This is also mentioned there that two countries are resolved to settle their differences by peaceful means through bilateral negotiations or by any other peaceful means mutually agreed upon between them. It was also mentioned in it that in J&K, the Line of Control resulting from the ceasefire of December 17, 1971, shall be respected by both sides without prejudice to the recognized position of either side.[65]

Almost three decades later, the Lahore Declaration signed between Atal Bihari Vajpayee and Nawaz Sharif on February 21, 1999, reiterated bilateralism enshrined in the Shimla Agreement. Similarly, January 6, 2004, Indo- Pakistan joint statement also makes similar commitments.[66]

However India's position was vindicated when cross border terrorism as a serious threat to stability was put on the agenda of the composite dialogue process in Male in 1997, but with very little success so far. In the last round of talks held on September 6, 2004, in New Delhi, no progress was made. India talked of 'cross-border terrorism' whereas Pakistan talked of 'human rights' abuses in J&K. The divergence in the interpretation of terrorism seems to be shaped up the two sides but larger stand on the Kashmir issue.

B. India's Kashmir Policy

In contrast to Pakistan's stand, India considers the J&K as an internal matter and focuses on addressing it internally. India's thrust has been to accommodate the grievances and demands of the people of J&K within the constitutional framework and deal with the 'problem in Kashmir'. Combating cross-border terrorism is the main ingredient of India's Kashmir policy. Weeding out terrorism is the core of India's multi pronged strategy in J&K. It has following characteristics:

1. Directly countering terrorism through security measure undertaken

---

Demands Convergence', Strategic Analysis, (January – March, 2005).

65 Jawed naqvi, 'Kashmir: a tragedy and a farce', available at **http://www.kashmirobserver. com/ opinion.htm,** (Last Viewed on October 11 2009).

66 'India Pakistan Joint Press Statement: Islamabad', available at http://meaindia.nic.in/ articles, (Last Viewed on January 6, 2004).

by J&K police and security forces.

2. Accelerating economic development, improved provision of services and good governance to maintain satisfaction level among the people of J&K.

3. Willingness to talk to the people of J&K, especially those who eschew the path of violence.

4. Strengthening the political process through elections at all prescribed levels and encouraging open debates.

India has sought to find solutions to the problems in J&K at the local level. It has adopted a range of measures to offset the impact of terrorism on the people with an emphasis on planned and balanced regional development, building/strengthening physical and social infrastructure and improving the productive potential of the state. Indian Government has taken several peace initiatives and also achieved to some extent.

i. Border Fencing: In a significant step towards checking infiltration of terrorists in J&K, a decision was taken to fence the LOC, which has turned out to be a very effective measure in countering terrorism. According to the Ministry of Home Affairs' annual report 2003-04, on the India – Pakistan border, out of 2,003 km, a length of 1,641 km has already been fenced.[67] Besides, fencing has been done in the Gujarat and Rajasthan sectors, while in Jammu it is about to be completed.

The Centre and the J&K Government jointly adopted several other measures also for combating terrorism. These include strengthening border management to check infiltration, pro-active action against terrorist within J&K, gearing up intelligence machinery, greater functional integration through an institutional framework of Operations Groups and Intelligence Groups of the unified headquarters at various levels, and improved technology, weapons and equipments for security forces and action as per law against ground supporters of the terrorists. Checking infiltration through improved border management has also been undertaken.

ii. Democracy: In spite of internal turmoil, democracy has prevailed in J&K. The conduct of municipal elections in January – February 2005, after a gap of 27 years in all the 14 districts, is another illustration of the

---

67 Ashutosh Mishra, 'The Problem of Kashmir and the Problem in Kashmir: Divergence Demands Convergence', Strategic Analysis, (January – March, 2005).

State's democratic success and the people's resolve to come out to vote in defiance of the boycott call from terrorist groups. It is also reaffirmed people's faith in democracy. The overall voter turnout was between 30-35 percent. Qazigund, in Anantnag, a distributed area, recorded 78.9 percent turnout. Pulhwama with 56.6 percent, Doru with 65.99 percent and Jammu with 65 percent showed much promise for the troubled state. In Srinagar, the terrorist groups boycotted elections and even gunned down several candidates, both before and after the elections yet, ignoring all this, people came out to vote and the turnout was recorded at around 20 percent. The positive outcome of these elections was that mainstream parties returned to the democratic fold.[68] Another striking feature of these elections was the large turnout of women voters. People's participation in this election gave a strong message – "freedom can wait but development cannot".

iii. Economic Development: Economic development of J&K has been another concern of the Centre. The Central Government envisaged planned and balanced regional development for building physical, economic and social infrastructure, thereby improving the productivity of the State. In 2003-2004, the State's annual plan outlay has been increased to Rs. 2,500 crores. Several important schemes have also been introduced in the infrastructure sector – railways, power, communication and roads.[69]

iv. India- Pakistan Rapprochement: Discussing Kashmir:

In the Year 1997 – May in Male, then Prim Minister Inder Kumar Gujral and Mr. Nawaz Sharif initiated the composite dialogue process which created eight baskets of issues (6 = 2) namely, J&K, Siachin, Wullar Barrage/Tulbul Navigation Project, Sir Creek, Terrorism and Drug Trafficking, Economic and commercial cooperation, peace and security, and promotion of Friendly Exchanges in various fields.[70]

In the year 1998 – under the composite dialogue process, the first round talks on J&K were held in Islamabad from October 15 -17, though they ended without success. Pakistan's insistence on third – party intervention was rejected by India, but the need to reduce the risk of a conflict by building mutual confidence in the nuclear and conventional

---

68 Jehangir Rashid, 'It's a Vote for Progress, Development in Phuwara' available at http:// www.kashmirtimes.com, (Last Viewed on October 18, 2008)

69 Supra note 60

70 Amar Chadel, 'India Pakistan Agree to Reduce Risk of War', *The Tribune*, October 19, 2008.

fields was reiterated.[71]

In the year 1999 - In early 1999, Prime Minister Atal Bihari Vajpayee undertook a historic bus trip to Lahore, where he signed the Lahore Declaration with his counterpart Nawaz Sharif on February 21, 1999. Among other issues, the Declaration also said that the two parties "shall intensify their efforts to resolve all issues, including the issue of J&K".

In the year 2001- India's policy decision of 'no talks' in the wake of the 'Kargil war', the military coup in Pakistan and terrorist attacks on the Indian Parliament, was reversed in July 2001, with Vajpayee inviting General Pervez Musharaff for talks in Agra. Unfortunately, in the absence of proper groundwork, disagreement, antagonism and brinkmanship wrecked the initiative with not even a joint declaration being produced.

Several place initiatives have been undertaken in recent years to address the Kashmir issue. Despite peace initiatives and international pressure on Pakistan to combat terrorism as a foreign policy instrument terrorist violence has been continuing to J&K. During year 2002, approximately 839 civilians and 469 security forces personnel were killed during the year and some 1,714 terrorist were killed by the security forces in counter-terrorism operations. This was a little less than the 1067 civilians, 590 security personnel and 2850 terrorist killed in 2001.[72]

These trends showed that peace initiatives do not necessarily imply a respite from violence. The increase in civilian causalities, however, was marginal, and there was also a decline in the total number of incidents recorded. The pattern continued in 2002 with terrorist violence erupting whenever peace moves were initiated. While 44 percent of the votes turned out to vote during the State Assembly election in October 2002, the State's cleanest elections were also its bloodiest. In 45 days of campaigning, 46 political activists were killed. Most of them including a state minister, belonged to the ruling National Conference Party. The 1996 elections had witnessed skeletal turnout with 13 political workers getting assassinated.[73]

v. Renewed Efforts for Peace

In the year 2003 – In April 2003, Prime Minister Atal Bihari

---

71 Ibid.

72 Sunil Sondhi, "Combating Terrorism in South Asia", South Asia Politics, Vol. III, New Delhi, (March, 2005).

73 Ibid.

Vajpayee again made an offer for talks, which was duly reciprocated by his counterpart, Zafarullah Khan Jamali. This time around the two sides chose to first do the groundwork. As a result, snapped rail, road, air and diplomatic links were resorted to boost mutual trust and confidence.

In the year 2004 – the ensuing rapprochement enabled the two sides to reserve talks on the eight baskets of issues. The talks were held on July 27-28, 2004, in New Delhi led by Indian Foreign Secretary Shashank and his counterpart Riaz Khokhar. The Pakistan Foreign Secretary termed the talks as "useful" and a "good first step", and Indian External Affairs Minister Natwar Singh described the talks as "positive and concrete". The joint statement reaffirmed the "need to promote, a stable environment of peace and security". The two sides also reaffirmed their commitment to the joint press statements of January 6, 2004, in Islamabad. The Foreign Secretaries expressed the hope that the dialogue would lead to a "peaceful settlement of all bilateral issues, including J&K, to the satisfaction of both sides.[74]

In the year 2004 – As part of composite dialogue between Pakistan and India, talks on combating terrorism and dealing with the menace of narcotics and drug cartels were held on 10-11 August 2004 at Islamabad. On these sensitive issues very little could be expected to emerge in the first round of talks. India and Pakistan reaffirmed their determination to combat terrorism and emphasized the need to eliminate this menace. As expected, there was no headway however on the issue of terrorism as both sides had divergent positions on what "terrorism" meant. Pakistan and India, for political reasons define "terrorism" in different ways and it was therefore difficult to arrive at a consensus in the first round of talks.

In November 2004, Prime Minister Manmohan Singh visited J&K to deliver 'peace and dignity' to the people.[75] He announced a Rs. 24,000 crore "Reconstruction Plan for J&K". Towards addressing grievances and concerns he said, "Outdoors are open to anybody who wants to talk to us". However, the most significant step was the announcement of the reduction of troops from South Kashmir, to boost people's confidence and also the peace process which was welcomed even by the Pakistan Foreign Ministry spokesman Masood Khan said, "This is a positive development and a good

74 Summit Ganguly (1997), *The Crisis in Kashmir: Proponents of War, Hopes for Peace,* p.92.

75 Indrani Bagchi, 'Central Promises Valley a Better Future – The Manmohan Mantra: Heal, Hope and Harmony', *The Times of India,* November 18, 2004

beginning".[76]

Nevertheless, in an effort to change the political climate that surrounds the issue, the two sides discussed confidence building measures, such as the bus services between Srinagar – Muzaffarabad bus service talks were stalled over the travel document issues. Pakistan insisted on UN documents and India proposed to carry passport as travel documents. The second round of talks on December 7-8, 2004, in New Delhi, was again derailed because of the same reason. This time, Pakistan also demanded that the bus service be kept exclusively for the Kashmiris, whereas India wanted it to be open for all Indians.

In the year 2005 – In February 2005, Natwar Singh and Kursheed Mahaud Kasuri in Islamabad resolved the row over the documents and gave the historic bus service a nod. It was agreed that passengers can travel with the entry permits, which would basically be their identity cards for travels. Both sides displayed considerable flexibility with Pakistan discarding the 'UN document' stand India, the 'Passport stance'. It clearly demonstrates the ability of the both sides to made concessions in the light of popular perceptions.

Despite the positive tone, differences still persisted. It is often said that you cannot choose your neighbours, and India has lived with this bitter truth for many years. No matter how hard we try as a nation to break away from the shackles of a bloody history and chart a new course in the region, we are always reminded of the problems on our borders. It happened once again. Militants struck at the heart of the Indo- Pakistan peace process on the eve of what was to be the boldest step between the two countries in a long time. The day before the opening of the Srinagar- Muzaffarabad bus route on April 6, 2005, the *fidayeen* attack on the tourist reception centre in the J&K capital sent out a clear message. The obstacles to peace still exist.[77]

The first bus journey across the LOC since partition was an attempt to build people contact and brings Kashmiris on both sides closer than they had been in decades. The bus route represented a possibility of hope that the issue of the troubled State could at least be dealt with in a conducive atmosphere without fear and hostility. The attack on the tourist reception

---

76 Sunil Sondhi, "Combating Terrorism in South Asia", *South Asia Politics*, Vol.III, New Delhi, March, 2005.

77 Ramesh Vinayak, 'Trial by Fire', India Today, (April 18, 2005).

centre, where the 24 passengers due to board the bus were sequestered, claimed no victims other than the terrorists. But it did leave us with the persistent feeling that India and Pakistan were back to where they had started. It also raised the questions, about the peace process as a whole, about cross- border terrorism and lapses in security.[78]

India raised the issue of terrorism, whereas Pakistan contended with a call for ending "human rights violations and troop reduction in the State". The failure to agree on a common 'definition of the problem' shows the complexity of the issues and the challenges it poses. The inability of the two sides to reach a common definition till date remains the primary challenge.

In the year 2009 - In a new milestone in the peace process, Pakistan has moved some of its troops from on its border with India to its western border. Movements of troops seen on Pakistan's eastern border with India would result in reduction of tension between the two neighbours. Pakistan is in the middle of a massive military offensive against the Taliban in the North West Frontier Province and is planning to extend the operation to Taliban. Pakistan has moved its troops from the east to the west and the northwest of the country to combat terrorism.[79]

Undoubtedly, Pakistan has achieved success also by adopting such a policy. The number of suicide bombings and attacks in Pakistan declined nearly 20 percent in 2010 as a result of Pakistani military operations, better surveillance and the death of key militants in US drone strikes. The number of attacks declined from 2,586 in 2009 to 2,013 in 2010, according to a report by the Pak Institute for Peace Studies. However, it said that attacks tripled in Karachi and Lahore, in a sign that militants are exporting the fight far from the Afghan border.[80]

In the year 2010 – The elections that were held after the Mumbai attack to the legislative Assemblies in some states, including J&K had seen a large voter turnout thereby reaffirming the faith of the people in a democratic polity. It is pertinent to note that general masses are identifying themselves as Indians first even though they are fighting on diverse

---

78 Ibid.

79 "Pakistan may Lessen Troops along India Border", IndiaToday. New Delhi, (June 16, 2009).

80 Editorial Column 'Fewer Terrorist Attacks in Pakistan', *Today*, Singapore, January 17, 2011.

agendas. These concepts militate against the very principle chosen to be followed in the journey as a free nation.

In the joint effort for peace, children of India ad Pakistan will try to mind the relationships and make new bonds, starting from January 2011, nearly 2,400 children from Delhi, Mumbai, Lahore and Karachi will write letters to each other across the border to learn more about their culture, cuisine and life style which shares a common history. Students from three schools in Delhi – Sanskriti, St. Paul's and BR Mehta Vidya Bhavan and Shishuvan School and Gandhi Memorial School in Mumbai will correspond with their counterparts in 5 Pakistani schools over 16 months as part of a project started by Indian NGO Routes 2 Roots and The Citizens Archives of Pakistan.[81]

In a frank conversation, a senior Indian diplomat, the point person for Af-Pak policy in the Foreign Ministry, offered a bleak long term assessment of Indian Pakistan tries saying that even if India were to "lop – off" Kashmir and hand it to its western neighbour, it would still not result in peace.[82]

Y. K Sinha, Joint Secretary in Ministry of External Affairs (MEA), told US Officials that, "call me a cynic, but even if India were to lop off Kashmir and hand it on a platter to Pakistan, they would still find a reason to make trouble for us". The official's assessment that the historical and civilization faultiness dividing India and Pakistan really run deep and could at a certain level be irreconcilable was offered in late 2009 and are part of a US embassy cable leaked by the WikiLeaks Cablegate. Displaying a fairly hard headed understanding of Pakistan's main motives, Sinha is reported to have said the US needed to 'recognise and resist Islamabad's game of promising cooperation in Afghanistan in return for US pressure on India to improve ties with Pakistan, while also exaggerating India's threat to Pakistan." Pakistan was only leveraging the 'threat' from India. If Islamabad really felt to improve its relations with India, it would never have moved on entire army corps away from the east to deploy it in the west. However, LeT was a creature of ISI and armed by that wing of the Pakistani military.[83] Since ISI as the root cause of terrorism in Pakistan,

---

81 Neha Pushkaran, 'Children Go Ahead for Peace Process across the Border', *The Times of India*, New Delhi, December 18, 2010.

82 Eitorial Column, 'Even Handing over Kashmir won't Bring Peace with Pak, MEA Official', *The Times of India*, New Delhi, December 20, 2010.

83 Ibid.

therefore it would have to be seriously reformed in order to address the problem effectively.

Many a time proposals had been made from the Indian side to enter into an extradition agreement with Pakistan. However, in the year, 2002, Pakistan offered to negotiate a bilateral treaty to provide a legal framework for the extradition of the criminals from both the sides. In the year, 2004, also the Pakistan government invited Deputy Prime Minister, L K Advani to work out an extradition treaty between two nations. But, it is to bear in mind that Pakistan negotiates for the sake of talks.

By taking into consideration the current circumstances between India and Pakistan, now any assumption about the extradition treaty between India and Pakistan seems to be unfeasible, because the tension has been mounting from the both sides and it has gone to an extent of a new South Asian cold war. India has handed over to Pakistan its itinerary of evidences on Mumbai terror attacks accompanying the request for Pakistan to extradite the suspects who were involved in the recent Mumbai attacks in India, so that they could be tried under the Indian legal system. Pakistan's response was that there is no extradition agreement between India and Pakistan, so the suspected terror mongers can't be handed over to India, rather, they must be prosecuted in Pakistan only which was initially supported by U.K but now U.S.A. is also supporting this fact that Pakistan should not extradite suspected criminals. Pakistan always wears the veil of "no extradition treaty" whenever such demand is made. The reason is very simple, the assorted terrorist activities are being carried out on Pakistan soil and it is a well- known fact to the whole world and even Pakistan for that particular matter. If any such agreement is made between these two countries, then, there will be a legal obligation for Pakistan to hand over the criminals to India. There is always an option of denial "that attackers are not from Pakistani land" which is always played by Pakistan and in such a condition even an extradition agreement can't do fair dealing. A blatant example of this is Ajmal Kasab,[84] whom Pakistan is

---

84 The main accused of a most brazen and prolonged terror strike on November 26,2008 by Pakistani terrorists belonging to the Lashkar-e-Toiba (LET) in the financial and entertainment capital of the India, targeting mainly the CST station, Oberoi, Trident, Taj Mahal Palace and Tower Hotel, killing and injuring number of people. Fire fighting with terrorists could have been stopped successfully after three days in a joint operation involving the Maharashtra Police, Indian Army and the National Security Guard. The attack occurred on the 10th anniversary of the demolition of the Babri Mosque in Ayodhya. This

incessantly denying that he is not from Pakistan, notwithstanding the fact that India has given firm proof of him being a Pakistani Citizen and he is also asserted the same during interrogations in India.

India longs for an extradition agreement, India seeks to try any suspect in India as it doesn't have any trust in the Pakistan government and its legal system. India is highly critical of Pakistan's devotion in fight against terrorist groups. Therefore, it is cynical that the Pakistani legal system would trail potential convictions for the crimes committed. If the prosecution happens in Pakistan, then obviously it will not be fair and it will be akin to the notion that "thieves are prosecuting the thieves."

Pakistan would have to fight terrorism for its own purpose or it will implode, and that India's interest was not in Pakistan's demise but in its stability.[85] India views its neighbour with increasing alarm after the militants' attacks in Mumbai and militants strikes in Lahore, which is close to the Indian border. However India is watching the developments in Pakistan with concern as these have direct impact on India as well, especially on cross-border terrorism which affects India directly.

In today's Kashmir and other bordering State's of India, fear and hope remain constant companions. Any progress in Indo-Pakistan relations comes with a rider: the road to peace, it seems; will be as bloody as any war. As such as the future the peace dialogue too has to negotiate the minefield of the past.

India and North East Region

Ever since independence, northeast India has witnessed ethnic border infiltration, which have political manifestations and aspirations. What initially began as a home- grown insurgency was sustained in the later years through support in India's neighbourhood.

India's economically underdeveloped northeast region shares its boundary with four countries and has suffered due to cross border terrorism, illegal influx of Bangladeshis, and cross- border terrorism backed by the ISI.[86]While India faces a constant threat from terrorism sponsored by its

---

was the worst attack in Mumbai since the 1993 Mumbai serial blasts that killed 257 and injured over 700 people

85 Editorial Column, 'India Talks tough with US on Pakistan', *The Hindu*, Chennai, December 18, 2010.

86 Dipanjan Roy Choudhury, 'Avoid another J&K like Problem', India Today, (January

Western neighbour, the country's northeast too faces an increasing threat of cross- border terrorism, also encouraged and abetted by state agencies of Pakistan.

India and Bangladesh

As India shares its longest border with Bangladesh which is highly porous, the issue of border management has been a very important one. India has been concerned with the presence and activities of IIGs in Bangladesh. It considers their activities a major security threat to both India and Bangladesh. The ineffective border management has also resulted into a large scale cross border illegal movement from Bangladesh. To instill greater confidence in Bangladesh about India, the Indian side expressed very clearly that they would like to see a stable, prosperous and secure Bangladesh. India would even be happy to cooperate with Bangladesh in its economic development. Both sides noted that the relations between India and Bangladesh are multifaceted and rich in its content and scope. They recognized that further strengthening of these relations will not only be in the larger interests of the two "friendly neighbouring countries," but also will make an important contribution to the peace, progress and prosperity of all their peoples.

India has been trying for a while to get its neighbours to close down the camps and flush out the militants from their sanctuaries. In December 2003, under considerable pressure from India, the Royal Bhutan Army launched military operations against camps in southern Bhutan along the India- Bhutan border. Some 30 camps belonging to the ULFA, NDFB and the KLO and others were closed down and about 600 insurgents were killed. But regimes in Bangladesh remain defiant. [87]

In the Sixth home secretary level talks between India and Bangladesh at New Delhi in 2005, both sides managed to maintain the cordial atmosphere during the talks while pursing their "national interests." But problems arose over the contentious issues. Differences between India and Bangladesh on security and illegal migration issues reportedly delayed the signing of the joint statement. According to internal security agencies and BSF, Bangladesh has roughly 190-200 camps of North East insurgent

---

10, 2009).

87 Anand Kumar, 'Indo-Bangladesh Home Secretary Level Talks: An Exercise In Preparing Ground For upcoming SAARC Summit', available at http://www.southasiaanalysis. org/paper/html, (Last Viewed on January 11, 2010).

and extremist outfits.[88] Many a times, the BSF handed over to Bangladesh Rifles a detailed list of these camps. But it's a charge that Dhaka has consistently denied.

Nevertheless, at the meeting, India raised the issue of camps of northeastern Indian militants in Bangladesh, to which the Bangladeshi delegation offered that Indian officials could visit their country and see for themselves if there was any such camp. But Bangladesh expressed reservations when India wanted the offer to be included in the minutes of the meeting.[89]

Indian side also brought up the issue of an extradition treaty with Bangladesh to enable New Delhi to get custody of key militants from the North-East region who are believed to be operating training camps for insurgents in that country. Regarding extradition treaty and agreement on Mutual Legal Assistance in Criminal Matters, Bangladesh agreed to expedite its response to the proposal. Dhaka, however, did not agree to Delhi's request for a "high-level" meeting to discuss and set up a mechanism to deal with illegal migration from Bangladesh.

However, there were some positive developments also related to security issues. Both sides agreed to provide consular access to the insurgents/ criminals arrested by either side and to share information about activities of insurgents. Both sides also agreed that all possible measures will be taken to prevent smuggling of arms and explosives. They stated that their Governments did not encourage any type of smuggling and are resolute in their determination to effectively curb smuggling.

The delay in signing of joint statement itself had confirmed that the issues involved between Bangladesh and India are too complex to be sorted out quickly. As both sides struggled to come to a point which is acceptable to both sides, it has clear that there was a desire to avoid acrimony though it was agreed that a proper solution of the long-standing problems would take time.

Even after making all attempts to plug the loopholes in the preventive mechanism, an attack could not be stopped in Assam, when Mr. P. Chidambaram made his maiden trip as the Home Minister. In 2008 alone over a thousand persons were killed in terrorist- related violence in the

---

88 Ibid.
89 Ibid.

northeastern states. The bulk of these deaths occurred in two states - Assam and Manipur. Assam reported 372 fatalities while the death toll in Manipur was just shy of 500, second only to Kashmir, which recorded 539 deaths. While the country has been preoccupied with Kashmir and escalating terrorist violence elsewhere, separatist related violence in the northeast has been on the rise. The total number of deaths in this region has increased from 640 in 2006 to 1,057 in 2008.[90]

Although success of varying degrees has been achieved by the government vis-à- vis various rebel groups from the region since 2003, groups like ULFA, aim to wage a relentless war void of any clear objective and with support from elements in the Bangladeshi establishment and Pakistan's Inter Services Intelligence. The ISI and the Directorate General of Field Intelligence (DGFI) of Bangladesh are agencies which reportedly facilitate the ULFA's presence and operations.[91]

However, groups in Manipur too show no signs of any compromise. Manipur, with the second highest number of terrorist related deaths after Kashmir, has remained below the national radar. All 59 police stations in the state have reported terrorist activities, and 32 of them have been placed in the high violence category. The number of terrorists killed in Northeast has increased from 317 in 2006 to 501 in 2007 and to 612 in 2008. But the civilian death toll too has risen from 231 in 2006 to 405 in 2008. Since 1994, an estimated 16,271 persons have been killed in this volatile region.[92]

The problem of illegal migration from Bangladesh to Assam and other parts of the northeast is not only a threat to the identity of the people of the region but also a threat to the nation. The infiltration from Bangladesh is also paving way for sneaking in of ISI operatives to the country. Expediting the fencing work particularly along Indo- Bangladesh border (over 4,000 km), issuing of multi- purpose I-cards and putting an end to political interference are imperative to check illegal migration.

---

90 Dipanjan Roy Choudhury, 'Avoid another J&K like Problem', India Today, (January 10, 2009).

91 'Terror Kills More in North East than J&K', available at http://timesofindia. indiatimes.com, (Last Viewed on December 9, 2009).

92 Anand Kumar, 'Indo-Bangladesh Home Secretary Level Talks: An Exercise In Preparing Ground For Upcoming SAARC Summit', available at http://www.southasiaanalysis. org//paper, (Last Viewed on January 11, 2010).

Bangladesh is being used to plan and execute terror attacks against India. Increasing use of its territory by religious extremists, pan- Islamist outfits, and insurgents operating in India's northeast, remains the most serious threat not only to the internal security of the country, but also to the regional security environment. A number of transnational Islamist terrorist groups, including the Al- Qaeda, have established a presence in Bangladesh in alliance with various indigenous militant fundamentalist organisations. Prominent among these is the Harkat- ul- Jehadi- e- Islami, Bangladesh (HuJI- BD), which was established with direct aid from Osama bin Laden in 1992. The HuJI- BD has very close links with the ISI. Indian insurgent groups like ULFA are working in close unison with HuJI- BD and according to US based intelligence think- tank Stratfor have outsourced terror operations to the latter.

A. Renewed Peace Efforts

India Cross border terrorism, infiltration, smuggling of fake currency and activities of Northeast militants will be high on the agenda both for India and Bangladesh. The Indian delegation led by Home Secretary G K Pillai, seeking cooperation from Bangladesh. The two sides were discussing sensitive issues relating to the border, smuggling of narcotics, fake currency and chalk out strategy how to deal with the problems

Illegal immigration is another issue that has been nagging the bilateral relations. India will ask the Bangladesh side, led by its Home Secretary Abdus Sobhan Sikder, to take steps for handing over of jailed militant like ULFA general secretary Anup Chetia.[93]New Delhi is believed to be happy over the "detention" of two top ULFA leaders - Sashadhar Choudhury and Chitraban Hazarika -- in Dhaka and subsequent "handing over" of them to BSF along Indo-Bangla border in Tripura.[94]However, India is hopeful about Sheik Haseena's government that Dhaka would adhere to its demand of dismantling the terror infrastructure and hand over the Insurgents group's members.

India and Nepal

India and Nepal also resolved not to allow use of their territories for activities directed against each other and agreed to strengthen cooperation

---

93 Editorial column, 'India Bangla Home Secretary Level Talks', India Today, (November 27, 2009).

94 Ibid

to control terrorist's activities across the border. This was decided at the fourth India-Nepal joint working group meeting on border management when the two sides also agreed to share intelligence to deal with terrorists and undesirable elements across the border.

The decision assumes significance in the context of apprehensions in New Delhi about the activities of anti-India elements in Nepal, which were suspected to be behind the hijacking of the Indian Airlines aircraft from Kathmandu. While agreeing to hold regular meetings of the Interpol units to expedite disposal of pending cases on both sides, the meeting also decided to commence expert-level discussions on a legal framework for cooperation in criminal and civil matters and to review extradition arrangements. The two sides also agreed to expedite the procedural aspects of improving infrastructural facilities at the border check posts[95]

India and Myanmar

India and Myanmar have also agreed to strengthen cooperation for tackling the activities of insurgents, arms smugglers, drug traffickers and other hostile elements along the border with Myanmar assuring that arms smugglers would be severely punished if caught on its soil.[96] At the 11th Home Secretary-level talks between the two countries at Yangon capital of Myanmar, the two sides also reviewed the status of various infrastructural projects in Myanmar, particularly in the road and power sectors, over which the two countries had agreed to cooperate. They also discussed issues relating to security, border trade, border management and proposed infrastructure projects in Myanmar.

The Indian delegation was led by Union Home Secretary V K Duggal while the Myanmar side was headed by Deputy Minister of Home Affairs, Brig-Gen Phone Swe. It was agreed that, when completed, these infrastructure projects would help in the economic development of border areas and promote greater movement and interaction among people across the border. The Myanmar side requested sympathetic consideration for their fishermen who cross the maritime boundary inadvertently. The Union Home Secretary suggested setting up of a working group, which can evolve a mechanism so that innocent fishermen from both sides who

---

95 Editorial column, 'India- Nepal Agree to Curb Terrorism,' *Times of West Bengal*, October 13, 2009.

96 S. Satyanarayanan, 'India, Myanmar Agree to Tackle Cross border Terrorism', *The Tribune Online News Services*, October 16, 2005.

drift into the territorial waters of the other side, are not put to hardship.

On India's request, the Myanmar side also agreed to look into the release of five Indian nationals who were arrested by the Myanmar's Army. Both sides agreed to further strengthen cooperation for curbing drug trafficking and cross border terrorism, which is certainly a step forward the international peace and harmony with cooperation.[97]

India and China

The border dispute of India and China triggered a brief and bloody war in 1962 that proved to be a defining moment in modern Indo-Chinese relations, and the basis for decades of mutual suspicion and mistrust that have yet to be fully shed. India claims for China's illegal occupation of 38,000sq km of its north-western territory, while Beijing claims a 90,000 sq km chunk of north-east India.[98] Perceptions are that China is taking a harder line on its claim have led New Delhi to beef up its military presence along the frontier with thousands of extra combat troops, armour and expanded front-line air bases.

In December 1988, Indian Prime Minister Rajiv Gandhi visited China. The Prime Ministers of the two countries agreed to settle the boundary questions through the guiding principle of "**Mutual Understanding and Mutual Adjustment**". Agreement also reached that while seeking for the mutually acceptable solution to the boundary questions; the two countries should develop their relations in other fields and make efforts to create the atmosphere and conditions conducive to the settlement of the boundary questions. The two sides agreed to establish a Joint Working Group (JWG) on the boundary questions at the Vice-Foreign Ministerial level.[99]

An **Agreement on the Maintenance of Peace and Tranquility** along the Line of Actual Control in the India-China Border Areas was signed on 7 September 1993. After more than thirty years of border tension and stalemate, high-level bilateral talks were held in New Delhi starting in February 1994 to foster "**confidence-building measures (CSBMs)**"

---

97 Ibid.

98 Pratap Chakravarty, 'Wen's India Trip Skirts Border Issue', *My Paper*, Singapore, December 27, 2010.

99 'India China Border Dispute' available at

http://www.globalsecurity.org/military/India-china_conflicts.htm,, (Last Viewed on April 12, 2009).

between the defence forces of India and China, and a new period of better relations began. In November 1995, the two sides dismantled the guard posts in close proximity to each other along the borderline in Wangdong area, making the situation in the border areas more stable. During President Jiang Zemin's visit to India at the end of November 1996, the Governments of China and India signed the **Agreement on Confidence Building Measures** in the Military Field along the LAC in the China-India border areas, which is an important step for the building of mutual trust between the two countries. These Agreements provide an institutional framework for the maintenance of peace and tranquility in the border areas.[100]

Though lot had been done during the Sino-Indian official border talks, with number of border related CSBMs put in place, the border issue remains mired in various bilateral and domestic compulsions and contradictions on both sides. Border 'encounters' between India and China are not rare. They arise from the very real disagreements that exist between the two sides in demarcating the LAC on the ground. Such incidents have usually been handled, not in full media glare, but by the two sides discreetly withdrawing to their earlier positions.

The two sides withdrew sentries along the eastern section that were considered to be too close to each other. During early 1990s, India unilaterally withdrew about 35,000 troops from its eastern sector. On the other hand, China maintains a force between 180,000 and 300,000 soldiers and has directly ruled Tibet from 1950 to 1976, and indirectly thereafter.[101] Tibet today is connected to other military regions through four-lane highways and strategic roads. And Beijing's capability to airlift troops from its other neighbouring military regions has advanced very far from its comparative inability to use air force in 1962.

However, during the Indian Prime Minister's visit to China in June 2003 India and China signed a **Memorandum on Expanding Border Trade**, which adds Nathula as another pass on the India-China border for conducting border trade. The Indian side has agreed to designate Changgu of Sikkim state as the venue for border trade market, while the Chinese side has agreed to designate region of the Tibet as an autonomous region, as the venue for border trade market.

During Chinese Premier Wen Jiabao's visit to India in April 2005,

100 Ibid.
101 Supra note 92.

the two sides signed an agreement on political settlement of the boundary issue, setting guidelines and principles. In the agreement, China and India affirmed their readiness to seek a fair, reasonable and mutually acceptable solution to the boundary issue through equal and friendly negotiations. India after 1962 adopted a policy not to develop the border areas. The idea was that if India developed the border areas, the Chinese can easily use these facilities in the event of a war. This policy had changed by 2008. To redress the situation arising out of poor road connectivity which has hampered the operational capability of the Border Guarding Forces deployed along the India-China border, the Government has decided to undertake phase-wise construction of 27 road links totaling 608 Km in the border areas along the India-China border in the States of Jammu & Kashmir, Himachal Pradesh, Uttarakhand, Sikkim and Arunachal Pradesh at an estimated cost of Rs.912.00 crores.[102]

In order to overcome the problem of Cross border infiltration, both sides carry out patrolling activity in the India-China border areas. Transgressions of the LAC are taken up through diplomatic channels and at Border Personnel Meetings/Flag Meetings. India and China seek a fair, reasonable and mutually acceptable settlement of the boundary question through peaceful consultations.

However, in the end of the year 2010, Chinese Premier Wen Jiabao's visit in India was remarkable and certainly helped in stabilizing India-China relations and ensuring that they remain on an even keel, but the returns are certainly disappointing when compared to Wen's last trip to India in 2005. That trip had been genuinely forward looking as a road map on settling the border issue, which included respecting settled areas, had been developed. Since then, there has been considerable backsliding on the Chinese side noticed. For instance, China's an increasingly assertive claim for Arunanchal Pradesh. Not only did Wen's current visit not yield any fresh initiatives on the border issue, the Chinese chose not to resolve even the minor issue of the stapling of the visas of J&K residents, while Beijing maintains a stony silence on India's bid for a permanent seat on the UN Security Council.[103]

Even the Chinese Government indicated that it would play no role in pressuring Pakistan to crack down on terrorist groups operating on its soil,

---

102 Ibid

103 Editorial column, 'Mostly Trade', *The Times of India*, December 20, 2010.

reiterating its position that cross border terrorism and Kashmir were issues for India and Pakistan to resolve. China's official policy is that Kashmir is an issue for India and Pakistan to resolve and it would maintain a position of neutrality over the dispute of Kashmir as China believed that it had no role to play.[104]

Simultaneously, China is also providing tacit support to Pakistan in its jihadi strategy with an aim to pin down half a million Indian troops in Kashmir. Beijing has provided direct protection to these terrorist groups at the UN Security Council's 1267 committee, blocking efforts against Jamaat-ud-Dawa (the Lashkar-e-Tayiba front)[105] China is trying to promote insurgency in India by helping sectarian forces -- including Islamic terrorists and Maoists -- carry out their nefarious activities against India.[106]

Undoubtedly, Chinese Government has put aside diplomatic tact which is clearly inferred from an interview of China's defense minister Liang Guanglie, published in state backed newspaper that Country's military will prepare itself for 'military conflict' in every strategic directions in the next five years. The military will speed up modernization and development of equipment. He further remarked that, "We may be living in the peaceful times but we can never forget war, never send the horses south or put the bayonets and guns away".[107] China's pace and scale of military modernization and construction of military related infrastructure has caused alarm among neighbours like India, South Korea and Japan.

India And Us Policies To Curb Border Terrorism

There was optimum in India after September 11, 2001 attack on twin towers at America that India will also be benefited by United States commitment to uproot international terrorism. Since Pakistan and Afghanistan have been the epicenter of terrorism, it was hoped that terrorism might get eliminated in Kashmir and other affected states of India. It was hoped

---

104 Amarnath Krishnan, 'It's for India, Pakistan to Resolve Terrorism, Kashmir: China', *The Hindu*, Friday, December 17, 2010.

105 'China Backing Kashmiri Terrorists', available at http://news.rediff.com/htm, (Last Viewed on January 27, 2011).

106 'How China Plans to Break up India', available at http://news.rediff.com/htm, (Last Viewed on January 27, 2011).

107 Saibal Das Gupta, 'China's Readying for Military Conflict from all Directions: says Minister', *The Times of India*, December 31, 2010.

that the United States fight against terrorism would fracture and gradually eliminate terrorism from the region. However, United States policy to use Pakistan as frontline state to fight terrorism in Afghanistan belied India's hope. Instead Pakistan feels benefited economically, politically, military, diplomatically and strategically.

However, the British Prime Minister, the US Secretary of State and all member states of the Security Council have no doubts about the linkage between the terrorist attack and the terrorist elements in Pakistan. In a remarkable effort in the year 2010, India and the US (US ambassador to India Timothy J Roemer signed the agreement along with Home Secretary G K Pillai) signed a **Counter Terrorism Initiative** that includes steps to check financing of terror activities, joint probe in cases of bomb blasts besides cooperation in cyber and border security. In this agreement, they agreed that both the countries will work closely in matters like intelligence sharing and probe into bomb blasts.[108]

The agreement seeks to further enhance the cooperation between two countries in counter terrorism as an important element of their bilateral strategic partnership. The initiative provides for strengthening capabilities to effectively combat terrorism; promotion of exchanges regarding modernisation of techniques; sharing of best practices on issues of mutual interest; development of investigative skills and promotion of cooperation in forensic science laboratories. Besides, it seeks to establish procedures to provide mutual investigative assistance; enhancing capabilities to act against money laundering, counterfeit currency and financing of terrorism; exchanging best practices on mass transit and rail security; increasing exchanges between Coast Guards and Navy on maritime security. Exchanging experience and expertise on port and border security; enhancing liaison and training between specialists Counter Terrorism Units including National Security Guard with their American counter parts are part of the agreement.

The US envoy described it as a historic day for the US and India as the pact would bring the two countries closer together on issues of intelligence sharing, border security, mega policing efforts and "to fight together on a global basis against a common enemy, against terrorism"." Terrorism has brutally attacked the US on September 11; terrorism has attacked the

---

108 Editorial column, 'India and US Sign Counter Terrorism Initiative', India Today (July 23, 2010).

people of India, particularly on 26/11 in Mumbai, where six Americans were killed. Thus, this effort symbolizes Prime Minister Singh's and President Obama's efforts to create this indispensable partnership for the 21 century. It is an exciting day, an unprecedented day and a very proud day for the people of US," US ambassador said.[109]

Nevertheless, the US may emerge as a key partner in counter terror efforts post Mumbai terror attack, but it has a very dim view of the capabilities of Indian security forces. It also felt that just a couple of years ago that India was reluctant to have an effective anti-terror partnership because of the suspicions about American policies towards Pakistan, its independent foreign policy stance and sensitivities over Muslim sentiments.[110] "India's Police and security forces are overworked and hampered by bad police practices including the widespread use of torture in interrogations, rampant corruption, poor training, and a general inability to conduct solid forensic investigations," the US embassy observed in a cable it sent on February 23, 2007, after a not satisfactory meeting of an Indo-US counter terrorism joint working group.[111]The memo further said, 'India's security forces also regularly cut coroners to avoid working through India's lagging justice system, which has approx. 13 judges per million people. Thus Indian police officials often do not respond to the request for information about attacks or our offers of support because they are coming up poor practices, rather than rejecting our help outright.[112]

Eventually, in the aftermath of the Mumabi terror attacks on November 26, 2008, top diplomats and officials did some tough talks with US on Pakistan, with the former foreign secretary, Shivshankar Menon, conveying in clear terms New Delhi's disagreement with Washington's assessment that the Pakistan army was not involved in the dastardly strike.[113]

---

109 Ibid.

110 Editorial column,' US Scathing about India's Security Forces: WikiLeaks', *Sunday Times*, December 19, 2010, p.1.

111 Ibid

112 The communication disclosed in the cable refers to the US unease over the arrest of a computer expert, Mukesh Saini, who was working with India's National Counter Terrorism Centre (NCTC), and was arrested on charges of spying for Americans, available in 'US Scathing About India's Security Forces: WikiLeaks', *Sunday Times*, December 19, 2010, p.1.

113 Editorial column, 'India Talks Tough with US on Pakistan', *The Hindu*, December 18, 2010, Chennai.

According to the US cables, Indian firms were also aiding Syria in its chemical and biological weapon programme. In March 2008, Washington shared with New Delhi information indicating that an Indian company, whose name has been blacked out by the WilkiLeaks, "had offered French – origin, MTCR – controlled graphite blocks to Iran's ward commercial company" which had been involved on behalf of Shahid Hemmat Industrial group, Iran's primary liquid propellant ballistic missile developer. The cable points out that the Indian government has a general obligation as a Chemical Weapons Convention State Party to never, under any circumstances, assist any more in the development of chemical weapons.[114]

However, there are certain set of appreciations by US on India's concern for Afghanistan. The Indian Government was pressing forward with a host of development related investments in Afghanistan despite a sense of deep concern surrounding potential attacks upon its staff by militants groups and blockades of transit agreements by Pakistan. India's assistance programme for small community based projects, to its deployment of "low cost" engineers for infrastructure development projects and training courses for Afghans in Indian institutions. Since 2002, India contributed over USD 1.2 billion in reconstruction assistance, putting it away the top ranks of Afghan donors. However, Indian officials expressed growing concern with the security situation in Afghanistan, US diplomats wrote, that "they have been increasingly critical of what they perceive as the Pakistani Government's inability or unwillingness to act in the border tribal belt.

In the context of above mentioned efforts of both India and US, they are looking forward to maintain good relations with each other as both the nations are the ultimate victims of terrorism. To have a decisive victory against Osama bin Laden and his supporters, India and the US have to come together in a big way and work both at the policy level as well as on the ground. Unless this is appreciated and implemented, the efforts of democratic regimes against Islamic fundamentalist forces and terrorists will be lopsided and misplaced.

---

114 Editorial column, 'US Suspected Indian cos Role in Iran N-Plan', *Sunday Times*, December 19, 2010, New Delhi, p.18.

India's Renewed Anti-Terrorism Policies

Regarding India's renewed anti terrorism policies, the reference of substantial agencies is vital like the National Investigation Agency (NIA), a federal body constituted to probe and prevent terrorist attacks, becomes operational. Along with this there are large-scale changes are done to the Multi-Agency Centre (MAC) in the Intelligence Bureau (IB), which is meant to collate intelligence inputs, assess them and disseminate its reports to security forces, among a slew of efforts to improve national security. The NIA will only investigate terror related offences. The BSF's additional director general A.P. Singh, a 1974- batch IPS officer, is tipped for the job.

Infact, the revamp of the MAC, will make it work along the lines of the US Office of the Director of National Intelligence (DNI). The centre will now function round-the-clock as a central hotline for intelligence. It will be duty-bound to share inputs with all the intelligence agencies, States and Union Territories (UTs). In turn, all intelligence agencies, states and UTs will be obliged to share inputs with MAC on a real-time basis.[115]

However, subsidiaries of MAC have already been set up in a number of state capitals, but now every capital will have one. Since Mac was not able to achieve its objective there fore it is recommended by Mr. Chidambram (Home Minister) that a legal colour should be given to MAC His admission confirmed allegations that infighting among various intelligence agencies had put paid to MAC's efficiency - particularly in the lead up to the November 26 Mumbai attack. Intelligence inputs indicating the possibility of the attack had been available, but the centre failed to collate and assess it to prevent the tragedy.[116]

Infact, Mr. Chidambaram said his daily meetings with the national security adviser and intelligence chiefs had helped him assess the gaps in the security infrastructure. He now wants to replicate the same system at the state level. Chidambaram asked all chief ministers to set up round-the clock control rooms under a senior superintendent of police-level officer to share intelligence inputs on terrorism on a real-time basis with the MAC. He also asked the CMs to meet state-level intelligence and security chiefs

---

115 Aman Sharma, "Anti–Terror Law and Investigative Agencies are Active", India Today, (January 1, 2009).

116 Ibid.

every day.

The Home Ministry will also bring a note before the Cabinet on establishing a coastal command and setting up National Security Guard (NSG) hubs in major cities around the country. These hubs will be established in four cities to begin with, and later spread to more cities to facilitate quicker deployment of NSG commandos in case of a terrorist attack.[117] There are certain possible changes in the protection system for VIPs. While leading corporate houses like Tata, Oberoi and Infosys have approached the home ministry for CISF cover in the wake of the Mumbai attack, there was also a demand that elite forces like the NSG should be freed from such duties. "Among other measures, the IB has been sanctioned to fill up executive cadre vacancies on an emergent basis. Ten officers of the SP/DIG/IG level have been appointed to the IB against vacancies. Work is in progress to set up 20 counter-insurgency schools. There is also the procurement of around 20,000 bullet proof jackets for paramilitary troops on an emergent basis.[118]

Conclusion

However, indeed, one of the greatest challenges is the role of major powers, from within and outside the region, in India's neighbourhood. Neither confrontation nor the collusion between major powers, whether between the US and China, is in India's own interest.

However, India's most critical engagement was with Pakistan and it was vital to reach out for dialogue to reduce tensions, resolve outstanding issues and foster friendship. "There have been periods of crises, but also moments of hope. The sense of cynicism about dialogue with Pakistan is understandable especially when those responsible for Mumbai 26/11 attacks roam freely. India needs to intensify its engagement with Pakistan, notwithstanding its fragile polity and uncertain interest in peace at this stage, because keeping away from it is not a wise choice

Nevertheless, India is always pressing for concrete action by neighbouring countries especially Pakistan to end cross border terrorism in the backdrop of renewed infiltration bids and terror attacks. The dialogue process of India with its neighbours has contributed so meaningfully to

---

117 Id.

118 Editorial column, 'Tatas, Oberois, Reliance seek CISF cover.' *The Times of India*, Jan 1, 2009.

the improvement of relations over last four years. India would always appreciate to carry the process forward. However, India is looking forward for a concrete action by Pakistan in ending cross border terrorism and Infiltration. India believes terrorism is a "common concern" for both the countries and that it is in the interest of Pakistan itself to clamp down on the scourge as it has lost former Prime Minister Benazir Bhutto to terrorism. The cross-Line of Control initiatives particularly has witnessed a lot of forward movement and a further push is likely to be given during the upcoming talks. Pakistan too wants the peaceful resolution of all contentious issues with India, including Kashmir, so that it can "entirely focus" on the western border with Afghanistan to eliminate terrorism. According to one of the remarkable statement made by the Prime minister of Pakistan Mr. Yousuf Raza Gilani during a meeting with a visiting delegation of US Senators in the year 2010,"Pakistan wants to have good neighbourly relations with India and seeks the peaceful resolution of all the contentious issues between the two countries, particularly Kashmir and water disputes, to be able to entirely focus its attention on its western border for rooting out terrorism.[119]

Therefore India always makes it clear that the atmosphere of peace is essential for the dialogue process to succeed. However, it is also clear that terror incidents in India will not stop the peace and dialogue process with any of its neighbour. Ultimately, with the help of these talks, agreements, negotiations and composite dialogues we can achieve the target of eliminating the terrorism from its roots once for all. The need of time is the collaborative actions by all the nations. Countries must own up to their responsibilities in defeating terrorism. Therefore, the international community is to take "decisive and united" action to combat terrorism, which poses a grave threat to the stability of the world as well.

---

119 Editorial column, 'Pak Wants Resolution of All Issues, Kashmir with India: PM', India Today, (July 9, 2010).

Chapter V

Anti Terrorist Laws And Judicial Response:
An Overview

Traditionally, terrorism was considered to be a coercive tactic, sometimes adopted as part of a larger guerrilla strategy, in that actions created threats of worse to come if political demands were not met, and these demands tended to be geared to end foreign occupation or to secure the objectives of a secessionist movement. The rise of modern terrorism, however, has been far more complex, tied to diverse ideological and political goals, and often astounding in the scale of violence and the ambitions of its practitioners. The weapons used in the modern terrorist attacks have grown deadlier and far more accurate than the archaic guns and daggers of the early revolutionary terrorist and as terrorist groups make increasingly persistent efforts to acquire radiological, biological and chemical and weapons of mass destruction, the future outlook becomes more ominous. The situation is compounded further by the availability of enormous financial resources and new communications equipment that has immensely empowered both the terrorist and his masters.

- Terrorism is the acts of unlawful violence and war. It feeds off the personal suffering by luring governments into actions that abandon hard-earned freedoms of modern civilization. All terrorist acts are motivated by two things:

- **Social and political injustice**: People choose terrorism when they are trying to right what they perceive to be a social or political or historical wrong—when they have been stripped of their land or rights, or denied these.

The belief that violence or its threat will be effective, and usher in change. Another way of saying this is: **The belief that violent means justify the ends**. Many terrorists in history said sincerely that they chose violence after long deliberation, because they felt they had no choice.[1]

Terrorism is the affected, use of violence to bring forth fear. Terrorists know what they are doing and their targets are planned in advance. Terrorism may be motivated by political, religious, or ideological ideas. The base of terrorism is to produce fear in someone to make a government change its political attitude. Although it is relatively new in the mainstream world, extremists have practiced terrorism to generate fear and compel a change in behavior throughout history. Before the nineteenth century, terrorists usually recognized innocents - people not involved in conflict - and made sure not to harm them. But now terrorist don't care who they hurt, they just want to get they point across like the acts of September 11, Mumbai bomb blasts etc.[2]

The ground realities in India are stark and statistics provide a grim reminder of the increasing threat that terrorism constitutes. India has lost over so many lives to terrorism over the last decade in the major irregular and sub-conventional wars that have afflicted the country. A majority of these fatalities have occurred in J&K and in the Northeast alone as a result of the proxy war in the former, and a range of separatist insurgencies in the latter. A significant number of deaths have also occurred due to Left wing extremism (referred to as Naxalism in India) and retaliatory violence in some areas of the States of Andhra Pradesh, Maharashtra, Madhya Pradesh, Orissa, Chhattisgarh, Jharkhand, Uttar Pradesh, West Bengal and Bihar.[3]

India's Anti-Terrorist Laws And Judicial Response

The authority and legitimacy of modern nation states has come under a severe challenge as a result of rising trends in terrorism. Confronted with one of the most brutal forms of violence, a suitable or adequate response to terrorism is still to be framed, even as a proper context of evaluation and a sufficient understanding of its causation and methodology remain elusive. The uniqueness of terrorism lies in its complex inner dimensions, its continuous and rapid adaptations, and its wide variations across different theatres. Significantly, the transformation of terrorism over the past twenty

---

1   Saji Cherian, 'Terrorism and Legal Policy in India', Vol.XV, available at http://www. satp.org/satporqtp/publication/faultiness, (Last Viewed on April 6, 2009).

2   Ibid.

3   Siddharth, 'Anti- Terrorism Laws in India & The Need of POTA', available at http:// www.legalserviceindia.com/articles/html, (Last Viewed on April 20, 2011).

years has been startling, with rising anxiety over its burgeoning lethality.

India is facing multifarious challenges in the management of its internal security. There is an upsurge of terrorist activities, intensification of cross border terrorist activities and insurgent groups in different parts of the country. Terrorism has now acquired global dimensions and has become the challenge for the whole world. The reach and methods adopted by terrorist groups and organisation take advantage of modern means of communication and technology using high tech facilities available in the form of communication system, transport, sophisticated arms and various other means. This has enabled them to strike and create terror among people at will. The criminal justice system was not designed to deal with such type of heinous crimes. In view of this situation it was felt necessary to enact legislation for the prevention of and for dealing with terrorist activities.

Counter-terrorism legislation is, moreover, entirely consistent with a jurisprudential history of special laws that have been enacted from time to time to deal with special situations, and India's record is no exception. The first preventive detention law was introduced by the British in 1793, and was aimed solely for the purpose of detaining anybody who was regarded as a threat to the British settlement in India. The East India Company in Bengal subsequently enacted the Bengal State Prisoner's Regulation, which was to have a long life as 'Regulation III of 1818'. An extra-Constitutional ordinance, opposed to all the fundamental liberties which the colonial state would later pretend to be bound by, Regulation III provided for the indefinite confinement of individuals against whom there was insufficient ground to institute any judicial proceeding. Regulation III was the most effective tool in the hands of the British to quell any political violence.[4]

The beginning of the 20th century witnessed an increase in the revolutionary movement in India, with the birth of many underground groups pursuing the goal of independence through violent means. The period also marked the emergence of several legislations to quell the rising tide. In 1908, the government passed the **Newspapers (Incitement to Offences) Act** and the **Explosive Substances Act** and, shortly thereafter, **the Indian Press Act, the Criminal Tribes Act**, and the **Prevention of Seditious Meetings Act**. A majority of these legislations were aimed at

---

4   Ibid

breaking the back of the revolutionary movements by curbing meetings, printing and circulation of seditious materials and propaganda, and by detaining suspects. The Foreigners Ordinance of 1914 sought to restrict the entry and movement of foreigners in India. **The Defence of India Act (1915)** allowed suspects to be tried by special tribunals, whose decisions were not subject to appeal.[5]

The Defence of India Act was to expire shortly after the end of the World War I and the British Government had to come up with a new law to counter new tendencies. Based on the recommendations of Justice Rowlatt, Chairman of the Committee appointed to curb seditious movements in India, the Rowlatt Act, also known as the **Anarchical and Revolutionary Crimes Act**, was passed in 1919, giving unbridled powers to the colonial Government to arrest and imprison suspects without trial and crush civil liberties. The violent movement was blunted in the 1930s by the tough regulations passed by the Government, including the Constitutional Reforms of 1935.

Terrorism has immensely affected India. The reasons for terrorism in India may vary vastly from religious to geographical to caste to history. The Indian Supreme Court took a note of it in *Kartar Singh v. State of Punjab*[6], where it observed that the country has been in the firm grip of spiraling terrorist violence and is caught between deadly pangs of disruptive activities. Apart from many skirmishes in various parts of the country, there were countless serious and horrendous events engulfing many cities with blood-bath, firing, looting, mad killing even without sparing women and children and reducing those areas into a graveyard, which brutal atrocities have rocked and shocked the whole nation Deplorably, determined youths lured by hard-core criminals and underground extremists and attracted by the ideology of terrorism are indulging in committing serious crimes against the humanity.

After attaining Independence, the violence witnessed during Partition forced the Government of Free India to pass the **Punjab Disturbed Areas Act, Bihar Maintenance of Public Order Act, Bombay Public Safety Act, and Madras Suppression of Disturbance Act**, aimed at curbing forces that were using religion to incite violence. The rise of the Naxalite (Left-wing extremist) movement prompted the West Bengal government

---

5   Supra note 1.

6   [1994] 3 SCC 569

to pass the **West Bengal (Prevention of Violent Activities) Act of 1970.** [7]

The last three decades have witnessed a number of legislations being enacted to tackle various specific contingencies: **Jammu and Kashmir Public Safety Act (1978); Assam Preventive Detention Act (1980); National Security Act (1980, amended 1984 and 1987); Anti-Hijacking Act (1982); Armed Forces (Punjab and Chandigarh) Special Powers Act (1983); Punjab Disturbed Areas Act (1983); Chandigarh Disturbed Areas Act (1983); Suppression of Unlawful Acts Against Safety of Civil Aviation Act (1982); Terrorist Affected Areas (Special Courts) Act (1984); National Security (Second Amendment) Ordinance (1984); Terrorist and Disruptive Activities (Prevention) Act (1985, amended 1987); National Security Guard Act (1986); Criminal Courts and Security Guard Courts Rules (1987) and the Special Protection Group Act (1988).**[8]

Preventive detention legislations both before and after independence has been in vogue to control crime and criminal activities for public benefit. Various legislations by Indian government were enacted to curb and control nefarious activities viz. **Punjab Distributed Areas Act, Bihar Maintenance of Public Order Act, Bombay Public Safety Act and Madras Suppression of Disturbances Act.** These Acts conferred wide power to security forces to detain and arrest any person in the name of public order. In 1950 the **Prevention Detention Act** was passed and in 1958 **Armed Forces Separate Powers Act** was passed to arrest unrest in North East region. In 1971 **Maintenance of Internal Security Act (MISA)** was passed. [9]

Although these laws were enacted to meet special situations, most of them were not directed against the larger menace of terrorism. Anti-terrorism laws in India have always been a subject of much controversy. One of the arguments is that these laws stand in the way of fundamental rights of citizens guaranteed by Part III of the Constitution. The anti-terrorist laws have been enacted before by the legislature and upheld by the judiciary though not without reluctance. The intention was to enact these

---

7   Saji Cherian, Terrorism and Legal Policy in India, Vol.15, available at http://www.satp. org/satporqtp/publication/faultiness

8   Siddharth, 'Anti- Terrorism Laws in India & The Need of POTA', available at http:// www.legalserviceindia.com/articles/html, (Last Viewed on April 20, 2011)

9   Surat Singh (2006), *Law Relating to Prevention of Terrorism*, New Delhi.

statutes and bring them in force till the situation improves. The intention was not to make these drastic measures a permanent feature of law of the land. But because of continuing terrorist activities, the statutes have been reintroduced with requisite modifications.

At present, the legislations in force to check terrorism in India are the **National Security Act, 1980** and the **Unlawful Activities (Prevention) Act, 1967**. There have been other anti-terrorism laws in force in this country a different points in time. Earlier, the following laws had been in force to counter and curb terrorism. The first law made in independent India to deal with terrorism and terrorist activities that came into force on 30 Dec 1967 was **The Unlawful Activities (Prevention) Act 1967 (UAPA).**[10] The UAPA was designed to deal with associations and activities that questioned the territorial integrity of India. When the Bill was debated in Parliament, leaders, and cutting across party affiliation, insisted that its ambit be so limited that the right to association remained unaffected and that the executive did not expose political parties to intrusion. So, the ambit of the Act was strictly limited to meeting the challenge to the territorial integrity of India. The Act was a self-contained code of provisions for declaring secessionist associations as unlawful, adjudication by a tribunal, control of funds and places of work of unlawful associations, penalties for their members etc. The Act has all along been worked holistically as such and is completely within the purview of the central list in the 7th Schedule of the Constitution.

Terrorist and Disruptive Activities (Prevention) Act, 1987 (TADA) was the second major act came into force on 3 September 1987. This act had much more stringent provisions then the UAPA and it was specifically designed to deal with terrorist activities in India. When TADA was enacted it came to be challenged before the Apex Court of the country as being unconstitutional. The Supreme Court of India upheld its constitutional validity on the assumption that those entrusted with such draconic statutory powers would act in good faith and for the public good in the case of Kartar Singh vs State of Punjab[11]

In 1994, the Supreme Court, in the landmark judgement of *Kartar Singh vs. State of Punjab* dealt with various provisions of the Terrorist and Disruptive Activities (Prevention) Act, 1987 and upheld the constitutional

---

10 Ibid.

11 (1994) *3 SCC 569*

validity of the Act. From the very outset, the Court, looked into the matter in a broad perspective. Acknowledging the fact that the existing situation in the country was peculiar, the Court observed that,

"deplorably, determined youths lured by hardcore criminals and underground extremists and attracted by the ideology of terrorism are indulging in committing serious crimes against humanity. In spite of the drastic actions taken and intense vigilance activated, the terrorists and the militants do not desist from triggering lawlessness if it suits their purpose." [12] Further, realising the severity of the situation, the Court noted: "No one can deny these stark facts and naked truth by adopting an ostrich like attitude completely ignoring the impending danger."[13]

However, there were many instances of misuse of power for collateral purposes. The rigorous provisions contained in the statute came to be abused in the hands of law enforcement officials. TADA lapsed in 1995. Other major Anti-terrorist law in India is **The Maharashtra Control of Organised Crime Act, 1999 (MCOCA)** which was enforced on 24th April 1999.[14] This law was specifically made to deal with rising organised crime in Maharashtra and especially in Mumbai due to the underworld. This legislation was passed by the Maharashtra Assembly in view of the growing menace of organised crime. 'Organised Crime' bears an uncanny resemblance to terrorism: neither phenomenon is confined by international borders; both organised crime and terrorism involve murder, kidnapping, arson, robbery, burglary, extortion, dealing in narcotics or dangerous drugs, intimidation and violence; finally, the support structures and sources of finance are often the same for both.

The MCOCA has been an extraordinary success in Maharashtra, with a conviction rate as high as 78 per cent in some years. Many of the provisions of MCOCA are similar to those under **Prevention of Terrorist Activities Act (POTA)**.[15] For example, both acts have identical provisions with respect to

i.   Procedures and powers of Special Court – Section 9 of MCOCA and Section 29 of POTA;

---

12 Ibid.

13 Ibid.

14 Surat Singh (2006), *Law Relating to Prevention of Terrorism*, New Delhi.

15 Awantika Manohar, 'Terrorism, How to Control it', Lawz, Vol.VI, (June, 2006).

ii.   Authorisation of interception of wire, electronic or oral communication – Sections 14 and 16 of MCOCA and Section 36 to 48 of POTA;

iii. Certain confessions made to police officer to be taken into consideration – Section 18 of MCOCA and Section 32 of POTA;

iv.   Protection of witnesses – Section 19 of MCOCA act and Section 30 of POTA;

v.   Forfeiture and attachment of property – Section 20 of MCOCA and Sections 6, 7 and 8 of POTA.

There can be no doubt that, if a clear anti-terrorism strategy involving the police, the executive and the judiciary could be formulated and executed on a national scale, the successes of MCOCA could be replicated under POTA.

In 2002 March session of the Indian parliament the **Prevention of Terrorist Activities Act (POTA)** was introduced. It was termed as Indian version of U.S Patriot Act. It was nothing more than the reincarnation of TADA with largely cosmetic changes. The Act was considered as a draconian piece of legislation as it curtailed various rights of a citizen which were recognized since long and were contrary to Article 21 of the Constitution. It was repealed in 2004 with **Unlawful Activities (Prevention) Amendment Act, 2004**.[16] The POTA had widespread opposition not even in the Indian parliament but throughout India especially with the human rights organisation because they thought that the act violated most of the fundamental rights provided in the Indian constitution. The protagonists of the Act have, however, hailed the legislation on the ground that it has been effective in ensuring the speedy trial of those accused of indulging in or abetting terrorism. POTA is useful in stemming "state-sponsored cross-border terrorism", as envisaged by the then Home Minister L.K. Advani. The Prevention of Terrorism Act, 2002 (POTA), was seen as a controversial piece of legislation ever since it was conceived as a weapon against terrorism.

For, POTA did not take note of organised crime as such while MCOCA not only mentions that but, what is more, includes 'promotion of insurgency' as a terrorist act. Again, the onus to prove a person guilty under POTA lies on the prosecution while under the Maharashtra law a person

16 Ibid.

is presumed guilty unless he is able to prove his innocence. MCOCA does not stipulate prosecution of police officers found guilty of its misuse. But POTA did. MCOCA does not stipulate prosecution of police officers found guilty of its misuse. But POTA did. Under POTA a police officer found guilty of malafide action could be jailed for up to two years but MCOCA offers no such protection.

Need of POTA

It is normally said that terrorism is a low intensity war. But the loss, which our country has suffered in the last two decades due to the rise of terrorist activities, has been on a very large scale. This country has fought four high intensity wars and in those wars we have lost more then 6000 people. We have already lost more then 70000 civilians. In an addition, we have lost more then 9000 security personnel. Almost six lakhs people in this country have become homeless as a result of terrorism. Outside the expenditure on our armed forces, merely for maintaining the entire set up to fight insurgency, to fight cross-border terrorism, the economic cost itself has been Rs 45000 crore. The budgetary increase itself in the last 15 years, because of terrorism or anti-insurgency activities, has been 26 times. We have no record of the explosives that have been used in various parts of the country. We have a record of crime. But the explosives that have been confiscated by our security agencies weigh 48000 kilos. If our security forces had not been vigilant enough to confiscate these explosives, they would probably have been enough to take care of every inch of Indian soil.[17]

Therefore it becomes very necessary in a country like India that if a law regarding terrorism is enacted it should be made so stringent that the culprit be bought to book and does not go scot-free just because of the loopholes and lacunas in the ordinary law because when our neighboring nation Pakistan which is the cause of perpetrating terrorism in India and can have such stringent then India should also have such laws.

---

17 Ibid

Analysis of some important sections of POTA[18]

In the case of *People's Union for Civil Liberties vs. Union of India (UOI)*[19] the constitutional validity of the Prevention of Terrorism Act, 2002 was discussed. The court said that the Parliament possesses power under Article 248 and entry 97 of list I of the Seventh Schedule of the Constitution of India to legislate the Act. Need for the Act is a matter of policy and the court cannot go into the same. Once legislation is passed, the Govt. has an obligation to exercise all available options to prevent terrorism within the bounds of the constitution. Mere possibility of abuse cannot be a ground for denying the vesting of powers or for declaring a statute unconstitutionally. Court upheld the constitutional validity of the various provisions of the Act.[20]

A. Section 3(a) Defining terrorist act

Whoever with the intent of threatening the unity, integrity, security and sovereignty of India or strike terror in the minds of people or any section of the people does any act or thing by using dynamite or explosive substances or inflammable substance or firearms or other lethal weapon or poisonous or noxious gases or other chemical or any substance of a hazardous nature in such a manner as to cause death or injuries to any person or loss or damage to property or disruption of any supplies or services essential for life.

Case Law- *Devender Pal Singh vs. State of N.C.T. of Delhi* [21]In a case where 9 person had died and several other injured on account of perpetrated acts The court said that such terrorist who have no respect for human life and people are killed due to there mindless killing. So any compassion to such person would frustrate the purpose of enactment of Tada and would amount to misplaced and unwarranted sympathy. Thus they should be given death sentence.

Argument against- Trade union activity would be affected because

---

18 Atin Kumar, 'Combating Terrorism and Protection of Human Rights: Striving Towards balance', available at http://www.lawyersclubindia.com/articles/html, (Last Viewed on May 8, 2010).

19 (2004) 9 SCC 580

20 Siddharth Malik, 'Should India Revamp Its Anti- Terrorism Laws After The July 11 Serial Explosions', available at http://www.legalserviceindia/articles/htm, (Last Viewed on June, 25, 2009).

21 (2002) *(1) SC (Cr.) 209*

whoever disrupts essential supplies would be covered under POTA.

Argument in favor- At least trade union leaders are nationalist leaders. Nobody has ever suggested that when trade union leaders go on strike, they threaten the unity, integrity, security and sovereignty of India.

B. Section 4 Possession of certain unauthorized arms

Where any person is in unauthorized possession of any- bombs, dynamite or hazardous explosive substance or other lethal weapons capable of mass destruction or biological or chemical substances of warfare in any area, whether notified or not.

Case Law- *Sanjay Duttt vs. State through C.B.I* [22]The expression possession though that of section 5 of Tada has been stated to mean a conscious possession introducing thereby involvement of a mental element i.e. conscious possession & not mere custody without awareness of nature of such possession and as regards unauthorized means and regards without any authority of law.

Argument against - That an offence coming under the Arms Act has been brought under POTA, irrespective of whether a person carrying such arms has any nexus with a terrorist.

Argument in favour - Firstly the section clearly says that any person who has unauthorized possession of arms that is does not possess a proper license for the arms. This section is only making the law stringent by stating that anybody who possesses arms should also possess proper license from the proper authority. Secondly it also states weapons should be capable of mass destruction or biological or chemical substances of warfare so why would any person without any reason possess such kind of weapons and that to unauthorized.

C. Section 7 Powers of investigating officers

If any officer (not below the rank of SP) investigating an offence committed under this act, has reason to believe that any property in relation to which an investigation is being conducted represents proceeds of terrorism he shall with prior approval in writing from Director General of Police of which the property is situated can make an order to seize or attach such property.

---

22 (1994) *SCC 410*

Argument against - The petition articulates the fear that permitting a police officer to act on the basis of his belief will be "draconian and unguided.

Argument in favour - Case Law - *T.T. Anthony vs. State of Kerala* [23]This plenary power of police to investigate a cognizable offence is not unlimited. It is subject to certain limitations such as if no cognizable offence is disclosed & still more if no offence of any kind is disclosed the police would have no authority to undertake an investigation.

D. Section 21 Offence relating to support given to a terrorist organisation-

    1. A person commits an offence if

        b. He invites support for a terrorist organisation , and

        c. The support is not, or is not restricted to, the provisions of money or other property

    2. A person commits an offence if he arranges, manages or assists in managing or arranging a meeting which he knows is-

        c. To support a terrorist organisation, or

        d. To further the activities of a terrorist organisation, or

        e. To be addressed by a person who belongs or professes to belong to a terrorist organisation.

    3. A person commits an offence if he addresses a meeting for the purpose of arranging support for a terrorist organisation or to further its activities.

Case Law - Vaiko's Case One of the petitions in this regard admitted by the Supreme Court has been filed by Vaiko, the general secretary of the (MDMK), a constituent of the ruling National Democratic Alliance at the Centre. Vaiko had defended POTA in Parliament during the debate on it. Therefore his petition challenging the validity of Section 21 of the Act assumes particular significance. Under this Section, a person commits an offence if he invites support for a terrorist organisation, and even if the support is not confined to the provision of money or other property. He is guilty if he arranges or addresses a meeting which he knows is meant

---

23 (2001) *Cri LJ 3329*

to support a terrorist organisation or to further its activities. Vaiko was arrested under this Section on the basis of certain remarks saying that "I was a supporter of LTTE once. I was a supporter of LTTE yesterday; I am a supporter of LTTE today and I will be a supporter of LTTE tomorrow." Then, he asked his audience whether the LTTE had engaged in terrorism for the sake of violence or had taken up arms to suppress a culture. Mr. Vaiko, was in detention for 17 months, did not choose to seek bail on a matter of principle.

When we looked at various chapters internationally, it was found that as far as membership of a terrorist group is concerned, the British law has an exclusive chapter on banning terrorist organisations. After banning a terrorist organisation, membership of a terrorist organisation, ipso facto, becomes a punishable act.

E. Section 22- Fund raising for a terrorist organisation to be an offence-

6. Whoever commits an offence if he-

   g. Invites, receives or provides money or other property

   h. Intends that it should be used, or has reasonable cause to suspect that it may be used, for the purposes of terrorism.

The second component that was not there in TADA is, if you try and earn money through a crime, that is, through terrorism, there are two offences which flow out of that. Whoever funds terrorism is also held guilty. By funding terrorism we are abetting terrorism. We are giving resources to terrorism. The old terrorist laws the world over never had a chapter on funding of terrorists. But now we must create a fear and scare in the minds of those who fund terrorists.

Whatever earned out of crime is not your private property; it is against public interest and must belong to the state. The UN passed a draft Money Laundering Bill which all is having been debating. The whole concept of money laundering is that profits out of crime must be confiscated because they cannot belong to an individual. It is an argument today that since India is now to have a provision where profits from terrorism will be confiscated, it is a draconian provision.

F.   Section 27 Powers to direct for samples, etc.

When a police officer investigating a case requests a Chief Metropolitan Magistrate to obtain hand writing, footprints, photographs, blood, saliva, semen, hair, voice of any accused person reasonably suspected to be involved in the commission of this act it will be lawful for the judge to give

Case Law - *S. Srinivasa Vs. M/s Deccan Petroleum Ltd.* [24]The court said where the order of refusal to issue summons for production of document was prejudicial to accused then such order is not sustainable. The most important part of the section says that the power to take samples is not given to the police authorities but when a police officer investigating a case requests a Chief Metropolitan Magistrate to obtain samples of any accused person reasonably suspected to be involved in the commission of this act and then if only the Chief Metropolitan Magistrate gives the order to obtain such samples its only then he can force the accused to give such samples. If any accused person refuses to give such samples the court shall only then draw adverse inference against the accused.

G.   Section 32 certain confessions made to police officers taken into consideration

A confession made by a person before a police officer not lower in rank than a S.P. and recorded by him out of whom sound or images could be reproduced shall be admissible in trial of such person for the offence under this act.

Case Law - *Devender Pal Singh vs. State of N.C.T. of Delhi* [25]The court said that it is entirely to the court trying the offence to decide the question of admissibility or reliability of a confession in its judicial wisdom strictly adhering to law it must while so deciding the question should satisfy itself that there was no trap. No track and no importance seeking evidence during the custodial interrogations and all the conditions required are fulfilled. If the court is satisfied then the confessional statement will be a part of the statement.

Confessions could be made admissible evidence. In respect of confessions, we have given the facility of video recording. After that, within 48 hours, the person should be produced before a magistrate. The

---

24 2001) *Cri LJ 659*

25 (2002) *(1) SC (Cr.) 209*

magistrate will ask whether it was voluntary or not. If the accused says that it was not voluntary, that he had been assaulted and coerced

If the accused says that it was not voluntary, that he had been assaulted and coerced, the magistrate will have a medical examination done. So, a safeguard has been put in.

State (N.C.T. of Delhi) Vs. Navjot Sandhu & Afsan Guru[26] this was an appeal against convictions in view of attacks made on parliament. The matter was relating to admissibility and evidentiary value of evidence that retracted confessions cannot be acted upon by Court unless it is voluntary and can be corroborated by other evidence. Confession of accused can be used against co-accused only if there is sufficient evidence pointing to his guilt confession made under POTA cannot be used against co-accused as POTA operates independently of Indian Evidence Act and Indian Penal Code. Section 10 of Evidence Act has no applicability as confessionary statement has not been relied on for rendering conviction.

Admissibility of intercepted phone calls, intercepted phone calls are admissible piece of evidence under ordinary laws even though provisions of POTA cannot be invoked as it presupposes investigation to be set in motion on date of its interception. Confession made involuntary is inadmissible evidence. If procedural safeguards have not been complied it will affect admissibility and evidentiary value of evidence being proved all charges beyond reasonable doubt convictions were upheld.

H. Section 45 Admissibility of evidence collected through the interception of communication

1. notwithstanding anything in the code or in any other law for the time being in force the evidence collected through the interception of wire, electronic or oral communication shall be admissible as evidence against the accused in the court during the trial of a case.

It is said that TADA was misused. Probably it was misused. However, one of the great weaknesses in TADA a structural defect was its dependence on witnesses; eyewitnesses and humble citizens appearing against terrorist groups. Anybody from Punjab, Mumbai or Kashmir will testify that the average citizen is scared of coming and honestly deposing before these institutions. This is a threat that the witnesses face against terrorist acts. So

---

26 (2005) *11 SCC 600*

a normal person cannot be able to give a statement before the court.

Therefore, there is a need bring in a provision that when terrorist gangs communicate with each other, intercepts of their communication should be allowed and these intercepts should become admissible evidence in court. So, when you arrest terrorists, you do not need a humble citizen to come and give evidence against them. You produce the recording of that intercept. At that moment, it becomes admissible evidence. Under normal law it is not admissible evidence. We examined the suggestion and accepted it. One of the strengths of this law is actually on the question of intercepts becoming admissible evidence. It is one reason why in Maharashtra, the conviction rate has reached 75% plus under MOCA.

A. **Bail provision**: This language of a bail provision, the CrPC normal bail provisions, will not apply: That no person will be released on bail unless the public prosecutor has an opportunity or where he opposes the application, there is a reasonable opportunity of believing that the person is innocent and shall not commit an offence. This was the language under TADA. The language was diluted under POTA.

B. **Action against police officer**: There is a provision that in case any police officer misuses this law for his own personal purposes or for collateral reasons, he will be prosecuted under POTA itself. Several safeguards have been incorporated in the Act to minimize the possibility of its misuse. Some of the main safeguards are as follows:

  i.   Investigation of an offence under the Act is to be done by an officer not below the rank of Deputy Superintendent of Police.

  ii. No court can take cognizance of an offence under the Act unless sanction of the State.

  iii. The Act provides safeguards against abuse of the provision relating to admissibility of confession made before a police officer.

  iv. Intimation of arrest of the accused will have to be provided to a family member immediately after arrest and this fact is to be recorded by the police officer

    v.   Provision for prosecution of police officers for malafide actions under the Act and compensation to affected persons in such cases.

The State Government/UT Administrations were advised to ensure that the provisions of this law are used only against the terrorists and not against the innocent. They were also advised to sensitize the police officers and others concerned with the implementation of POTA on the need to ensure its fair and transparent operation and to also install a mechanism to oversee the implementation of the Act.

Our Constitutional ethos requires Parliament to enact laws, which on the one hand should be effective instruments in dealing with terrorists and on the other hand, ensure that the foundation of our constitutional values and our adherence to the rule of law does not falter. Basically, the reason for repealing POTA was because of rampant misuse of its provisions for setting political scores, targeting minority community and arresting innocent citizens,. Tamil Naidu Chief Minister, Jayalalitha invoked the POTA for booking MDMK leader Vaiko, UP Chief Minister, Mayawati used it against Raghuraj Pratap Singh and Gujrat Chief Minister, Narender Modi used it as a tool to book persons belonging to a particular community. In Jharkhand, more than 300 persons were arrested under the POTA, which included women and children.[27]

Consequences of repeal of POTA

Finally on September 17, 2004 the Union Cabinet in keeping with the UPA government's Common Minimum Programme, approved ordinances to repeal the controversial Prevention of Terrorism Act, 2002 and amend the Unlawful Activities (Prevention) Act, 1967.[28] By the promulgation of

1.   Ordinance No.1 of 2004, it repealed POTA, a law specially designed to deal with the menace of terrorism with its repeal, the state apparatus combating terrorism has been debilitated.

2.   By Ordinance No 2 promulgated on the same day, virtually all the penal provisions of POTA concerning terrorist organisations and activities were transferred to the pre-existing milder sounding

---

27 Kapil Sibal, 'Action and Reaction – The Threat of Terrorism is real', available at http://.www.sabrang.com/html, (Last Viewed on March 30, 2009).

28 Siddharth Malik , 'Repeal Of POTA - Justified', available at http://www. legalserviceindia.com/articles, (Last Viewed on October 16, 2009).

Unlawful Activities (Prevention) Act, 1967 (UAPA). Even with the repeal of POTA, India can, under the present legal framework of the Act of 2004, claim to have the harshest law dealing with terrorists. However, it would however be simplistic to suggest, as some critics did, that the new law has retained all the operational teeth of POTA or it has made only cosmetic changes. The difference between POTA and UAPA is substantial even as a lot of provisions are in common. By Ordinance No 2, the definition of unlawful association has been expanded to also include any association which has for its object any activity which is punishable under Section 153A of the Indian Penal Code, or which encourages or aids persons to undertake any such activity, or of which the members undertake any such activity. Section 153A is about promoting enmity between different groups on grounds of religion, race, place of birth, residence, language, etc.

3. There would be no arrests made after the ordinance is promulgated.

4. Among the special provisions dropped are those restricting release on bail and allowing longer periods of police remand for the accused. Now suspected terrorists may roam free under the bail a rule, jail an exception dictum. The police will not get sufficient time to interrogate the accused to investigate the cases which, by their very nature, are complex. In POTA, as in Tada earlier, confessions made before a police officer of the rank of superintendent were admitted as evidence.

5. All terrorist organisations banned under POTA would continue to remain banned, under the Unlawful Activities Act, after the repeal of the Act.

6. Some of the clauses contained in POTA, which will be completely dropped in the amended Unlawful Activities Act, are: the onus on the accused to prove his innocence, compulsory denial of bail to accused and admission as evidence in the court of law the confession made by the accused before the police officer.

7. In another major departure from POTA, the government has removed all traces of strict liability. Meaning, the burden of proof has shifted from the accused to the police. There is no presumption of guilt under UAPA. Like under any other ordinary criminal law,

the police will have to establish that the accused person had a criminal intention for committing the offence in question.

8. As reported recently in the Indian Express, UAPA is more draconian than POTA when it comes to the admissibility in evidence of telephone and e-mail intercepts. The police can now produce intercepts in the court without abiding by any of the elaborate safeguards provided by the repealed law. Thus, if the police cannot anymore extract a confession in custody, they have been given more scope than before to plant evidence in the form of interceptions.[29]

9. Another glaring shortcoming in the new law pertains to the dichotomy in the provision for banning terrorist organisations and unlawful organisations. UAPA was originally meant only for banning unlawful organisations. Now it has a separate chapter for banning terrorist organisations as well. Thus, the procedures prescribed by the same law for the two kinds of bans are different. But the problem is that the procedure for banning a group on the charge of terrorism is easier than to ban it on the milder charge of unlawful activities. The government cannot, for instance, ban any group for unlawful activities without having its decision ratified within six months by a judicial tribunal headed by a sitting high court judge. There is no such requirement if the ban is on the charge of terrorism. This anomaly has arisen because of the strategy adopted by the UPA government to hide special provisions in an ordinary law.

The UAPA was designed to deal with associations and activities that questioned the territorial integrity of India.[30] When the Bill was debated in Parliament, leaders, cutting across party affiliation, insisted that its ambit be so limited that the right to association remained unaffected and those political parties were not exposed to intrusion by the executive. So, the ambit of the Act was strictly limited to meeting the challenge to the territorial integrity of India.

---

29 Editorial column, 'What We Talk About Law When We Talk About Law', *The Indian Express*, September 25, 2008

30 'The New POTA: Spot the Dangers', available at http:// www.iecolumnists. expressindia.com, (Last Viewed on June 17, 2009).

Unlawful Activities (Prevention) Amendment Act, 2004

A. The Act does not define the word terrorist in its definition clause
    but defines a terrorist act. The word terrorist is to be construed
    according the definition of the terrorist act. Terrorist act is defined
    in the Act as "Whoever, with intent to threaten the unity, integrity,
    security or sovereignty of India or to strike terror in the people or
    any section of the people in India or in any foreign country, does
    any act by using bombs, dynamite or other explosive substances
    or inflammable substances or firearms or other lethal weapons
    or poisons or noxious gases or other chemicals or by any other
    substances (whether biological or otherwise) of a hazardous
    nature, in such a manner as to cause, or likely to cause, death of,
    or injuries to any person or persons or loss of, or damage to, or
    destruction of, property or disruption of any supplies or services
    essential to the life of the community in India or in any foreign
    country or causes damage or destruction of any property or
    equipment used or intended to be used for the defence of India
    or in connection with any other purposes of the Government of
    India, any State Government or any of their agencies, or detains
    any person and threatens to kill or injure such person in order to
    compel the Government in India or the Government of a foreign
    country or any other person to do or abstain from doing any act,
    commits a terrorist act" (Section 15).The above definition did not
    exist in the 1967 Act. The previous Act only defined and dealt with
    unlawful activity. An unlawful activity includes "an activity which
    intends to bring about cession of a part of the territory of India or
    the secession of a part of the territory of India from the Union, or
    which incites any individual or group of individuals to bring about
    such cession or secession; or which disclaims, questions, disrupts
    or is intended to disrupt the sovereignty and territorial integrity of
    India, or which causes or is intended to cause disaffection against
    India" (Section 2(o)).

B. Whether an association is unlawful is to be declared by the Central
    government by giving the grounds for such a declaration. Section
    3 Thereafter; it is referred to the Tribunal Section 4. A notice is
    issued by the Tribunal to the association concerned to show cause
    why it should not be declared unlawful. To ascertain whether there
    is sufficient cause for declaring the association unlawful.

C. For taking cognizance of any offence under this Act prior sanction of the Central or the State government, as the case may be, is necessary. Criminal Procedure Code, 1973, is made applicable in matters of arrest, bail, confessions and burden of proof. Those arrested are to be brought before a magistrate within 24 hours, confessions are no longer admissible before police officers and bail need not be denied for the first three months. The presumption of innocence leaving the burden of proof on the prosecution has also been restored. The evidence collected through interception of wireless, electronic or oral communication under the provisions of the Indian Telegraph Act or the Information Technology Act or any law being in force has been made admissible as evidence against the accused in the court Section 46. The amended Act provides for following penalties: Offence Includes Penalty

D. Being a member of an unlawful association; A person who is and continues to be a member of such association, takes part in meetings, contributes to, or receives or solicits any contribution for the purposes of the association or in any way assists the operations of such association. If such person is in possession of unlicensed firearms, ammunition, explosive, etc, capable of causing mass destruction and commits any act resulting in loss of human life or grievous injury to any person or causes significant damage to any property, and if such act has resulted in the death of any person. In any other case Imprisonment for a term which may extend to two years and fine.

E. Death or imprisonment for life: Imprisonment for not less than five years. Dealing with funds of an unlawful association includes an association declared unlawful by the central government. Such association is prohibited from dealing in any manner with moneys, securities or credits pays, and imprisonment upto three years, or fine, or both. Contravention of an order made in respect of a notified place includes use of articles for unlawful activities found in a notified place (i.e. a place used for unlawful association and so notified by the central government), imprisonment upto one year. Unlawful activities Includes taking part in or committing an unlawful act, advocating, abetting, advising or inciting the commission of any unlawful activity. Assisting an unlawful organisation in its activities then a term of seven years and fine.

F.   The amended law now contains new provisions dealing with terrorist acts, the offences and their punishments. Chapter IV, sections 15-22. The following table summarises these provisions:

1.   Terrorist act resulting in death of any person in any other case, death or imprisonment for life. A term for not less than five years.

2.   Raising funds for a terrorist act, term not less than five years.

3.   Conspiracy, term not less than five years.

4.   Harbouring, imprisonment for not less than three years.

5.   Being a member of a terrorist organisation, the term may extend upto imprisonment for life.

6.   Holding proceeds of terrorism may extend to imprisonment for life.

7.   Threatening witnesses, imprisonment upto three years.

8.   There is a provision in the Act which provides for enhanced penalties. Any person aiding a terrorist or acting in contravention to Explosives Act, 1884, the Explosive Substances Act, 1908 or the Inflammable Substances Act, 1952 or the Arms Act, 1959, or has unauthorized possession of bombs, explosives, etc, will be punished with a term not less than three years and may extend for life (Section 23).

9.   The Act also gives power to the Central and the State Governments, as the case may be, to forfeiture the proceeds of terrorism. The investigating officer is empowered to seize the concerned property with the prior approval of the Director General of the police of the State (Section 24 and 25). Cash (including monetary instruments) can also be seized if it is intended to be used for purposes of terrorism. The Court confirms the seized property and orders its forfeiture Section 26. An appeal to the High Court against the forfeiture is allowed within one month from the date of receipt of such order.

Chapter VI of the amended Act gives power to the Central government under section 35 to add or remove an organisation in the schedule as a terrorist organisation. Under section 36, an application can also be made to remove an organisation from the schedule. Such an application can be made by an organisation or any affected person. The offences and penalties under this chapter as given below:

1. Membership of a terrorist organisation (S. 38), imprisonment not exceeding ten years.

2. Supporting a terrorist organisation (S. 39), imprisonment not exceeding ten years.

3. Raising funds for terrorist organisation (S. 40), a term not exceeding fourteen years.

The Act also provides for protection of witnesses under section 44 such as keeping the their identities secret even in orders, judgments and records of the Court, issuing directions to secure the identity of the witnesses and by imposing punishment for contravention of any such directions.

Various suspicion and voices have been raised by people NGO's under the pretext of constitution, constitutional provisions, and equality before law and civil rights. All these organisations must keep in mind that provisions are there in the constitution where reasonable restrictions can be enforced even upon the liberty of people and in view of the increasing terrorist activities in the nation more particularly in view of the 9/11 attacks on the World Trade Center which killed more then 3000 people and 13 December attack on the Indian Parliament and large number of terrorist activities not only in J&K, North East., Arunachal Pradesh., and other areas of our country need for promulgation of POTA type legislation becomes the need of the hour.

However there are numerous safeguards to prevent the abuse of above legislation by unscrupulous investigating officers, which are being ignored by various organisations professing the repeal of such law. The attention of those who are against this legislation is invited to object and reason for which POTA was enacted. The repeal of POTA is just party politics to gain for their party's vote bank. If security forces and investigative forces are not given the legal power, human rights violations will be much worse. Therefore, if one wants, out of concern for human rights, the powers not to be misused, one cannot sustain a situation where no one is giving powers to the police but putting pressure on it to deliver. Hence that would be considered as a situation of anarchy.

Conclusion

The fault lies, not in the legislation, but in the system that implements the law. Delays are chronic, right from the stage of issuing summons to the defendant, which, in some cases, can take several months, as processes are delayed on flimsy grounds. Delays in civil cases hurt particular individuals and institutions; but the failure to expedite the prosecution of the accused in criminal cases–especially of serious criminal offences such as terrorism–is a cause of alarm, as it constitutes a threat to the life of the individual and to the security and stability of the state.

Therefore, it should be understood that the problem we are now dealing with requires various kinds of provisions. Legitimate power has to be given because this is an extraordinary situation. Extraordinary situations require extraordinary remedies. Terrorism has several consequences that have to be faced in the context of a growing threat to the country. References have repeatedly been made to laws in other countries. It is very dangerous to quote selectively. Therefore, the situation of terrorism should be dealt with it under the normal procedure. Learning from this experience, the people who are opposing this law to once again reconsider their stand because posterity eventually will decide that this country, for its integrity, sovereignty and unity certainly needs this law. Quite clearly, there is a crying need to fight the menace of terrorism united. Partisanship of any sort in dealing with the ISI-sponsored terror attacks in India should be abandoned forthwith. Today terrorism has reached the heart of India in New Delhi's Parliament House, and capital city of Mumbai. Preventive detention laws without any safeguards whatsoever against their misuse were required in those relatively peaceful times in the Seventies and Eighties but are not required now, even with safeguards against their misuse, is to betray a sickening streak of partisanship.

To the extent it detracts from presenting a united front against terrorists, the government's myopic stand on POTO and MCOCA in Delhi represents a greater threat to national unity than even the threat of the ISI-sponsored terror. So it becomes very necessary in a country like India that if a law regarding terrorism is enacted it should be made so stringent that the culprit be bought to book and does not go scot-free just because of the loopholes and lacunae's in the ordinary law because when our neighboring nation Pakistan which is the cause of perpetrating terrorism in India can have such stringent laws then India should also we have such laws. Indian law as it stands today has come around in strange circumstances as the earlier legislation was found capable of being misuse. This law is less harsh than the previous anti-terrorism laws in India and is not equipped by way of express provision for discretion to deal with a vast variety of terrorist activity or other activities connected with perpetration of terrorism. Therefore stringent legislation should be either made or brought back for curbing terrorism and such like activities with a strong arm, which may help in preventing and deterring such activities.

The conceptual confusion is that when we deal with terrorists through laws like POTA, we effectively combat terrorism, terror still continues. Terrorism which has roots everywhere needs to be combated with determination. The strategy is two folded. One, enact laws which allow combating terror by use of technology, electronic devices, interceptions, satellite networks and management systems. These institutional arrangements would allow various security agencies to share information. These mechanisms need to be strengthened.[31] Besides, we need to invest hugely in building human resource capacities within our security personnel, establishment of specialized forces with unique skills to deal with terror and forensic abilities, which can prevent incidents of this nature. Two, having access to such information, to deal with terrorist through a legislation which is effective and inspires public confidence consistent with our constitutional ethos. And last not the least, the protection and promotion of Human Rights under the rule of law is essential in the prevention of terrorism. If human rights are violated in the process of combating terrorism, it will be self- defeating. As lack of hope for justice can also provides breeding grounds for terrorism. The threat is really. The remedy requires mature response.

Much of the reluctance in accepting the need for special anti-terrorism legislation is based on the fallacy of equating 'terrorism' with other forms of violence, and the consequent argument that the prevailing or 'ordinary' laws that have been enacted to deal with the latter are sufficient to take care of the former. However, it was widely believed that terrorism was a response to injustice and that the terrorists were people driven to desperate actions by intolerable conditions, be it poverty, hopelessness, or political or social oppression. Following this reasoning, the only way to remove

---

31 Kapil Sibal, 'Action and Reaction – The Threat of Terrorism is real', available at http://.www.sabrang.com/html, (Last Viewed on March 30, 2009).

or at least to reduce terrorism is to tackle its sources, to deal with the grievances and frustrations of the terrorists, rather than simply trying to suppress terrorism by brute force.

Chapter VI

Conclusion And Suggestions

Terrorism, the "cancer of the modern world", a growing threat to the maintenance of an orderly society and a scourge which undermines development, economic and political stability and democratic institution is one of the most challenging problems of the modern times. An unethical, low cost, surrogate war undermines the full exercise of human rights and threatens the stability of many societies in the world.

India is located in a region which "harbours the epicenter of terrorism" and has been a victim of the menace over the last two decades. Over the last two years, terrorism and violence, natural disasters, volatility in oil and food prices besides the global meltdown had tested the inherent success and highlighted the need for monitoring and response mechanisms.[1]

Terrorism is largely sponsored from outside the country, mainly Pakistan and China which has utilised terrorism as an instrument of state policy. Nevertheless, India's external policies have been dictated by a desire to have a supportive neighbourhood. Unfortunately, we cannot choose our neighbours, and some countries like Pakistan have in the past encouraged and given sanctuary to terrorists and other forces that are antagonistic to India. India tried to minimise the impact of such hostility by fencing the border along LOC in J&K and Bangladesh from where the vast majority of the infiltrations into India tended to take place.[2]

As far as the matter of eruption of militancy in Kashmir during late 1980's is concerned, this was not a sudden outburst but the cumulative result of various twists and turns in the state's politics since long. If one wants to understand the growth of militancy in Kashmir, one has to bear

1   Editorial column, 'Indo-Pak War of Words Hots Up', *Statesman*, January 7, 2009.

2   'Nepal, B'desh being used to push militants' Pak using terrorism as state policy: PM", available at http://www.dailyexcelsior.com/html, (Last Viewed on April 21, 2009).

in mind that it is both spontaneous as well as result of some external planning. The denial of basic human needs like genuine decent livelihood, civil liberties and federal autonomy to other people of Kashmir alienated them from the Indian nation and they finally crossed over to the side of militancy.

Pakistan, a traditional rival in the dispute of Kashmir, took advantage of the situation. It not only gave military training to young Kashmiri Muslims but also provided sophisticated weapons. After their return, these young men started an armed struggle in Kashmir.

Pakistan's sponsored cross border terrorism brought both the countries on the brink of war in 2002 when India had deployed large number of troops on its international borders and severe all diplomatic relations with Pakistan. Terrorist's attack on the Kashmir Assembly and Indian Parliament, followed by attack on an army camp in Jammu suggest that Pakistan is pursuing a dual policy. In response to such threats, maxima lists in India pressurized the Indian government that it must take decisive action. It was argued that if United States has right to defend itself. India should also deal with such security threats firmly. However, the tit-for-tat kind of tactics cannot be fought between nuclear countries. In case of war each side would be in hurry to launch all its nuclear systems before they regretted by its adversary. Thus, the logic of mutual destruction in case of war stands firm even in the case of limited nuclear countries like India and Pakistan. There is however one factor which cannot be avoided in striving at reconciliation between the two hostile neighbours in twenty first century – this is the nuclear factor. Neither India nor Pakistan could afford to ignore the realities and overwhelmed by the past prejudices and perceptions. There is concrete evidence that the global changes had put pressures on both countries to settle their differences.

The Way Forward

India and Pakistan still hesitate to make any significant concessions over Kashmir even while they propose to break away from the past. The only progress thus far could be that India has agreed to bring Jammu & Kashmir on the agenda of the composite dialogue process and Pakistan has expressed its willingness to explore options other than the United Nations resolutions. The progress has only been placed on the table and does not promise much beyond the current stage. [3]

---

3   Ashutosh Mishra, 'Problems in Kashmir, Divergence Demands Convergence',

However, one significant step forward has been the **agreement over the Srinagar- Muzaffarabad bus service** and with the first bus on the Srinagar- Muzaffarabad road rolling out against the backdrop of a militant attack in Srinagar on April 6, 2005, India and Pakistan have initiated the biggest gamble ever on Kashmir.[4]

The decision to settle the **'United Nations document'** and **'passport'** issues show that both sides have the capacity to make adjustments. The two discarded options had a linkage with their respective official stands on the status of Kashmir.[5] Many more such mutual concessions would be required from both sides in future talks. It would not be an exaggeration to say that the historic agreement over the bus service is one step forward towards converging the 'problem of Kashmir' and the 'problem is Kashmir' approaches at some mutually agreed positions.

The peace process does show mutual willingness to move toward. However, there remains a challenge to convert the willingness into settlements on other issues. The wounds of Kargil and terrorist strikes in J&K prevent India from showing flexibility beyond its stated positions. In such a situation, Pakistan's periodic outbursts of going back to its 'fall back' position on J&K will undoubtedly stymie the rapprochement underway. The ongoing controversy over the Baghliar Dam in Doda district and Pakistan's decision to approach the World Bank rather than seeking a solution bilaterally could prove detrimental to the future of the peace process.

Given India's willingness to discuss the Kashmir issue, Pakistan must be open, to discuss proposals such as 'greater autonomy' and an 'integrated Kashmir', to be followed by demilitarization of the area and free movement of people and trade from the two sides. All concerned parties including the All Party Huriyat Conference (APHC) would require molding their official's positions to facilitate solutions that could improve the lives of the people of Jammu and Kashmir. The situation demands flexibility by all acting on such lives could eventually be a 'win-win' situation for all.[6] The concepts of 'autonomy', 'integration' and 'soft border' are worth a try. The

---

Strategic Analysis, Vol. XXIX, (January- March, 2005).

4   Ramesh Vinayak, 'Trial by Fire', India Today, (April 18, 2005).

5   Ashutosh Mishra, 'The Problem of Kashmir and the Problem in Kashmir: Divergence Demands Convergence', Strategic Analysis, (January – March, 2005).

6   Ibid.

concept of a 'linked' Kashmir (through bus services and trade exchanges) with a 'soft border' give Pakistan the satisfaction of changing the status quo; to the people of Jammu and Kashmir dividends of the linking are in the form of trade, family reunions and peaceful backwards; and to India it provides a solution within the parameters of the constitution.

India wants from Pakistan--dismantling of terrorist camps, taking action against those involved in terror attacks and handing over of fugitives of Indian laws like the chief of the banned Jaish-e-Mohammed (JeM) Masood Azhar.[7] The Indian authorities have claimed that they have the intercepts of telephone conversations between the terrorists operating in Mumbai during the attack and their handlers in Pakistan. It would seem the US and UK authorities, who operate world-wide signal intelligence services, have the same evidence. Possibly, the Russians and Chinese, too, have similar intercept evidence. The Pakistanis are in a position to investigate these them and they do not need any evidence from outside if they are honest in their intention. But by demanding evidence and casting doubts on Pakistani and British media disclosures about Ajmal Kasab, the Pakistani Government and sections of the Pakistani media have revealed themselves to be helpless pawns in the hands of the ISI.[8]

It is certain that India has to carry out many internal reforms and address many political and administrative shortcomings in the wake of this attack. However, there can be no doubt that the most immediate task to be attended to is to ensure that future attacks of this type are reduced to a minimum and the damage they can do to the country and society are limited to the extent possible.

Suggestions

Terrorist strikes will continue and so will be the killing unabated, till we really, honestly, sincerely and unselfishly decide to protect mankind and abhor the ambition for one-upmanship.

Following suggestions are being made to face the grave threat posed by cross border terrorism at national level:

1. **Economic Development**: As discussed in the previous chapters,

---

7   Editorial column, 'Stop Creating War Hysteria : Pranab Tells Pak', India Times, (December 30, 2008).

8   K Subhramanyum, 'Bleeding India is Part of Pakistan's Long Term Plan', India Times, (December 20, 2008).

Economic factors are one of the serious causes of turmoil in most developing societies. Since the bordering nations are completely ignored with respect to their overall development, reason being nearer to the borders and usually the disturbed areas. Perhaps this is the time for neighbouring countries especially Pakistan and India to focus more on their economic growth and keep the contentious political and territorial issues in cold freeze.

In Kashmir, the development programmes devolution of fiscal powers allow for handling the problems more effectively. No doubt India had been spending enormous resources to support Kashmir but the results never reached the masses. Even the Central Government's economic grant consisting of mega project was never used for development. Kashmir requires a decentralized economic programme so that the people at the grass roots level can directly receive resources for development and are empowered to formulate, approve and implement development projects. India could become a global economic power in the years to come. Being a matured democracy, India had a clear edge over Pakistan in this respect. Politically, Pakistan had been and remains on the edge of failure and this created uncertainty about its economic future. Much of its present economic growth is due to the trade in narcotics which brings in easy money for the country and its people. It needs to consolidate its position in the manufacturing and services sectors to remain on the high growth trajectory. Peaceful relations with India could go a long way in stabilizing the Pakistani economy and integrating it into a globalizing world

2. **Strengthening the Administrative Institutions:** It is difficult to resist the temptation to think that the problem is rooted in the culture of the Border States, or perhaps of the nation, and that there is not much anyone can do about it. It is true that the states will neither develop its economy nor consolidate its democratic system until its cultural changes, but it is wrong to presume that cultural changes must lead the way out of the predatory trap.

Cultures changes only slowly, but institutions can be changed rapidly. And culture will adapt to new institutional incentives if the institutions work effectively to generate new expectations and norms. Through civic education and organisational efforts new, more civic norms can be generated. But these will be sustainable only if the institutions of a civic community come into place. The state of J&K needs to be completely overhauled institutionally.

The institutions that generate a rule of law and a climate of peace, predictability and order are: an independent and professional judicial system; a transparent and efficient banking system (including an independent central bank); effective rules, regulations and oversight agencies governing banking, capital markets and commerce; rules and institutions to restrain corruption by monitoring and when necessary punishing the conduct of public officials, a system of domestic policing that enables people to invest, produce and exchange free of extortion from the state or criminals; and a tax system that collects sufficient revenue to finance these and other public good.

3. Effective Governance

One major challenge ahead is to ensure effective and good governance in Bordering States in India. There is a need for an action plan on good governance. This includes the following:

- A comprehensive legal framework that is defended and enforced by an impartial and component judicial system.

- A framework that would be accountable and open

- A transparent executive decision – making apparatus.

- A system coupled with a capable, efficient and people- friendly bureaucracy.

- Lastly, a strong civil-society.

According to some independent reports, effective governance especially in J&K requires the following:

- To make power generation a key priority

- Give more emphasis too primary and vocational education

- Energize the state civil services, including the judiciary and legal profession

- Strengthen the states human rights commission

- Rehabilitate Kashmiri Pandits

There is need of an accountable, streamlined and people – sensitive administration machinery, a speedy grievance redressal system that includes an upright and effective judiciary and of course a revival of Kashmir's traditionally tolerant society and its expression in the form of Kashmiriyat is required. All these factors have been absent in the state for most of the last decade. Only if these are in place we can hope for a politically and socially stable J&K.

In the Kashmir valley, there is an over whelming sentiments against violence irrespective of its origin and intent. Militancy has clearly lost its popular legitimacy. Several surveys and opinion polls have proved that over 90 percent of the Kashmir is disapproved of violence. Good governance involves not merely maintenance of law and order but also taking into account the basic needs of human beings and protecting their constitutional and other rights. Human rights protection in Jammu and Kashmir requires that they should enjoy economic, social and political right. Only good governance can lead to the revival of Kashmiri's traditionally tolerant society and its expression in the form of Kashmiriyat. All these factors were nursing in Kashmir in last decade.

The war on terrorism cannot stop at military victories. India must help and induce predatory and messy administration in J&K to develop civic institutions and norms. Only then will the state be able to sustain good governance and development progress, and there by regain the confidence of the people. Only then can India achieve a lasting victory in the war against terrorism.

4. Abrogation of Article 370[9] of Indian Constitution

This article specifies that except for Defence, Foreign Affairs, Finance and Communications, (matters specified in the instrument of accession) the **Indian Parliament** needs the State Government's concurrence for applying all other laws. Thus the state's residents lived under a separate set of laws, including those related to citizenship, ownership of property, and fundamental rights, as compared to Indians.

Similar protections for unique status exist in tribal areas of India including those in **Himachal Pradesh, Arunachal Pradesh**, and **Nagaland** however it is only for the state of Jammu and Kashmir that

---

9   Reference of Appendix D

the accession of the state to India is still a matter of dispute between India and Pakistan still on the agenda of the UN Security Council and where the Government of India vide **1974 Indira-Sheikh accord** committed itself to keeping the relationship between the Union and J&K State within the ambit of this article .The **1974 Indira-Sheikh accord** mentions that "The State of Jammu and Kashmir which is a constituent unit of the Union of India, shall, in its relation with the Union, continue to be governed by Article 370 of the Constitution of India."

For instance, Indian citizens from other states and women from J&K who marry men from other states can not purchase land or **property** in J&K. Some argue that the President may, by public notification under article 370(3), declare that Article 370 shall cease to be operative and no recommendation of the Constituent Assembly is needed as it does not exist any longer. Others say it can be amended by an amendment Act under Article 368 of the Constitution and the amendment extended under Article 370(1). Art. 147 of the Constitution of J&K states no Bill or amendment seeking to make any change in the provisions of the constitution of India as applicable in relation to the State; shall be introduced or moved in either house of the Legislature. As per Art. 5 of the Constitution of J&K the executive and legislative power of the State extends to all matters except those with respect to which Parliament has power to make laws for the State under the provisions of the Constitution of India as applicable in relation to this state.

Nevertheless, this Article 370 has created certain psychological barriers, as it is considered to be the root cause of all the problems in J&K. Further believe is that this Article 370 encouraged secessionist activities within J&K and other parts of the country. However, at the time of enactment, it was a temporary arrangement which was supposed to erode gradually. But it has strengthened its roots. Therefore there is a demand of abrogation of this article. Abrogation will lead to some serious consequences like it will encourage masses to demand plebiscite which will lead to internationalisation of the issue of J&K at international platforms like UN one more time. It would not only provide India the freedom from the solemn undertaking given by India through the instrument of accession, but would also discourage the unnecessary misgivings in the minds of the people of J&K, making the issue more sensitive.

5. Rehabilitation of Kashmiri Pandits and Immigrants from across the borders

January 19 is an insignificant day for most of the people around the world. It comes and goes and nobody notices. But for the last 21 years, for one community, it is the day that brings back frightening and dreadful memories. It is the day when 21 years ago final nail in the coffin of forsaken community of Kashmiri Hindus was hammered. It was the day when Islamic terrorists and their sympathisers gave 24 hours eviction notice to Kashmiri Hindus. It was the day when the threats of *Raliv, Galiv Ya Chaliv* (Convert, die or escape) replaced the sounds of evening Azaan (prayers) from majority of mosques in the valley of Kashmir. [10]

On this day the so-called secularism died in Kashmir. It was the day that will remain etched in the memories of Kashmiri Hindus worldwide because on this day they lost the most precious thing they had -- their homeland. It has been 21 years since first shots of Kashmiri Hindus' ethnic cleansing were fired loud and clear from the ramparts of mosques in the Kashmir valley. And it has been 21 long years of neglect, apathy and carelessness on the part of all the successive governments both in the state of Jammu and Kashmir and the capital Delhi.

Kashmiri Hindu refugees who were overnight made homeless on January 19, 1990 have been moving from pillar to post, demanding their fundamental rights. But no one cares. No one has time for this community because they are too small a number to matter. It is a shame that the one and only symbol of India in the valley, the Kashmiri Hindus, are treated as pariahs by the government. [11]

If it were not for Kashmiri Hindus and their steadfast belief in the Indian constitution and tricolour, Kashmir would have been lost two decades ago. Sadly that stark realisation is lost on the Indian polity and government. It is not mere governments that have ignored this refugee community of patriots and nationalists. Even the media has forgotten its responsibility of highlighting the cause of those who do not have a voice. These days, the mainstream media is more interested in knowing what

---

10 Lalit Kaul, President of Indo-American Kashmir Forum and editor of *Kashmir Herald*, 'Kashmir Hindus: Forsaken, forgotten for 21 years', available at http://Rediff.com/India/news, (Last Viewed on January 19, 2011).

11 Ibid.

goes on inside the four walls of the *Big Boss'* house than fighting for the fundamental rights of those who have been wronged.

Some leading journalists instead of focusing on ethnic cleansing issues like those of Kashmiri Hindus' have converted the noble profession of journalism into tabloid yellow journalism and are busy lobbying for political parties. It is shameful to mention that in a free country like ours with free press, half a million Kashmiri Hindus have been hounded out of their homes and hearths and mainstream media has continued to ignore this for 21 years.

Nevertheless, the Kashmiri Hindu is a survivor. Islamic terrorists thought they could annihilate and eradicate Kashmiri Hindu community from the face of this earth but they miserably failed in their mission. The Kashmiri Hindu community despite homeless ness and horrendous ethnic cleansing survived and will survive. It is the Kashmiri Hindu's tenacity to weather any storm and belief in its values and morals that has kept the Kashmiri Hindu alive. While Kashmiri Hindus are starting their 22nd year in exile, they will never give up their dream and demand of reclaiming their homeland.

In spite of extreme apathy shown by the world, Kashmiri Hindus will continue to fight for their fundamental rights and homeland in the Vale of Kashmir. Indian governments, Human Rights organisations, the media, and other world bodies might continue to ignore one of the largest ethnic cleansing in the recent times, but that will not shake off Kashmiri Hindus from their just path to their dream.

The government was implementing a programme for the rehabilitation of Kashmiri Pandits by offering them employment avenues, transit and accommodation facilities. But this is a very small step. Until and unless the sense of security that was snatched away from Kashmiri Pandits is given back, probably they won't come back home. There is an urgency to give them that sense of security. [12]This is one approach which is applicable to all the immigrants residing at the Border States, which need the kind attention of the government.

6. Border Management

The Indo–China and Indo–Pak borders gravely impacting upon the security of the country and thus posing challenge to management of

---

12 Editorial column, 'Without Pandits , Kashmir is Incomplete: Omar', *The Press Trust of India Ltd (PTI)*, January 19, 2011.

borders. The Indo- Pakistan border is a long one and heavily inhabited and inhabitants have a common history of growth, culture, language and rich heritage. Today most of the problems are the manifestation of this fact. The problem of border management on this border is not just one securing the border but of doing so without causing harm to the economic interest of the people, long dependent on mutual trade and various other forms of interdependence. Being on the extreme corner of the country, the border areas have remained underdeveloped and were economically and politically ignored for a long time. The negligence by mainland forced the people of the border area to indulge in and depend on the traditional systems for their survival and this gave rise to cross border movements. Those in-charges of terrorism infrastructure in Pakistan have resorted to other stratagems to infiltrate terrorists into India via Nepal and Bangladesh though it has not totally ceased via the LOC.[13] Therefore proper management of borders is vitally important for the national security. There are certain suggestion for the border management:

- **Electric Fencing**: India has to first manage its soft borders that help in smuggling of arms, narcotic and cross border infiltration. It is not possible to fence the entire border. The deployment of land mines in some of the difficult area has also has also been criticized on the ground of violation of human rights. One of the suggestions put forward in this regard is that the border can be electronically fenced in order to prevent any kind of objectionable infiltration in India.

- **Modern Security Measures**: India needs to change its old structure and procedures of border patrolling. It needs to introduce modernized surveillance and communication systems of that India can detect the problem before it is too late. There has to be coordinated command, control and communication and intelligence systems in order to avoid any delay in action. It seems that Indian security forces are not trained or equipped to deal with protracted insurgency. Indian forces should be provided light weight weapons, proper clothing suitable to the alpine type climatic conditions.

---

13 Editorial column, 'Terrorism as a State Policy for Pakistan: PM', India Today, (January 6, 2009).

- **Internationalisation of Border**: Both India and Pakistan should ideally arrive at a mutually acceptable solution. One of the suggestions is that the LOC can be converted into an international border. Since people in two parts of Kashmir have lived under two different states for last 50 years, the status quo can be maintained and it can be used as a solution. In this regard, the international community can play a significant role by pressurizing Pakistan to stop this cross border terrorism in Kashmir.

- **Development of Border Areas**: Without peaceful borders with its neighbours, India can hardly play its legitimate role in global affairs at this time of seminal global change. Since borders are with neighbours and neighbours are people, we have to take into consideration the people and the state when we talk about borders and its management.

To integrate the border with the mainland, economic and infrastructure development of the border areas must be done. It is also equally important to ensure political satisfaction of the border people, provision of adequate security, closing the cultural and communication gaps between the border people and the national mainstream and developing friendly relations with their border people. Above all, people should be informed about the security issues in order to mobilize their support to defence preparations and government policies

7. Criminal Justice

Government can treat cross border terrorism as a heinous crime and therefore pursue the extradition, prosecution and incarceration of suspects. The law framed by the various governments should not be misused by prosecuting ordinary criminals as was done in India under TADA and POTA. Enforcement machinery of these laws should be firstly trained how to apply these strict laws otherwise police misuses wide powers given to them under anti terrorist law. Secondly, while framing anti-terror laws government should try to build consensus and welcome the views from all sections of society. Indian government while framing POTA ignored all the suggestions and offers for discussion by various human rights groups and ignored the advice of various parliamentarians to refer the Bill to Joint Committee of Parliament so that it can be thoroughly discussed and it is not misused.

Further, it is submitted that there is an urgency of enactment of a **uniform civil code**. All the citizens should have just one set of law. No self respecting nation emasculates itself in the name of religious tolerance to the extent that different laws for different religions are allowed.

There should be the provision of **fast-track courts** for trying terrorists. No terrorism related case should be allowed to gather the dust of time and thereby an obscurity which allows us to forget. Mercy petitions of terrorists sentenced to death should be speedily dealt with. In this connection, it may be mentioned that the mercy petition of Afzal Guru who has been sentenced to death by the Supreme Court, has not been disposed of even after a number of years. The same thing can happen with Azmal Kasab, the single culprit of Mumbai terror attacks. Any fine morning there may be another attack to set free a terrorist.

The researcher acknowledges that any terrorist–perpetrator or abettor–must get the death sentence, nothing less. There should be revision of the President of the mercy option if the person has indulged in anything related to terrorism. It should be made clear to everyone in the country that there is something called treason. If the treason related laws do not make his utterances inclusive, modify the treason laws and make them more stringent.

8. Evaluation of the Working of Non Government Organisations

There are large numbers of schemes and projects for women and children full funded by the Central Government but implemented by the State Government in all the states of India, including Jammu and Kashmir, Assam, Sikkim, Arunachal Pradesh. Many of these are implemented by Non- governmental organisations (NGOs). There is a strong need for an evaluation of these schemes and projects, especially in view of the persistent reports of non- implementation and non- performance by both the State Government and the NGOs concerned. In Srinagar, there are a number of NGOs which receive government funding but are not said to exist on the ground. As a recent study mentioned estimated figures of 8000 widows and 8000 orphans for the valley region. Surely, the number of orphans must be more unless one assumes only one orphan per widow. The study indicates further that government assistance has reached only about 50 percent of the sample surveyed.[14] Therefore, there is a requirement of

14 K. S Subramanian, 'Jammu and Kashmir Conflict Saturation and Human Rights of

proper evaluation of the work of such type of social groups organised for doing the welfare work out there.

9. Harmony among Armed Forces and Civilians

In general terms, a pervasive atmosphere of anger, bitterness, suspicion, dissatisfaction and unhappiness prevails among the people along with widespread mistrust and suspicion of the State and Central Governments in the cities of Jammu and Srinagar. In Srinagar, there is deep resentment and a feeling of being oppressed and brutalized among the people. Mainly as result of the excesses perpetrated by the armed forces deployed in the State, mostly non-Kashmiris. Incidents involving heated exchanges between the civilians and the men in military uniform are a daily feature. The pressure under which these men in uniforms work spending hours upon hours in their lonely bunkers with weapons on the ready against a population perceived to be hostile to outsiders is to be appreciated.

The morale and motivation of those guarding the borders has to be ensured in terms of welfare, incentives and promotions. These men no doubt work under the most trying conditions. In inhospitable terrain, remain away from their families throughout the year and are under constant mental stress. If these men are not motivated, no amount of instructions and measures towards border management will yield the desired results and simultaneously, there is need to give clear instructions to the armed forces to respect the human rights of the ordinary people also.

10. Organisational support:

Organisational support to the security forces should be given which is an important aspect to be considered and this include some substantive recommendations:

- Reforming and energising the state police forces.

- Having specially trained forces to tackle terrorism.

- Intelligence coordination and sharing.

    i.   **State Police Forces:** The state police forces should be strong enough to deal with terrorist movements in the initial stages. Unfortunately, this is not the case in India with the result that the paramilitary forces get sucked in from the very start and, before long; even the Army is called in. Political interference in the day to day administration has played havoc with the morale and objectivity of the police. The National Police Commission had recommended comprehensive measures to insulate the police from political influences and transform it into an instrument of service to the people accountable to the laws of the land and the Constitution of the country. These recommendations must be implemented.

ii. **Specially Trained Forces**: In US, each branch of the armed forces has its own elite units: Army Rangers, Green Berets, Navy SEALs, Delta Force, and the USAF Special Ops. Some of these units were deployed in Afghanistan and are reported to have given a good account of them.

In India, there is an element of overlap in the anti-terrorist operations. Forces are deployed not so much according to their suitability for a particular terrain or the nature of operations called for but more according to their availability. It is essential that we have the right force for the right situation. The Rashtriya Rifles should be principally utilised for counter-insurgency duties. The government has already decided to double the present strength of the RR by raising another 30 battalions. That would take the total strength of RR to well over 85,000. The expansion is sought to be achieved by 2005. The government should think more about the security of the common man than the security of politicians and ministers. The irony of our security system is, most of the NSG commandos in India are employed to provide security to the ministers. Since they are busy with their duties, they are not trained on the latest techniques of rescue. All the main cities should have a terror rescue team containing trained defence people.

During the Mumbai terror attacks on November 26, 2008, the NSG team had to come from Delhi. Though Mumbai is attacked so many times, there is no team of NSG commandos in Mumbai. There should be proper co-ordination between all the security and defence departments like Aviation security, home security, Army.[15]

---

15 Hari Jai Singh,'Countering Terrorism', available at http://www..tribuneindia.com/ mens-issues-articles/how-to-stop-terrorism-in-india/html, (Last Viewed on October 25, 2010).

iii. **Intelligence:** There are usually a plethora of intelligence agencies. In India, we have the Intelligence Bureau, Research & Analysis Wing, Military Intelligence, BSF G-branch, Revenue Intelligence, etc. However, in the event of a crisis we are always told that there was failure of intelligence. In the USA also, there was definitely failure of intelligence which enabled the terrorists to destroy the WTC and damage the Pentagon. The range of instruments to deal with internal security threat was not sufficiently sophisticated. Clearly, there is need to review the effectiveness of our set up for the collection of technical signal and human intelligence. The training and equipment provided to our security forces also requires a careful review.

11. Discouragement to Corruption

Rampant corruption, which is the root cause of a number of problems and bottlenecks which India is facing, is also responsible for increasing terrorist activities. How a person does enter a secured area with arms and ammunition, either out of ignorance and lack of responsibility or due to corruption and greed at grass root level. The strategy to combat terrorism should include all these issues. It is not a standalone problem but a summation of diverse political, social and economic factors. Clamp down heavily on Hawala trade. It is money that comes from this route that ends up in RDX and ammonium nitrate.

Increase the pay package and pension for the police force and the army substantially so that they do not have to look at the necessity (bribe) to make two ends meet. Discourage corruption at all levels. When there is evidence of corruption in spite of these measures, deal with it very harshly. It is to be noted that it is in the carrion of corruption that the worms of terrorism squirm and grow.

12. Awareness among Citizens of India

We must locate those people who are in India and are arranging shelter, help, money, men, boarding and lodging, ammunition, local information and then hiding places after the operation and till those people are not identified, a few people shall be coming from abroad and shall be playing havoc with us. Any information related with any suspected person is to be disclosed to the police

Being as an Indian national, this is a fundamental duty to co operates fully with the cops who are struggling day and night to safeguard our borders, so that everyone could sleep in their homes peacefully. All Indians must be directed to get permission from the local authorities when they allow a stranger to stay in their house even for one night. For some period there should be the ban on arms and ammunition and none should be allowed to carry with him any type of arm. We should close entry of Pakistani even by permission and if we allow, we should allow them without anything in their possession. There is an urgency to examine the case of supply of arms and ammunition to terrorists and also to locate the people who are supplying arms and ammunition to terrorists because they use arms and ammunition and there are people who are supplying these things to them. Similar actions are taken against Naxals and Maoists because they are also outfits of a neighbouring country. They are also terrorists.

However, the common public can contribute towards our security. Public should help these departments by informing them of suspicious incidents. Our political parties should stop their dog fights and taking political advantage of this situation and should sit together and make some stringent laws to curb terrorism. Among the relevant steps undertaken by an aware national are educating our neighborhood, connecting & communicating with the Government, being a leader at our workplace/ community/area, generating funds/donations, if required rallying / creating agenda's taking up Community Service, planning new indicatives & driving them, writing content for flyers/ objectives/ blogs etc., supporting the victims/casualty's family. Unless every one of us put our sincere efforts to fight terrorism, we will see many such Mumbai terror attack throughout our country.

13. Encouragement to International Efforts

Domestic measures alone are not capable in combating the acts of terrorism unless all the States themselves are not enthusiastic in suppressing it. The General Assembly on realizing the importance of the role of the States in this regard has called on States to take 'appropriate measures' at the international level and to co-operate with each other to eliminate terrorism. A question arises as t what could be the 'appropriate measures' which may be taken by the States at international level. The Assembly has not precisely elaborated it. The following measures may be taken by States in this regard.

a. **International Symposium and Researches on Terrorism**:
    Efforts may be made to organise an international symposium
    on terrorism and exchange information, one in a year, where
    all countries participate, while the sub- committee can meet
    more often. This will give more meaningful attention to this
    ulcer by all concerned. It is equally important that, more
    researchers are carried out, comprehensively, throughout
    the areas most affected to arrive at realistic estimation of
    the needs, resources and actions needed on the international
    platform

b. **Terrorists Enforcement Group:** The terrorists enforcement
    group in the Interpol secretariat could suitably strengthened
    by the induction of more staff in view of the increasing
    magnitude of the terrorist problem faced world wide so that
    it is able to provide more effective assistance to different
    countries in their fight against terrorism.

c. **Professional Functioning of Interpol**: There is need
    for adhering to the Article 3 of the Interpol constitution
    to facilitate the undiluted and professional functioning
    of Interpol. Regarding complaints of countries, Interpol
    has found that these were mostly due to lack of clear and
    adequate information. Hence, blaming another country for
    lack of cooperation was not proper when the information
    itself was lacking. If full facts were given, it could be quickly
    examined whether the information filled in the penal laws
    of the concerned country and necessary cooperation could
    be provided.

14. Diplomatic Initiatives

There should be a proactive approach by India on the diplomatic front
so that it could create a favorable international environment to realize
its objective. Government should consider its entering into negotiations
with terrorists groups and make concessions in exchange for the group's
renunciation of violence. While governments are often reluctant to do so
at the beginning of terror campaigns, negotiation may be the only way
to resolve some long-standing disputes. Therefore negotiations are to be

considered as the best policy in fighting terrorism. Unless we address the roots of terrorism we cannot fight terrorism even by military power. India should also pursue maximum negotiations with China, Bangladesh and Pakistan for the peaceful settlement of their disputes

15. Adoption of Foreign Policies

The Patterns of Global Terrorism, an annual publication brought out by the US State Department, lays down the four basic tenets which guide US policy:

- Make no concession to terrorists and strikes no deals.

- Bring terrorists to justice for their crimes

- Isolate and apply pressure on states that sponsor terrorism.

Bolster the counter-terrorist capabilities of countries that work with the US.

It should be possible for the Government of India to formulate its policy on the above lines with such changes as may be necessary, keeping in view the local conditions and the specific nature of the threat.

16. Ratification of International Conventions

Although no comprehensive "single convention" for combating cross border terrorism has been formulated as yet due to various problems of both a practical and theoretical nature, in the past a few conventions have been adopted in order to curb specific forms of terrorism. They are required to be ratified by all the States. Further, States are required to enact legislation to ensure the violations of various anti-terrorism instruments are brought to trial.

17. Extradition or Prosecution

Extradition of an offender normally takes only when there exists an extradition treaty between the territorial State and the requesting State. Persons involved in the act of terrorism therefore cannot be extradited if, after committing an offence of terrorism, they flee to a State which does not have an extradition treaty with the State where the offence has been committed. This rule of International Law ha sled the terrorists to flee only to such Sates. However, a limitation has been imposed on this rule by a few conventions which have been concluded to curb specific forms of terrorism. For instance, the Hague Convention 1970 has made a provision that the offence shall be deemed to be included as an extraditable offence in any existing treaty. The above provisions imply that a person who commits the offence shall be extradited by the contracting parties, even if extradition treaty does not exist. Further, such offence shall not be regarded as a political offence even if the act is committed with a political motive or purpose. Montreal Convention 1971 also provides, similarly, for the suppression of unlawful acts against the safety of international aviation. It is submitted that the persons charged for the offences of terrorism should be extradited by the States for their other acts as well. If the terrorists began to realize that they will be extradited and convicted by a State where the offence has been committed, terrorism can be eliminated substantially.

In those cases where a State fails to extradite a person charged with an offence of terrorism, because of technicalities of law or because of different interpretations, it should prosecute the offender by its component authorities. The authorities must take their decision in the same manner as in the case of any ordinary offence of a serious nature under the law of that State. It is desirable that prosecution takes place without delay. Speedy trial is likely to help in avoiding the repetition of similar acts. When the Indian aircraft was hijacked to Pakistan in 1981, the latter decided to prosecute the offenders but before the initiation of the prosecution proceedings, in 1984 another Indian aircraft was hijacked to Pakistan. Had the accused involved in 1981 air hijacking case been prosecuted or convicted earlier, perhaps hijacking of aircraft in 1984 would not have taken place. Punishment is required to be more serious and a wide publicity is required to be given to the decisions so that they may have deterrent effect.

18. Conclusion of Bilateral Treaties

In the absence of any multilateral treaty to curb terrorism, States are required to conclude bilateral treaties with as many States as possible for the extradition of the persons accused or convicted for the offence of terrorism. Such treaties are required to contain a list of acts of violence which constitute terrorism. In February 1992, India and Britain concluded the Indo-Britain Extradition Treaty and the Agreement to confiscate on reciprocal basis the assets of terrorists and drug–runners in either country. The Confiscation Agreement is the first of its kind in the world and is likely to have great impact on the activities of the terrorists.

19. Mutual Co-operation

Mutual co-operation among the States in Exchange of relevant information and apprehension of terrorists' acts is of paramount importance. It will also be helpful in the conclusion of special treaties and in the prosecution or extradition of perpetrators of terrorists' acts.

20. Protection of Human Rights

However, it is also observed that in those cases where the acts of terrorists do not affect the interest of the society, States are required to treat them differently. Their acts should be treated as an ordinary crime and therefore their human rights may not be violated by the States. It will be regarded as an unwarranted infringements on civil liberties if rights such as presumption of innocence, the right to fair trial, freedom from torture, privacy rights, freedom of expression and assembly and the right to seek asylum are suppressed or restricted in such cases. Such intended and undesirable consequence of the global efforts against terrorism should be avoided. Bacre Ndiaye, the Director of the New York Office of the UN. High Commissioner for Human Rights (OUNHCHR) has lightly stated that 'in some countries, non violent activities have been considered as terrorism, and excessive measures have been taken to suppress or restrict individual rights, including the presumption of innocence, the right to a fair trial, freedom from torture, privacy rights, freedom of expression and assembly, and the right to seek asylum. It is unwarranted and could lead to unwarranted infringements of civil liberties. And therefore such intended and undesirable consequences of the global effort against terrorism should be avoided.' Thus, availability of the human rights to the terrorists depends upon the severity of acts and its impact on the society and the State. The question of human rights to terrorists therefore is required to be considered by the States themselves according to the circumstances existing at the time when the act is committed. Hence, derogations of human rights are permissible if they are proportionate to the dangers that those events represent.

These are some of the areas which are likely to reduce frequency and intensity to terrorism. Although it is difficult to say that these measures would eliminate all possible acts, they would indeed be helpful in combating terrorism to a large extent. There can be many more options.

But these above are those that scream for our immediate attention. These are some minimum actions which government of India must take to stop terrorism. They may take up this point in public and the public can suggest some more points and those could be considered in the Parliament. We have already wasted much time and further wastage of time must be avoided.

Conclusion

There is little doubt that with force, vigilance and some luck, India will be able to substantially destroy and disrupts the existing cross border network of terrorism operating in its bordering states. But no amount of military force, territorial vigilance and operational genius can contain a group of suicide attackers that stretches endlessly across borders and over time. India must ultimately undermine their capacity to recruit and indoctrinate new true believers. That requires dealing with the factors that help in spreading terrorism. And one of the principal factors is chronically bad governance.

The researcher submits in the present study that the plain and even brutal fact is that the political and administrative system in J&K, north east states and several other states in India has been a failure. Political parties have used all means and broken rules at will in their quest for power and wealth. Ministers worry first about the money they can collect and second about whether their decisions have any value for their public legislators are known to have collected bribes to vote for bills. Even military officers are alleged to have ordered weapons on the basis of how large the kickback will be. There are instances where soldiers and policemen have extorted rather than defend the public. In Kashmir, the line between the police and the criminals in a thin one, and at times may not exist at all.

Most institutions of civil governance in the state, already weakened by inefficiency and corruption, have suffered a complete breakdown in the face of terrorist onslaught. In fact, in the state of J&K several government institutions are a façade. The police do not enforce the law. Judges do not decide the law. Custom officials do not inspect the goods. Manufacturers do not produce, bankers do not invest, borrowers do not repay and contracts do not get enforced. Most transactions are twisted to take immediate advantage. Time horizons are extremely short because no one has any confidence in the collectivity and its future. Government does not seem like a public enterprise but a criminal conspiracy, and organised crime heavily penetrates politics and government. In this content, neither democracy nor development can be sustained. Kashmir is clear example of lack of civic traditions which are so essential to make democracy work.

It is then, no coincidence that ethnic violence, religious blood letting and civil unrest are tightly entwined with the corruption of cynical leaders. The incapacitated states in India cannot sustain democracy, for sustainable democracy requires constitutionalism and respect for law. Nor can it generate sustainable economic growth, for that requires people with financial capital to invest it in productive activity and honest enterprise. They get rich by manipulating power and privilege, by stealing from the state, exploiting the weak and shirking the law. Thus it is not wonder that such weak and porous Border States have not been very successful in combating terrorism.

Member States of United Nations in September 2006 embarked upon a new phase in their counter-terrorism efforts by agreeing on a global strategy to counter terrorism. We in India need a National Strategy to combat terrorism. There are some issues worth mentioning with regard to India. We are struggling with a wide range of terrorist attacks. Our problem in India is all our enemies are within the country. Our borders are porous and we do not know who is an Indian. In most of the countries it is mandatory to have an Identity card while we Indians use it only as a documentary need. The new scheme of Unique Identification (UID) is a welcome step. Everybody should have a standard and common identification. Steps should also be taken to deny the use of web, which has become a hostile environment for terrorists.

Role of police, investigative agencies and intelligence agencies should be discussed at high level and we need to know the flaws behind them for their unsuccessful ness and how they can work together and give better results. The strategy to combat terrorism should focus at all the facilitating factors, motivational factors as well as structural factors creating a socio-economic environment in which the radical message seems appealing. It needs not only awareness of people but also their participation in society and democracy. They should feel their stake in society. Further, they must have trust on police and justice which is lacking.

The researcher acknowledges that people of India have maintained their communal harmony and peace during the incidents of terrorist activities in Jaipur, Bangalore, Mumbai and Pune. The same spirit should be upheld and we all should stand united against terrorism. But at the same time, it is submitted that anti terrorist laws provisions need to focus at all the facilitating factors, motivational factors as well as structural factors creating a socio-economic environment. In the ultimate analysis, there can be no two opinions about the need for stringent laws, sensitive judiciary, effective law and enforcement machinery to deal with such atrocious crime. But what is needed more than anything else is responsible behaviour of a citizen in which he is aware of his surroundings. The society sometimes gives shelter and support to evil practices which must be dry up to control terrorism. Therefore it needs not only awareness of people but also their participation in society and democracy. They should undertake the responsibility, feel stake in society and they must have trust in administration and justice, which is lacking. A determined, coordinated and concerted approach by all masses to tackle this menace of terrorism is necessary. Time has come when; the people of India must have introspection that we must stop terrorism in India. The menace has stopped from going ahead on the progress path because of its aftermaths. Therefore, we must come forward to stop this by taking a united vow.........

"Be Vigilant, Be Resilient

Be United Against Terrorism.

Be as One"

Annexure A

List of Worst Terrorist Acts and Incidents of Mass Casualty Terrorism in the World[1]

1. 13 Dec 1921: bombing of Bolgard palace in Bessarabia (modern Moldova) (100)

2. 16 Apr 1925: bombing of cathedral in Sophia, Bulgaria (160)

3. 18 May 1973: mid-air bombing of Aeroflot airliner, Siberia (100)

4. 4 Dec 1977: crash of hijacked Malaysian airliner near Malaysia (100)

5. 20 Aug 1978: arson of theater in Abadan, Iran (477)

6. 20 Nov-5 Dec 1979: hostage taking at Grand Mosque in Mecca, Saudi Arabia (includes 87 terrorists killed) (240)

7. 23 Sep 1983: crash of Gulf Air flight following mid-air bombing over the UAE (112)

8. 23 Oct 1983: truck bombings of U.S. Marine and French barracks, Beirut, Lebanon (301)

9. 14 May 1985: armed attack on crowds in Anuradhapura, Sri Lanka (150)

10. 23 Jun 1985: mid-air bombing of Air India flight off Ireland, and attempted bombing of second flight in Canada (331)

11. 18 Apr 1987: roadway ambush near Alut Oya, Sri Lanka (127)

12. 21 Apr 1987: bombing of bus depot in Columbo, Sri Lanka (106)

13. 29 Nov 1987: mid-air bombing of Korean Air flight near Burma (115)

14. 21 Dec 1988: mid-air bombing of Pan Am flight over Lockerbie, Scotland (270)

---

1   Available at http://www.johnstonsarchive.net/terrorism/globalterrorism/.html updated on May 31, 2010

15. 19 Sep 1989: mid-air bombing of French UTA flight near Bilma, Niger (171)

16. 27 Nov 1989: mid-air bombing of Avianca flight in Bogota, Columbia (110)

17. 3 Aug 1990: armed attack at two mosques in Kathankudy, Sri Lanka (140)

18. 13 Aug 1990: armed attack at mosque in Eravur, Sri Lanka (122)

19. 2 Oct 1990: crash of hijacked PRC airliner in Guangzhou, PRC (132)

20. 12 Mar 1993: 15 bombings in Bombay, India (317)

21. 22 Sep 1993: crash of airliner struck by missile in Sukhumi, Georgia (106)

22. 19 Apr 1995: truck bombing of federal building, Oklahoma City, Oklahoma, USA (169)

23. 14-19 June 1996: hostage taking in Budennovsk, Russia, and two failed rescue attempts (143)

24. 23 Nov 1996: crash of hijacked Ethiopian Air flight off Comoros (127)

25. 29 Aug 1997: attacks at Sidi Moussa and Hais Rais, Algeria (238)

26. 22 Sep 1997: attack at Ben Talha, Algeria (277)

27. 30 Dec 1997: attack at Ami Moussa, Algeria (272)

28. 4 Jan 1998: attacks at Had Chekala, Remka, and Ain Tarik, Algeria (172)

29. 11 Jan 1998: attack on movie theater and mosque at Sidi Hamed, Algeria (103)

30. 8 Aug 1998: truck bombings of U.S. embassies in Nairobi, Kenya, and Dar es Saalam, Tanzania (303)

31. 13 Sep 1999: bombing of apartment building in Moscow, Russia (130)

32. 31 Oct 1999: intentional crash of Egypt Air flight off Massachusetts, USA, by pilot (217)

33. 10 Aug 2001: attack on train south of Luanda, Angola (152)

34. 11 Sep 2001: crashing of hijacked planes into World Trade Center, New York City, New York, Pentagon in Alexandria, Virginia, and site in Pennsylvania, USA (2,993)

35. 12 Oct 2002: car bombing outside nightclub in Kuta, Indonesia (202)

36. 26 Oct 2002: hostage taking and attempted rescue in theater in Moscow, Russia (includes 41 terrorists killed) (170)

37. 29 Aug 2003: car bombing outside mosque in Najaf, Iraq (125)

38. 1 Feb 2004: two suicide bombings of political party offices in Irbil, Iraq (109)

39. 21 Feb 2004: armed attack and arson at refugee camp, Uganda (239)

40. 27 Feb 2004: bombing and fire on ferry near Manila, Philippines (118)

41. 2 Mar 2004: multiple suicide bombings at shrines in Kadhimiya and Karbala, Iraq (188)

42. 11 Mar 2004: bombings of four trains in Madrid, Spain (191)

43. 24 Jun 2004: multiple bombings and armed attacks in several cities in Iraq (103)

44. 1-3 Sep 2004: hostage taking at school in Beslan, Russia (includes 30 terrorists killed) (366)

45. 28 Feb 2005: car bombing outside medical clinic in Hilla, Iraq (135)

46. 14 Sep 2005: multiple suicide bombings and shooting attacks in Baghdad, Iraq (182)

47. 5 Jan 2006: bombings in Karbala, Ramadi, and Baghdad, Iraq (124)

48. 11 Jul 2006: multiple bombings on commuter trains in Mumbai, India (200)

49. 16 Oct 2006: truck bombing of military convoy near Habarana, Sri Lanka (103)

50. 23 Nov 2006: multiple car bombings in Baghdad, Iraq (202)

51. 22 Jan 2007: multiple bombings in Baghdad area, Iraq (101)

52. 3 Feb 2007: truck bombing in market place in Baghdad, Iraq (137)

53. 6 Mar 2007: two bombings and other attacks on pilgrims, Hilla, Iraq (137)

54. 27 Mar 2007: two truck bombings in Tal Afar, Iraq (152)

55. 18 Apr 2007: bombings in Baghdad, Iraq (193)

56. 3-10 Jul 2007: hostage taking and subsequent storming of mosque in Islamabad, Pakistan (102)

57. 7 Jul 2007: bombings in Baghdad and Armili, Iraq (182)

58. 14 Aug 2007: multiple truck bombings in Al-Qataniyah and Al-Adnaniyah, Iraq (520)

59. 18 Oct 2007: bombing of motorcade in Karachi, Pakistan (137)

60. 17 Feb 2008: bombing at dogfighting festival in Kandahar, Afghanistan (105)

61. 26-29 Nov 2008: multiple gun and grenade attacks and hostage takings in Mumbai, India (174)

62. 19 Aug 2009: multiple bombings at government sites in Baghdad, Iraq (102)

63. 25 Oct 2009: two vehicle bombings at government buildings in Baghdad, Iraq (155)

64. 28 Oct 2009: bombing at marketplace in Pakistan (118)

65. 8 Dec 2009: five car bombings in Baghdad, Iraq (127)

66. 10 May 2010: multiple bombings in Hilla, Basra, al-Suwayra, and other cities, Iraq (102)

Annexure B

Major Attacks by Islamic Terrorists in India[2]

March 12, 1993: 257 killed and more than 1,000 injured in 15 co-ordinated bomb attacks in Bombay. The blasts were orchestrated by an Islamic group headed by Dawood Ibrahim.

February 14, 1998: 46 people were killed and more than 200 injured in 13 car bombs in the city of Coimbatore, Tamil Nadu. The attacks were blamed on the "Al Umma" Islamist group

October 1, 2001: Militants belonging to Jaish-e-Mohammed, a Kashmiri group, attacked Jammu and Kashmir Assembly complex in Srinagar, killing 35 people.

December 13, 2001: Attack on the Indian Parliament complex in New Delhi led to the killing of a dozen people and 18 injured. Four members of the Pakistan-based Islamist group Jaish-e-Mohammed were later convicted for their part in the plot

September 24, 2002: 31 people killed, 79 wounded at Akshardham temple in Gujarat

May 14, 2002: Islamic attackers killed more than 30 people in an Army camp near Jammu.

March 13, 2003: A bomb attack on a commuter train in Mumbai killed 11.

Aug. 25, 2003: Twin car bombings in Mumbai killed at least 52 people and injured 150. Indian authorities blamed the Kashmiri Islamist group Lashkar-e-Taiba

---

2 Dr. Srdja Trifkovic, an expert on foreign affairs, is the author of The Sword of the Prophet and Defeating Jihad. His latest book is The Krajina Chronicle: A History of the Serbs in Croatia, Slavonia and Dalmatia

July 5, 2005: Attack on the Ram Janmabhoomi complex, the site of the destroyed Babri Mosque at Ayodhya in Uttar Pradesh.

Oct. 29, 2005: Three explosions in busy shopping areas of south Delhi, two days before the Hindu festival of Diwali, killed 59 and injured 200. Islami Inqilabi Mahaz (Islamic Revolutionary Group) claimed responsibility, but authorities blamed Lashkar-e-Taiba

March 7, 2006: A series of bombings in the holy city of Varanasi killed at least 28 and injured over a hundred. Indian investigators blamed Pakistan-based Islamic terrorists.

July 11, 2006: Seven bomb blasts on the Mumbai Suburban Railway killed over 200 people. Police blamed Lashkar-e-Taiba and Students Islamic Movement of India.

Sept. 8, 2006: At least 37 people were killed and 125 were injured in a series of explosions near a mosque in Malegaon, Maharashtra. The Islamic Movement of India claimed responsibility.

Aug. 25, 2007: Forty-two people killed and 50 injured in twin explosions at a crowded park in Hyderabad by Harkat-ul-Jehad-i-Islami (HuJI).

May 13, 2008: A series of six explosions in Jaipur killed 63 people and injured more than 150.

July 26, 2008: Serial explosions in the western Indian city of Ahmedabad killed 45 people and injured more than 150. The Indian Mujahideen claimed responsibility.

Sept. 13, 2008: Five bomb blasts in New Delhi's popular shopping centers left 21 people dead and more than 100 injured. The Indian Mujahideen claimed responsibility.

Annexure C

Terrorist Organisations Banned in India

1. Babbar Khalsa International

2. Khalistan Commando Force

3. Khalistan Zindabad Force

4. International Sikh Youth Federation

5. Lashkar–E–Taiba/Pasban- E- Ahle Hadis

6. Jaish-E-Mohammad

7. Harkat-Ul-Mujahideen/Harkat-Ul-Ansar/Harkat Ul-Jehad-E-Islami

8. Hizb-Ul-Kujahideen

9. Al-Umar-Mujahideen

10. Jammu and Kashmir Islamik Front

11. United Liberation Front of Assam (ULFA)

12. National Democratic Front of Bodoland (NDFB)

13. Peoples Liberation Army (PLA)

14. United National Liberation Front (UNLF)

15. Peoples Revolutionary Party of Kangleipak (PREPAK)

16. Kangleipak Communist Party (KCP)

17. Kanglei Yaol Kanba Lup (KYKL)

18. Manipur Peoples Liberation Front (MPLF)

19. All Tripura Tiger Force

20. National Liberation Front of Tripura

21. Liberation Tigers of Tamil Elam (LTTE)

22. Students Islamic Movement of India

23. Deendar Anjuman

24. Communist Party of India (M-L)- Peoples War Group and all its formations and front organisations

25. Maoist Communist Centre (MCC) and all its formations and front organisations

26. Albadr

27. Jamiat-Ul-Mujahideen

28. Al-qaida

29. Dukhtaran-E-Millat (DEM)

30. Tamil Nadu Liberation Army (TNLA)

31. Tamil National retrieval Troops (TNRT)

32. Akhil Bharat Nepali Ekta Samaj (ABNES)

Annexure D

Article 370 of the Constitution of India

1. Notwithstanding anything in this Constitution:

a. the provisions of article 238 shall not apply in relation to the State of Jammu and Kashmir,

b. the power of Parliament to make laws for the said State shall be limited to;

i. those matters in the Union List and the Concurrent List which, in consultation with the Government of the State, are declared by the President to correspond to matters specified in the Instrument of Accession governing the accession of the State to the Dominion of India as the matters with respect to which the Dominion Legislature may make laws for that State; and

ii. such other matters in the said Lists, as, with the concurrence of the Government of the State, the President may by order specify.

Explanation—For the purpose of this article, the Government of the State means the person for the time being recognised by the President as the Maharaja of Jammu and Kashmir acting on the advice of the Council of Ministers for the time being in office under the Maharaja's Proclamation dated the fifth day of March, 1948;

c. the provisions of article 1 and of this article shall apply in relation to this State;

d. such of the other provisions of this Constitution shall apply in relation to that State subject to such exceptions and modifications as the President may by order specify

i. Provided that no such order which relates to the matters specified in the Instrument of Accession of the State referred to in paragraph (i) of sub-clause (b) shall be issued except in consultation with the Government of the State:

ii. Provided further that no such order which relates to matters other than those referred to in the last preceding proviso shall be issued except with the concurrence of the Government.

2. If the concurrence of the Government of the State referred to in paragraph

(ii) of sub-clause (b) of clause

(1) or in second proviso to sub-clause

(d) of that clause be given before the Constituent Assembly for the purpose of framing the Constitution of the State is convened, it shall be placed before such Assembly for such decision as it may take thereon.

3. Notwithstanding anything in the foregoing provisions of the article, the President may, by public notification, declare that this article shall cease to be operative or shall be operative only with such exceptions and modifications and from such date as he may notify: Provided that the recommendation of the Constituent Assembly of the State referred to in clause (2) shall be necessary before the President issues such a notification.

4. In exercise of the powers conferred by this article the President, on the recommendation of the Constituent Assembly of the State of Jammu and Kashmir, declared that, as from the 17th day of November, 1952, the said art. 370 shall be operative with the modification that for the explanation in cl.(1) thereof the following Explanation is substituted namely:

Explanation—For the purpose of this Article, the Government of the State means the person for the time being recognised by the

President on the recommendation of the Legislative Assembly of the State as the *Sadar-I-Riyasat of Jammu and Kashmir, acting on the advice of Council of Ministers of the State for the time being in office

Selected Bibliography

Primary Sources

Acts

1. Anti Hijacking Act, 1982

2. Anti- Terrorism Act, 1997 (Pakistan)

3. Anti Terrorism, Crime and Security Act, 2001(UK)

4. Armed Forces (Punjab and Chandigarh) Special Powers Act, 1983

5. Armed Forces Separate Powers Act, 1958

6. Assam Preventive Detention Act, 1980

7. Bihar Maintenance of Public order Act, 1947

8. Bihar Maintenance of Public Order Act, 1948

9. Bombay Public Safety Act, 1947

10. Chandigarh Distributed Areas Act, 1983

11. Criminal Courts and Security Guard Courts Rules.1987

12. Explosive Substances Act, 1908

13. Internal Security Act (Singapore), 1960

14. Internal Security Act (South Africa), 1982

15. Jammu and Kashmir Public Safety Act, 1978

16. Madras Suppression of Disturbance Act, 1948

17. Maintenance of Internal Security Act, 1971

18. National Security (Second Amendment) Ordinance, 1984

19. National Security Act, 1980

20. National Security Guard Act, 1986

21. Newspapers (Incitement to Offences) Act, 1908

22. Prevention of Terrorism Act, 2005 (UK)

23. Punjab Disturbed Areas Act,1983

24. Suppression of Unlawful Acts Against Safety of Civil Aviation Act, 1982

25. Terrorism Act, 2006 (UK)

26. Terrorists Affected Areas, 1984

27. The Anarchical and Revolutionary Crimes Act, 1919

28. The Criminal Procedure Code, 1973

29. The Criminal Tribes Act, 1817

30. The Defence of India Act, 1915

31. The Indian Penal Code, 1860

32. The Indian Press Act, 1910

33. The Maharashtra Control of Organised Crime Act, 1999

34. The Prevention of Seditious Meetings Act, 1911

35. The Prevention of Terrorist Activities Act, 2002

36. The Special Protection Groups Act, 1988

37. The Terrorist and Disruptive Activities (Prevention) Act, 1985

38. The Terrorist and Disruptive Activities (Prevention) Act, 1987

39. Unlawful Activities (Prevention) Amendment Act, 2004

40. US Patriot Act, 2001

41. West Bengal (Prevention of Violent Activities) Act, 1970

United Nations Documents – International Conventions and Declarations

1. Convention for the Suppression of Financing of Terrorism, 1999

2. Convention on Prevention of Punishment of Crimes against Internationally Protected Persons including Diplomatic agents, 1973

3. Convention on the Physical Protection of Nuclear Material, 1980

4. Convention on the Prevention and Punishment of Terrorism, 1937

5. Convention the Safety of UN and Associated Personnel, 1994

6. Convention to Ensure the Safety and Security of the UN and Associated Personnel, 1994

7. European Convention on the Suppression of Terrorism, 1977

8. General Assembly Resolution 3034, 1972

9. General Assembly Resolution 38/130, 1979.

10. General Assembly Resolution 49/60 of December 9, 1994.

11. General Assembly Resolution 51/20 of December 17, 1996.

12. Human Rights Today United Nations priority Un briefing papers, 1998

13. International Convention for the Suppression of Terrorism Bombings, 1997

14. International Convention for the Suppression of Terrorism Bombings, 1997

15. Security Council Resolution 1373/2001

16. The International Convention against the taking of Hostages, 1979

17. United Nations Charter, 1945

18. Universal Declaration on Human Rights (UDHR), 1948

Secondary Sources

Books

1. Aggarwal, H.O (2006), *International Law & Human Rights*, Central Law Publications, Allahabad.

2. Alexander, Yonah (1982), *Terrorism in Europe*, Croom Helm Publications, London.

3. Anand, V.K (1984), *Terrorism and Security*, Deep & Deep Publications, New Delhi.

4. Arora, Chander (1999), *Strategies to Combat Terrorism*, Haranand Publications, New Delhi.

5. Burton, Authony.M (1975), *Urban Terrorism: Theory, Practice and response*, Lee Cooper Publications, London.

6. Cassese, Antonio (1989), *Terrorism, Politics and Law: The Achille Lauro Affairs*, Polity Press, Cambridge.

7. Chand, Attar (1992), *Pakistan Terrorism in Punjab and Kashmir*, Amar Prakashan Publications, New Delhi.

8. Chari P.R (1999), *Perspectives on National Security in South Asia*, Manohar Publications, New Delhi.

9. CHari, P.R.(1999), *Perspectives on National Security in South Asia*, Manohar Publications, New Delhi.

10. Conte Alex (2010), *Counter-Terrorism Law in Australia, Human Rights in the Prevention and Punishment of Terrorism*, MacMillan Publications, USA

11. Dhokalia, R.D (1989), *Terrorism and International Law*, Indian Society of International Law, New Delhi.

12. Dobson, Christopher (2001), *The Weapons of Terror*, Macmillan Publications, London.

13. Freedman, Lawrence (1986), *Terrorism and International Order*, Routledge and Kegen Paul Publications, London.

14. Ganguly, Summit (2005), *The Crisis in Kashmir: Proponents of War, Hopes for Peace, Woodrow Wilson Centre Series*, Cambridge University Press, New Delhi.

15. Gill, K.P.S (2001), *Terrorism and Containment Perspectives of India's Internal Security*, Gyan publications, Delhi.

16. Gutteridge, William (1986), *The New Terrorism*, The Mansell Publications, London.

17. Jankins, Brian (2002), *International Terrorism: A New Code of Conflict*, Mac Millan Publications, Los Angles.

18. Kansakar, Vidya Bir Singh (2001), **Nepal India Open Border: Nature, Pattern and Socio- Cultural Implication**, Kalinga Publications, Delhi.

19. Kapoor, S. K (2008), *International Law*, Central Law Agency, Allahabad.

20. Khanna, H.R (1987), *Terrorism in Punjab: Cause and Cure*, Panchnand Research Institute, Chandigarh.

21. Kohli, Manorma (2003), **From Dependency to Independence- A Study of Indo- Bhutan Relations**, Vikas Publishing House, New Delhi.

22. Lam, Alistair (1992), *Kashmir – A Disputed Legacy 1846-1990*, Oxford University Press, Karachi.

23. Laqueur, Walter (1977), *Terrorism*, Little Brown Publications, Boston.

24. Lodge, Julient (1981), *Terrorism: A Challenge to the State*, Martin Robertson publications, Oxford.

25. Mahata, Ashok K. (2005), *Problem of Terrorism and Other Illegal Activities on Indo- Nepal Border: Issues in Effective Border Management*, Kalinga Publications, Delhi, 2005.

26. Mani, V.S (2003), *International Terrorism and the Quest for Legal Controls*, International Studies, New Delhi

27. Markers, Keriskari (1996), *International terrorism: Unsolved Problems of International Community*, Macmillan publications, New York.

28. Matto, Amitabh (2007), *India and Pakistan*, Knowledge World Publications, Jammu.

29. Mehta, Ashok (2001), *Problem of Terrorism and Other Illegal Activities on Indo- Nepal Border: Issues in Effective Border Management*, Kalinga Publications, Delhi.

30. Narang, S.K (2001), *Terrorism: The Global Perspective*, Kanishka Publications, New Delhi.

31. Nath, Shaleshwar (1980), *Terrorism in India*, national Press, New Delhi.

32. Pachnanda, Ranjit. K (2002), *Terrorism and Response to Terrorist Threat*, UBS Publisher's Distribution Ltd., New Delhi.

33. Pachnanda, Ranjit.k (2002), *Terrorism and Responses to Terrorism Threat*, UBS Publishers, New Delhi.

34. Permanand (2007), *The Politics of Bhutan*, Pragati Publications, Delhi.

35. Puri, Harish.K (1999), *Terrorism in Punjab: Understanding Grassroots Reality*, Har Anad Publication, New Delhi.

36. Ray, Jayanta Kumar (1997), *India- Nepal Cooperation: Broadening Measures*, KP Bagchi & Company Publication, Calcutta.

37. Saksena, N.S (1985), *Terrorism, History and Facets in the World and in India*, Abhinav Publications, New Delhi.

38. Sarkar, Bhaskar (1998), *Tackling Insurgency and Terrorism: Blue Print for Action*, Vision Publications, New Delhi.

39. Saxena, J.N (1988), *International Terrorism: State Terror and Human Rights in Terrorism and International Law*, Central Law Publications, Allahabad.

40. Schimd, Alex P. and Jongman, Albert J. (1988), *Political Terrorism: A New Guide to Actors, Authors, Concepts, Data Base, Theories and Literature*, North Holland publishing Company, New Brunswick, Amsterdam.

41. Sehgal, B.P Singh (1995), *Global Terrorism: Social-Politico and Legal Dimensions*, Deep and Deep Publications, New Delhi.

42. Sexena, J.N (1998), *International Terrorism: State Terror and Human Rights*, Central Law Publications Allahabad.

43. Singh Surat (2006), *Law Relating to Prevention of Terrorism*, Universal Law Publishing Co., New Delhi.

44. Singh, Surat(2007), *Law Relating to Prevention of Terrorism*, Universal Law Publishing Co., New Delhi.

45. Singh, Surinder (1999), *Evolution and Growth of Border Security Force of India*, Trikuta Radiant Publications, Jammu.

46. Singh, Surjit Man (1998), *Geographic settings*, Vikas Publishing House, New Delhi.

47. Sinha, R.K (2005), *Crimes effecting State Security Problems and Recent Trends*, New Delhi.

48. Sinha, S.K (2001), *Terrorism in the New Millenium*, Authors Press, Delhi.

49. Stohl, Michael (1988), The *Politics of Terrorism*, Marcel Dekker Publications Ltd., New York.

50. Sukhwal, B.L (1991), *India: A Political Geography* Allied Publishers, New Delhi.

51. Sukhwal, B.L (2001), *India: A Political Geography* Allied Publishers, New Delhi.

52. Sverdlov. Y (1984), *Terrorism and International Law*, Progress Publishers, USSR.

53. Tajuddin, Muhammed (2001), *Foreign Policy of Bangladesh Liberation War to Sheikh Hasina, National Book Organisation*, New Delhi.

54. Thornton, T.P (1989), *Terror as a Weapon of Political Agitation: International War*, Free Press, New York.

55. Vas, E.A (1986), *Terrorism and Insurgency: The Challenge of Modernisation*, Natraj Publishers, Dehra Dun.

56. Wilkinson Paul (1990), *Political Terrorism*, Macmillan publishers, London.

57. Wilkinson Paul (1999), *Terrorism and The Liberal State*, Macmillan Publishers, London.

Articles

1. Bagachi, Indrani, 'Centre Promises Vallry a Better Fututre- The Manmohan Mantra: Heal, Hope, Harmony', *The Times of India*, 2004.

2. Chadel, Amar, 'India-Pakistan to reduce Risk of War', *The Tribune*, 1998.

3. Cloke, Kenneth, 'Mediating Evil, War and Terrorism the Politics of Conflict', *Settle it Now! Dispute Resolution Journal*, 2005.

4. Godbole, Madhav, 'Management of India's International Borders: Some Challenges Ahead', *Economic and Political Weekly*, 2001.

5. Grant, N.B, 'Terrorism in Search of a Definition', *The Indian Express*, 2005.

6. Jamwal, N.S. 'Management of Land Borders', *Strategic Analysis*, 2002.

7. Jindal, Nirmal, 'Kashmir Issue in Nucleotides South Asia', *Foreign Affairs*, 2005.

8. Katha, Tara, 'Countering Transnational Terrorism', *Strategic Analysis*, 2005.

9. Lowis, Prakash, 'POTA Must Go Lock, Stock and Barrel', *Mainstream*, 2004.

10. Mallin, Jay, 'Terrorism as a Military Weapon, **Air University, Review**, 20004.

11. Manohar, Awantika, 'Terrorism, How to Control it', *Lawz*, New Delhi.

12. Marwaha, Shalini Marwaha, 'Delimitation of Right of Self determination', *JUILS*, Chandigarh, 2007.

13. Mishra, Ashutosh, 'Problems in Kashmir, Divergence Demands Convergence', *Strategic Analysis*, 2005.

14. Puri, Balraj, 'Security Situation in Jammu and Kashmir', *Strategic Analysis*, 2003.

15. Rao, T. S Rama, 'State Terrorism a Response to Terrorism: National and International Dimensions', *Indian Journal of International Law*, 1987, p.183

16. Rapport, David Rapport, 'Fear and Trembling – Terrorism in Three Religious Traditions', *American Political Science Review*, 1984, 668-672.

17. Salathe, Radhika, 'Right of Self Determination of People in National Context: Kashmir Issue', *JUILS*, Chandigarh, 2007.

18. Singh, Jasjit, 'Cross Border Terrorism in South Asia', *Strategic Analysis*, New Delhi, 2004.

19. Singh, Prakash, 'Border Management', *BSF Journal*, BSF Academy, Takenpur, 2002.

20. Siwach, R.S, 'US Strategy to Counter Global Terrorism', *Mainstream*, New Delhi, 2003.

21. Sondhi, Sunil, 'Combating Terrorism in South Asia', *South Asia Politics*, New Delhi, 2005.

22. Vinayak, Ramesh, 'Trial by Fire', *India Today*, 2005.

23. Yoder, Amos, 'United Nations Resolutions Against International Terrorism', *Studies in Conflict & Terrorism Journal*, (1983).

Magazines

1. *Azad Kashmir*, Jammu and Kashmir
2. *Chanakya Civil Services Chronicles*, New Delhi
3. *Competition Success Review*, New Delhi
4. *Economic and Political Weekly*, Mumbai
5. *Frontline,* New Delhi
6. *India Today*, New Delhi
7. *Indian Defence Comments,* New Delhi

8. *Indian Defence review*, New Delhi

9. *Indian Defence Review*, New Delhi

10. *Lawz*, New Delhi.

11. *Mainstream*, New Delhi

12. *Reader Digest*, India

13. *South Asia Politics*, India

14. *Strategic Analysis*, New Delhi

15. *The Outlook*, New Delhi

16. *The Pioneer*, New Delhi

17. *The Week*, New Delhi

18. *UN Chronicles*, Geneva

19. *United Nations Juridical Year Book*, Geneva

Newspapers

1. *Ajit*, Jullandhar

2. *Amar Ujjala*, Chandigarh

3. *Dainik Bhaskar*, Chandhigarh and New Delhi

4. *Dainik Tribune*, Chandigarh

5. *My Paper*, Singapore

6. *Sainik Samachar*, New Delhi

7. *Sindh Today Online*, Sindh

8. *The Assam Tribune*, Guwahati

9. *The Daily Star*, New Delhi

10. *The Hindu*, Chennai

11. *The Indian Express*, Chandigarh

12. *The Press Trust of India*, New Delhi

13. *The Statesman*, Singapore

14. *The Summer*, New York

15. *The Tehelka*, New Delhi

16. *The Times of India,* New Delhi and Chandigarh

17. *The Times of West Bengal,* West Bengal

18. *The Tribune,* New Delhi

19. *Today,* Singapore

Dictionaries & Encyclopedia

1. Al-Bakshit, L.Bazin and S.m. Eissoko (2000), eds,. *History of Humanity*, Vol.IV, UNESCO.

2. Chandrachud, Y.V. (2007), *The Law lexicon: Encyclopedic Law Dictionary with Legal Maxims, Latin Terms, Words & Phrases*, Wadhwa, Nagpur.

3. *Collins Cobuild English Language Dictionary*.

4. *Encyclopaedia Britannica* (1985)

5. *Everyman's Encyclopaedia* (1967), 12 Vols, London

6. *Hardman Encyclopedia on Social Sciences*, New Delhi

7. *Hughes, Thomas Patrick (1999), Dictionaryof Islam,* New Delhi.

8. *Microsoft Encarta Encyclopaedia* (1993-2001Computer edition)

9. Smith, Bonnie G. (2008), *Encyclopaedia*, 4 Vols., Oxford University Press, New Delhi.

10. *The Oxford English Dictionary.*

Websites and Search Engines

1. http// www.usiofindia.org/html

2. http:// www.nagalim.nl

3. http://.in.news.yahoo.com/htm,

4. http://.mea.gov.in,

5. http://.www.alertnet.org

6. http://.www.Asiapacificforum.net

7. http://.www.geocities.com

8. http://.www.ipcs.org

9. http://.www.kashmirmedia.wordpress.com,

10. http://.www.lawcommissionofindia.nic.in

11. http://.www.sindhtoday.net

12. http://.www.un.org

13. http://.www.unhchr.ch

14. http://.www.unhchr.ch,

15. http://:www.News.indiamart.comanalysis

16. http://asianage.com

17. http://drdivas.wordpress.com

18. http://en.wikipedia.org

19. http://ikashmir.org,

20. http://law.nus.edu.sg

21. http://leninist.biz/htm

22. http://saaq.org

23. http://untreaty.un.org

24. http://www.aljazeerah.info

25. http://www.asthabharthi.org

26. http://www.dailyexcelsior.com

27. http://www.dailystarnews.com

28. http://www.globalct.org

29. http://www.globalct.org

30. http://www.globalpolicy.org

31. http://www.globalsecurity.org

32. http://www.idsa.in

33. http://www.india-defence.com,

34. http://www.indiandefencereview.com

35. http://www.ipripak.org

36. http://www.kashmirobserver.com

37. http://www.kashmirtimes.com

38. http://www.lawyersclubindia.com

39. http://www.legalserviceindia.com

40. http://www.Magnacartaplus.org.

41. http://www.mod.nic.in

42. http://www.nepaldemocracy.org

43. http://www.nepaldemocracy.org

44. http://www.rediff.com/news

45. http://www.rediff.com/news

46. http://www.satp.org

47. http://www.satp.org

48. http://www.southasiaanalysis.org

49. http://www.st-andrews.ac.uk

50. http://www.state.gov

51. http://www.tribuneindia.com

52. http://www.unafei.or.in

53. http://www.server.law.wits.ac.za,

Index

www.ingramcontent.com/pod-product-compliance
Lightning Source LLC
Chambersburg PA
CBHW070809300326

41914CB00078B/1916/J